Fodor's InFocus

BARBADOS &
SAINT LUCIA

KT-433-960

Welcome to Barbados and Saint Lucia

While each island has its own personality, you can't go wrong with either one, especially if you're looking for a toes-in-the-sand, sun-drenched vacation. But, if you're hoping for a little more adventure, you'll find an abundance of sea and shore experiences at your disposal, from diving and snorkeling to golf and hiking. Whatever you choose, the tropical warmth and relaxed pace guarantee an enchanting vacation. As you plan your upcoming travels to Barbados or Saint Lucia, please confirm that places are still open and let us know when we need to make updates by writing to us at editors@fodors.com.

TOP REASONS TO GO

★ **The Beaches:** Beautiful white sand awaits you on either island.

★ **The Resorts:** You'll find everything from luxurious beachfront hideaways to simple inns.

★ **The Activities:** Diving, sailing, snorkeling, golfing, and fishing can be enjoyed year-round.

★ **The Food:** Great food ranges from street-party barbecue to world-class dining.

★ **The People:** Bajans and Saint Lucians love sharing their islands and local culture.

Contents

MAPS

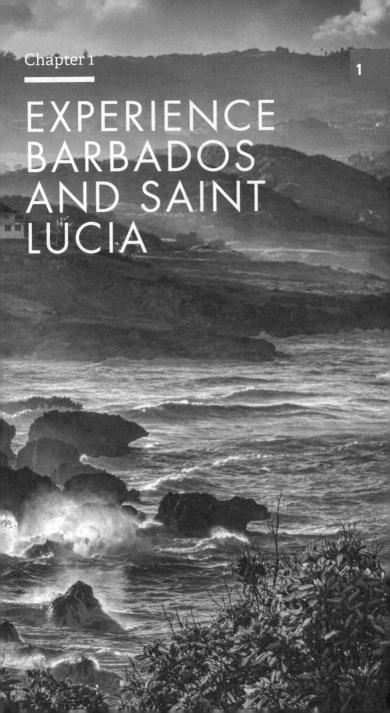

Chapter 1

EXPERIENCE BARBADOS AND SAINT LUCIA

13 ULTIMATE EXPERIENCES

Barbados and Saint Lucia offer terrific experiences that should be on every traveler's list. Here are Fodor's top picks for a memorable trip.

1 Marigot Bay, Saint Lucia

Spend a relaxing day at one of the Caribbean's most beautiful natural harbors. Marigot Bay is a small marina community with restaurants, boutiques, inns, a small beach, and tranquil waters. (Ch. 4)

2 Spa Day, Saint Lucia

Resorts such as Body Holiday, Sandals Grande St. Lucian, and Sugar, a Viceroy Resort have gorgeous spas that make the most of their tropical island settings. (Ch. 4)

3 Waterfalls and Mineral Baths, Saint Lucia

Brilliant flowers and towering trees line the pathways that lead to the splendid Diamond Falls and mineral baths deep within botanical gardens. (Ch. 4)

4 Local Food and Music, Barbados

In Holetown and the area known as "The Gap" on the south coast, you can hear live reggae, soca, pop, and jazz at various venues including the Friday Night Fish Fry in Oistins. (Ch. 3)

5 Sailing, Saint Lucia

Sail around on a resort's Sunfish, join a day sail along the coast, or charter a boat at Rodney Bay Marina. (Ch. 4)

6 Swim with Sea Turtles, Barbados

The waters off Barbados are home to adorable hawksbill and leatherback sea turtles. To spot them, book a dive with Barbados Blue, snorkel from Dottins Reef, or just swim from the Treasure Beach Hotel. (Ch. 3)

7 Rum Tasting, Barbados

Established in 1703, Mount Gay Rum is the world's oldest rum company. They take great pride in their history, offering fascinating tours with plenty of samples. (Ch. 3)

8 Rainforest Hikes, Saint Lucia

Edmund Forest Reserve has an abundance of exotic flowers and rare birds. A trek through this lush landscape also offers spectacular views of mountains, valleys, and the sea. (Ch. 4)

9 The Pitons, Saint Lucia

Rising above Soufrière Bay, these distinctive peaks are the symbol of Saint Lucia. Stay right between them at Viceroy's Sugar Beach resort, climb them with a guide, or simply marvel at their beauty. (Ch. 4)

10 Harrison's Cave, Barbados

This extensive cave system winds its way through the limestone underneath Barbados. There's even a 40-foot waterfall. It's a very popular sight, so plan your visit in advance. (Ch. 3)

11 Coco Hill Forest, Barbados

The island's lush, 52-acre tropical forest is ideal for nature walks, hiking, and forest bathing. The trails are fairly easy to hike and the views are incredible. (Ch. 3)

12 Golf at Sandy Lane, Barbados

On an island with spectacular courses, Sandy Lane Resort has three of the best. The famous Green Monkey Course is reserved for guests, but the Old Nine and Country Club courses are open to everyone. (Ch. 3)

13 Scuba and Snorkeling, Saint Lucia

Anse Chastanet, around the bend from the Pitons, has a colorful coral-lined wall that drops more than 140 feet. Other great spots include Anse Cochon and points along the western shore. (Ch. 4)

WHAT'S WHERE

1 Barbados. Broad vistas, sweeping seascapes, craggy cliffs, and acre upon acre of sugarcane make up the island's varied landscape. The warm Bajan hospitality, welcoming hotels and resorts, sophisticated dining, lively nightspots, and, of course, magnificent sunny beaches have forged a long, successful history of tourism.

2 Saint Lucia. One of the greenest and most beautiful islands in the Caribbean is, arguably, the most romantic. The scenic southern and central regions are mountainous and lush, with dense rain forest, endless banana plantations, and fascinating natural attractions and historic sites. Along the west coast and in the far north, picturesque and distinctively appealing resorts are interspersed with dozens of delightful inns that appeal to families, lovers, and adventurers.

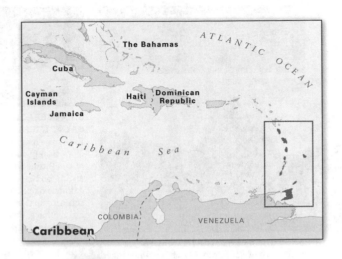

Barbados

Bridgetown

Scarborough

Tobago

ATLANTIC OCEAN

0   50 mi

0   50 km

Best Beaches

SUGAR BEACH, SAINT LUCIA

Enjoy the magnificent background of the Pitons while sitting on the Jalousie dock and soaking up the atmosphere. Visitors and locals alike enjoy the scenery. Pack snorkeling gear for the Anse Piton Marine Reserve.

ANSE CHASTANET, SAINT LUCIA

Just north of Soufrière Bay, this palm-fringed beach has calm waters for swimming, and some of the island's best reefs for snorkeling and diving right from shore. Anse Chastanet Resort's dive shop, restaurant, and bar are open to the public.

REDUIT BEACH, SAINT LUCIA

This long strand of golden sand is the focal point of Rodney Bay Village in the north of Saint Lucia. Three resorts line most of the beachfront, but that doesn't preclude public access. Splash Island Water Park, an open-water inflatable playground near Bay Gardens Beach Resort, is a highlight.

BOTTOM BAY BEACH, BARBADOS

Barbados has many top-notch beaches, but this secluded spot at the island's southeastern tip is the star. Surrounded by coral cliffs, the beach's pure white sand is soft and studded with palm trees.

CRANE BEACH, BARBADOS

Expect a steady breeze and lightly rolling surf—perfect for bodysurfing— at this exquisite crescent of pink sand on the southeast coast. Beach access is either down 98 steps or via a cliffside, glass-walled elevator at The Crane resort.

Pebbles Beach, Barbados

ANSE COCHON, SAINT LUCIA

Part of the National Marine Reserve, this dark-sand beach—accessible by boat or by jeep via Ti Kaye Resort's mile-long access road—is great for swimming, diving, and snorkeling. Most catamaran cruises to Soufrière stop here.

CATTLEWASH, BARBADOS

The rugged East Coast of Barbados is one of its best kept secrets. Though it's often too rough to swim in the water, you can dip in one of the natural pools during low tide. It's also one of the island's longest beaches, making it perfect for long walks and sea shell collecting.

MIAMI BEACH, BARBADOS

Just east of Oistins, this slice of pure white sand has shallow and calm water on one side, deeper water with small waves on the other, and cliffs on either side. There's palm-shaded parking area, snack carts, and chair rentals.

GIBBS BEACH, BARBADOS

When picturing a pristine, tree-lined beach in Barbados, you're probably picturing this one. The tranquil waters and shade make it a favorite among locals and boating enthusiasts.

PEBBLES BEACH, BARBADOS

Just south of Bridgetown, this broad half circle of white sand is one of the island's best family-friendly beaches. Umbrellas, beach chairs, and refreshments are available.

Best Outdoor Activities

BIKES, SCOOTERS, AND ATVS

Many hotels have cruising bikes available for guests, and scooters can be rented. More adventurous folks can join an ATV excursion in Saint Lucia, or rent mountain bikes on either island.

GOLF

Barbados has great golf, including Sandy Lane's Country Club and Green Monkey courses. Saint Lucia isn't as well-known for golf, but it does have the Sandals St. Lucia Golf & Country Club, and the highly anticipated Cabot Saint Lucia.

DIVING AND SNORKELING

Barbados and Saint Lucia have clear water, lots of marine life, and numerous wrecks. Divers in Barbados can explore more than two dozen sites; Saint Lucia's best diving is found between the Pitons and Anse Cochon.

HIKING

Hiking in the Caribbean is often associated with lush rain forests, and that wouldn't be wrong in Barbados and Saint Lucia. But Saint Lucia also has the Pitons, which offer spellbinding views.

WATER SPORTS

The Caribbean is the place for water sports—kayaking, paddleboarding, windsurfing, kitesurfing, snorkeling—and rates at beachfront lodgings usually include free use of nonmotorized equipment. Saint Lucia's southern tip is one of the world's prime locations for windsurfing—and its cousin, kitesurfing.

HORSEBACK RIDING

Horseback riding on the beach while the sun sets is a quintessential Caribbean dream that can be made possible in Saint Lucia.

Sea excursions

BEACHES

The south-coast beaches of Barbados are broad, with white sand and low-to-medium surf; on the west coast, beaches can become quite narrow after autumn storms. Reduit Beach at Rodney Bay is the longest, broadest beach on Saint Lucia; but tiny beaches in quiet coves are equally appealing.

SEA EXCURSIONS

Take a day cruise on a catamaran in Barbados and snorkel and swim with the turtles, a romantic sunset cruise with dinner and cocktails, or a spirited voyage on a pirate ship. A day sail along the Saint Lucian coast between Rodney Bay and Soufrière is a perfect way to visit the island's natural attractions and historic sites.

SPORT FISHING

Fish—barracuda, bonefish, billfish, dolphin, kingfish, marlin, sailfish, swordfish, tarpon, wahoo, yellowfin tuna, or the ravenous lionfish (a threat to local species, but delicious)—are biting year-round. Generally catch-and-release, the charter captain may let you bring a fish ashore for you (or the hotel chef) to prepare for your dinner.

ZIPLINING

Fly with the birds above the rain forest canopy, passing occasional waterfalls and wildlife as you zip from platform to platform tethered to a zipline in Saint Lucia.

Best Romantic Hotels

SANDPIPER HOTEL, BARBADOS
Fancy colonial cottages set among the most lush gardens you'll ever see provide a romantic setting. The private pool, superb dining, and fresh cocktails help to enhance the mood.

JADE MOUNTAIN, SAINT LUCIA
The crème de la crème—adjacent to Anse Chastanet—every open-plan "sanctuary" has an infinity pool from which to enjoy the full glory of Saint Lucia's Pitons World Heritage Site and the Caribbean Sea.

SWEETFIELD MANOR, BARBADOS
Perched on a ridge overlooking Carlisle Bay, this restored manor is a delightful bed-and-breakfast inn set in a lush garden. The resident peacock pride complement peaceful and entertaining outdoor walks.

TI KAYE VILLAGE, SAINT LUCIA
Quiet and remote, your private, rustically elegant cottage—each with a garden shower—peeps out of the hillside high above Anse Cochon. To truly get away from it all, this remote spot on the island's west coast is perfect.

SERENITY AT COCONUT BAY, SAINT LUCIA
At this upscale, adults-only enclave, the luxe accommodations have private garden patios, king beds, fine dining, 24-hour room service, saltwater plunge pools, and personal butlers.

CAP MAISON, SAINT LUCIA
The villas at this intimate resort have large private balconies (perfect for spa treatments), and most units have increible sea views as well as private plunge pools.

Ladera, Saint Lucia

ECO LIFESTYLE AND LODGE, BARBADOS

Blending an eco-chic atmosphere with a forested cliffside location on the rugged east coast is a perfect combination. The divine farm-to-table menu, on-site yoga classes, and hiking trails add to the relaxing getaway.

THE CRANE, BARBADOS

The ocean views are spectacular and the fresh, salty Atlantic sea-spray is pure magic helping couples to truly switch off and get away from it all.

SUGAR BAY, BARBADOS

This family-run, all inclusive and sustainable beach-front boutique hotel offers a great combination of on-site indulgences like the secluded Karma Spa, swim-up pool bar, and four restaurants.

LADERA, SAINT LUCIA

This sophisticated, elegantly rustic, small inn is perched on a volcano ridge-line 1,000 feet above the Caribbean Sea. Each suite has an "open wall" that allows for stunning views of the Pitons.

RENDEZVOUS, SAINT LUCIA

For couples only, this all-inclusive resort is set on the shores of the white-sand Malabar Beach in Castries. It offers a variety of accommodations and lots of activities, including a new on-site spa.

THE ATLANTIS HISTORIC INN, BARBADOS

The secluded location overlooking the Atlantic Ocean in Tent Bay is the perfect spot for those looking for a few days of peace and quiet.

What to Buy

ANTIQUES, BARBADOS

Antique hunters will find British antiques and some local pieces, particularly mahogany furniture at weekly auctions. Look especially for planters' chairs and the classic Barbadian rocking chair, as well as old prints and paintings.

ART, BARBADOS

The colorful flowers, picturesque villages, beautiful seascapes, and fascinating cultural experiences are great inspiration for local artists who have translated these onto canvas and into photographs, sculpture, and other mediums. Gift shops and even some restaurants display local artwork for sale, but the broadest array of artwork will be found in the island's various galleries.

BAJAN SOUVENIRS

Typical crafts include pottery from Earthworks and Hamilton Pottery, shell and glass art, and wood carvings. My Collection Barbados offers a wide range of locally made gifts and souvenirs.

BATIK AND SILKSCREEN, SAINT LUCIA

You'll find locally made batik clothing and wall hangings by Caribelle Batik in Morne Fortune and Joan Alexander-Stowe in Soufrière.

DUTY-FREE GOODS, BARBADOS

Duty-free luxury goods—crystal, cameras, porcelain, leather items, electronics, jewelry, perfume, clothing—are available at various stores on Broadstreet in Bridgetown, Limegrove Lifestyle Centre in Holetown, and the Grantley Adams International Airport departure lounge. Prices are often 30% to 40% less than retail.

DUTY-FREE SHOPPING, SAINT LUCIA

Pointe Seraphine and La Place Carenage in Castries and the Royal St. Lucia Resort arcade in Rodney Bay offer duty-free shopping, as does the Hewanorra International Airport departure lounge.

HANDMADE CRAFTS, SAINT LUCIA

Straw mats, straw hats, straw baskets, oh my! There's also wood carvings, leather work, clay pottery, and a zillion other items to bring home.

LOCALLY GROWN PRODUCTS, SAINT LUCIA

At Castries Market on Saturday morning, buy hot pepper sauce, vanilla extract, coffee, chocolate, and bags of spices such as fresh nutmeg, cinnamon, saffron, masala, Caribbean pepper spice, and cocoa sticks.

Carnival

Nothing brings West Indians together like partying and celebrating their culture. Barbados and Saint Lucia are two of the best places to celebrate Carnival, complete with costumes, music, dancing, and great food.

BARBADOS

After the decline of the sugar-cane industry, the festival was transformed into what we now know as Crop Over, one of the Caribbean's most popular celebrations. The festival, which begins in May (or June, it varies) and runs until the first Monday in August, includes Bridgetown's massive craft and food market, competitions to determine the festival's King and Queen, and the finale, The Grand Kadooment parade.

SAINT LUCIA

Saint Lucian Carnival is a month-long summer celebration that starts in June with a host of parties and events such as steel band competitions, pageants, and a Junior Carnival. Most revelers and spectators look forward to the last two days of Carnival, in mid-July, when the two-day costumes parade and Road March competition take place. There's a flurry of jewels, beads, and feathers as performers dance to the sounds of soca, reggae, and calypso music.

Weddings and Honeymoons

Choosing the Perfect Place. You have two choices to make: the ceremony location and where to have the reception (if you're having one). There are beaches, bluffs overlooking beaches, gardens, private residences, resort lawns, restaurants, and, of course, places of worship. If you decide to go outdoors, remember the seasons—yes, the Caribbean has seasons—and be sure to have a backup plan in case it rains. If you're planning an outdoor wedding at sunset—which is very popular—be sure to keep in mind when the sun sets—about 6 pm year-round.

Finding a Wedding Planner. If you're planning to invite more than an officiant to your ceremony, seriously consider an on-island wedding planner who can help select a location, coordinate the event, recommend a florist and a photographer, help plan the menu, and suggest local traditions to incorporate. Alternatively, many resorts have an on-site wedding planner and some, such as the three Sandals resorts on Saint Lucia and the one on Barbados, offer free weddings with a honeymoon package.

Wedding Attire. In the Caribbean basically anything goes, from long, formal dresses with trains to white bikinis. Men can wear tuxedos or a simple pair of solid-color slacks with a nice white linen shirt. If you want formal dress and tuxedo, it's best to bring your own.

Photographs. Deciding whether to use the resort's photographer or an independent photographer is an important choice. Resorts that host a lot of weddings usually have their own photographers, but you can also find independent, professional island-based photographers; an independent wedding planner will know the best in the area. Make sure you see proofs and order prints before leaving the island.

BARBADOS

Barbados makes weddings relatively simple for nonresidents, as there are no minimum residency requirements. Most resorts—and many smaller hotels and inns—offer wedding packages and have on-site wedding coordinators to help you secure a marriage license and plan your ceremony and reception. Alternatively, you may wish to have your wedding at a scenic historic site or botanical garden, or at sunset on a quiet beach.

To obtain a marriage license ($100 plus $13 for a stamp), which often can be completed in less than a half hour, both partners must apply in person and present valid passports to the Ministry of Home Affairs (located in the General Post Office building, Cheapside, Bridgetown, ☎ *246/621–0227*, open 8:15–4:30 weekdays). If either party was previously married, you'll need a certified copy of the marriage certificate and a certified copy of the official divorce decree or death certificate. For a civil marriage, a separate fee of $125 is payable to the Court; for an alternative venue, $175. All fees must be paid in cash, and an authorized marriage officer (a magistrate or minister) must perform the ceremony.

SAINT LUCIA

Saint Lucia may be the most popular Caribbean island for weddings and honeymoons. Nearly all of the island's resort hotels and most of its small inns offer wedding-honeymoon packages, along with coordinators to plan the event and handle the legalities. Several resorts, including Saint Lucia's three Sandals resorts, offer complimentary weddings if a minimum-stay honeymoon is booked. The most striking setting, though, may be between the Pitons at Ladera or Sugar Beach, A Viceroy Resort—or at one of the nearby resorts that also offer spectacular Piton views, such as Jade Mountain, Anse Chastanet, Ladera, or several smaller properties. Alternatively, botanical gardens, historical sites, or breezy boat trips are all romantic settings.

Most couples opt for the standard marriage license ($125), which requires three days of residence on the island prior to the wedding ceremony. You can marry on the day you arrive, but you'll need a "special" marriage license ($200), and have all the necessary documents mailed in advance. In either case, you can expect additional registrar and certificate fees ($60), and you must present valid passports, birth certificates, and a divorce decree (if necessary) or death certificate (if either party is widowed).

THE HONEYMOON

Do you want Champagne and strawberries delivered to your room each morning? A maze of a swimming pool in which to float? A five-star restaurant in which to dine? Then a resort is the way to go, and both Barbados and Saint Lucia have options in various price ranges. Whether you want a luxurious experience or a more modest one, you'll certainly find a perfect romantic escape. *Check out the Best Romantic Hotels feature in this chapter for places to stay.*

Family Travel

Both islands have plenty to keep children of all ages (and their parents) entertained. Some resorts and hotels welcome children, others don't, and still others restrict kids to off-season visits. Most restaurants, from casual dining to luxury, are kid-friendly.

BARBADOS

Sandy Lane and **Fairmont Royal Pavilion** welcome children at any time with programs for kids of all ages. Somewhat less pricey, **Crystal Cove Hotel, Mango Bay Hotel,** and **Tamarind** have children's programs, a great beach, and lots of water sports. On the south coast, **Turtle Beach Resort, Divi Southwinds Beach Resort, Sugar Bay Barbados,** and **Bougainvillea Beach Resort** are large resorts with great beaches and kids' activities. There are also professional childcare agencies such as **Island Sitters.**

Barbados has more restaurants than you can count, serving any type of cuisine you have in mind, but the Friday-night **Oistins Fish Fry** is definitely family-friendly.

Top children's activities include the tram ride through **Harrison's Cave**; a visit to the **Barbados Wildlife Reserve** during feeding times; a visit to **PEG Farm and Nature Reserve** to see the animals; and a train ride at **St. Nicholas Abbey.** There's also

George Washington House with its network of secret tunnels that are sure to fascinate kids. A catamaran cruise, which includes snorkeling with sea turtles, is always a highlight, as is a submarine ride with **Atlantis Submarines.**

SAINT LUCIA

While Saint Lucia has earned its "most romantic" reputation, children are welcome at most Saint Lucia resorts, hotels, and villa communities. **Windjammer Landing** is a good choice, and **St. James's Club Morgan Bay** is an all-inclusive resort with kid-friendly sports and activities. **Bay Gardens Beach Resort,** though, may be the best bet; it's right on Reduit Beach, with Splash Water Park just offshore and reasonably priced. In the south, **Sugar Beach, A Viceroy Resort** in Soufrière has children's programs; **Coconut Bay Beach Resort,** near the airport in Vieux Fort, devotes half the property to vacationing families and incorporates a water park.

Take a **catamaran cruise** to Soufrière from Rodney Bay, or visit **Pigeon Island National Landmark,** which has a beach, restaurant, museum, 18th-century garrison, and lots of space to run around. Teens will be thrilled by a **zipline** ride through the rain forest or **horseback riding** on the beach.

What to Watch and Read

Barbados

CAPTAIN BLOOD
This classic novel, by Rafael Sabatini, is about high-seas adventure.

THE POLISHED HOE: A NOVEL
Written by Austin Clark, this award-winning story is a personal confession that reflects national history.

IN THE CASTLE OF MY SKIN
A coming-of-age novel by George Lemming set on the island during the 1930s–'40s.

THERE ONCE WAS A LITTLE ENGLAND: A STORY ABOUT MAN'S OBSESSION WITH COLOUR AND CLASS
In this novel, Enrico Downer discusses how a youngster's mysterious death exposed racial, cultural, and class attitudes in 1950s Barbados.

THE SUGAR BARONS
Matthew Parker writes of family, corruption, empire, and war in the West Indies.

ISLAND IN THE SUN
A 1957 film about interracial romance, starring Harry Belafonte and Dorothy Dandridge.

THE STORY OF ADELE H.
A French historical drama film by Truffaut (1975).

THE TAMARIND SEED
A love story about expats on Barbados during the Cold War, starring Julie Andrews and Omar Sharif (1974).

Saint Lucia

OMEROS
An epic work by the Saint Lucian Nobel Prize–winning poet and playwright, Derek Walcott.

VOLCANO
A steamy, drama-filled love story set in Saint Lucia, by Patricia Rice.

TAKE ME THERE
Written by Leslie Esdaile, this is another steamy romance novel set on Saint Lucia.

DOCTOR DOOLITTLE
The original 1967 film starring Rex Harrison was filmed in Marigot Bay.

FIREPOWER
Scenes from this 1979 British thriller, starring Sophia Loren and James Coburn, were filmed in Saint Lucia.

WATER
A 1985 British comedy, starring Michael Caine and highlighting Eddy Grant's reggae music, was filmed in Soufrière.

Chapter 2

TRAVEL SMART

Updated by
Malou Morgan

Know Before You Go

Which island is best for me? Can I get by with English? When should I go? Do I need to bring my passport? Can I use American dollars? Will my smart phone work? You may have a few questions before your vacation in Barbados or Saint Lucia. Here's what you need to know before you embark for this tropical paradise so your next sunny holiday runs smoothly.

CORAL-REEF-SAFE SUNSCREEN IS A MUST

Coral reefs are dying at an alarming rate, and one of the major contributors is sunscreen, more specifically the chemicals oxybenzone and octinoxate. Luckily, numerous companies like Sun Bum, Blue Lizard, and Thinksport offer reef-safe alternatives. So check those labels before you buy your next bottle. It's the reef thing to do.

COVID-19

The Caribbean was gravely impacted by COVID-19 in 2020. Restaurants, hotels, shops, bars, and even cultural institutions were forced to close. Remember to call ahead to verify open hours, and to make sure the property is open.

ENGLISH IS WIDELY SPOKEN

English is understood, spoken, and written on both islands, though you will also hear a French Creole patois spoken in Saint Lucia.

BRING YOUR PASSPORT ... AND U.S. DOLLARS

A valid passport is needed to enter Barbados and Saint Lucia—and to reenter the U.S. But you won't have to worry about the local currency as U.S. dollars—but not coins—are widely accepted. Remember to bring small bills, though, as you'll almost always get change in local money—including from an ATM.

THE LEGAL DRINKING AGE

If you're traveling with older kids, it's good to note that the minimum legal drinking age in Barbados and Saint Lucia is 18.

TAXES AND CHARGES

In Barbados, a 7.5% government tax is added to all hotel bills, and a 7.5% V.A.T. is imposed on restaurant meals, admissions to attractions, and merchandise sales (other than duty-free items). Prices are often tax-inclusive; if not, the V.A.T. will be added to your bill. It's also good to know that a 10% service charge is often added to restaurant checks; otherwise, tip 10%–15%. Some hotels add a 10% service charge, as well.

In Saint Lucia, a 10% government V.A.T. is added to all hotel and restaurant bills. A 10% service charge is usually added to restaurant bills; otherwise, tip 10%–15%. Tip bellboys $1 per bag, maids $2 per night, and taxi drivers 10% of the fare. In both countries, tipping is greatly appreciated as hospitality industry wages are often very low.

DON'T JUST VACATION IN "HIGH SEASON"

A Caribbean vacation is a great way to escape winter in much of the U.S., but this is also "high season"—December 15 through April 15, especially the year-end holiday weeks. But wait! Caribbean weather doesn't change much from month to month, although late summer and early fall are generally more humid. So whenever you're in the mood to escape, don't hesitate. "Low season," which is really most of the year, can be quiet, but with lower prices for accommodations and flights. Both islands also celebrate Carnival during the summer, so there's lots of partying happening! The only caveat: hurricanes are at their peak in September and October.

ARE THERE HURRICANES?

When those storms come roaring across the Atlantic in the fall, they usually aim directly at the Leeward Islands. However, Saint Lucia and Barbados normally escape the storms, although the islands can experience periods of torrential rain and flooding in the fall.

WILL MY PHONE CHARGER WORK?

Electricity in Barbados is 110 volts, just as in the U.S., so converters or transformers are **not** needed.

However, electricity in Saint Lucia is 220 volts, 50 cycles. U.S. appliances will require a plug adaptor (square, three-pin) and, if they are not dual-voltage, a transformer.

WHAT ABOUT WI-FI?

Wi-Fi is available— and usually free—at most resorts, hotels, cafés, restaurants, and even beach facilities. Your phone will work, too, but beware: Roaming charges for calls, whether local or overseas, are prohibitively high unless you've arranged an international plan with your provider.

BEACHES—IT'S WHAT YOU CAME FOR

You may be expecting pristine white-sand Caribbean beaches, but you'll find the sand is more golden in color in Saint Lucia. As for pink-sand beaches, you'll find them in Barbados.

THERE'S MORE TO DO THAN LIE ON THE BEACH

Beaches in Barbados and Saint Lucia are a must, but there's also hiking, ziplining, horseback riding, mountain biking, and bird-watching. There are rain forests, underground caves, botanical gardens, volcanoes (yes, volcanoes), and a plethora of golf courses. And if you dare, try an ATV safari for an exhilarating hour or two.

Getting Here and Around

Barbados and Saint Lucia are two popular destinations in the eastern Caribbean's southern arc. Saint Lucia is situated between Martinique to the north and St. Vincent to the south. Barbados is about 108 miles (174 km) east of Saint Lucia. The two islands are about 20 or 30 minutes apart by air.

 Air

BARBADOS

You can fly nonstop to Barbados from Miami and Charlotte (American); Boston, Fort Lauderdale, and New York–JFK (JetBlue); Toronto (Air Canada, Westjet); London Heathrow (BA), London Gatwick, and Manchester (Virgin Atlantic); and Frankfurt (Lufthansa).

Caribbean Airlines offers connecting service from Fort Lauderdale, Miami, Orlando, and New York–JFK via Port of Spain, Trinidad, but this adds at least two hours to your flight time even in the best of circumstances and may not be the best option for most Americans. Barbados is also well connected to other Caribbean islands via LIAT airline. Grenadines Air Alliance (Mustique Airways and SVG Air) connects Barbados with St. Vincent and with Bequia,

Canouan, Mustique, and Union Island in the Grenadines. Many passengers use Barbados as a transit hub, often spending the night each way. Not all airlines flying into Barbados have local numbers. If your airline doesn't have a local contact number on the island, you may have to pay for the call.

AIRPORTS AND TRANSFERS

Grantley Adams International Airport (BGI) is a stunning, relatively modern facility located in Christ Church Parish, on the south coast. The airport is about 15 minutes from most hotels situated along the south or east coast, 45 minutes from the west coast, and about 30 minutes from Bridgetown. If your hotel does not offer airport transfers, you can take a taxi or a shared van service to your resort. There is duty free available on arrival, though limited, but the departure lounge is set up like a small mall.

SAINT LUCIA

American Airlines flies nonstop from Charlotte, Chicago, Philadelphia (PHL), and Miami to Hewanorra (UVF) in Vieux Fort, with connecting service from New York and other major cities. Delta flies nonstop from Atlanta to UVF. JetBlue flies nonstop to UVF from Boston and New York (JFK). United flies nonstop to UVF from New York (Newark) and Chicago.

LIAT flies to George F. L. Charles Airport (SLU) in Castries from several neighboring islands. Air Canada and Westjet both offer direct flights from Toronto. BA flies directly from London Gatwick.

AIRPORTS AND TRANSFERS

Saint Lucia has two airports. Hewanorra International Airport (UVF), which accommodates large jet aircraft, is at the southeastern tip of the island in Vieux Fort. George F. L. Charles Airport (SLU), also referred to as Vigie Airport, is at Vigie Point in Castries in the northwestern part of the island and accommodates only small prop aircraft due to its location and runway limitations.

Some large resorts—particularly the all-inclusive ones—and package tour operators provide round-trip airport transfers. That's a significant amenity if you're landing at Hewanorra, as the one-way taxi fare is expensive: about $80 to $100 for four passengers for the 90-minute ride to Castries and the north; about $75–$80 for the 45-minute ride to Soufrière. Taxis are always available at the airports.

If you land at George F. L. Charles Airport, it's a short drive to resorts in the north and about 20 minutes to Marigot Bay but more than an hour on a winding road to Soufrière.

Some people opt for a helicopter transfer between Hewanorra and Castries, a quick 12-minute ride with a beautiful view at a one-way cost of $165 per passenger. Helicopters operate in daylight hours only and carry up to six passengers; luggage usually follows by ground transportation.

🚤 Boat and Ferry

BARBADOS

No ferries provide interisland service to or from Barbados at this writing. However, you can charter a private yacht to travel to the other islands; namely Saint Lucia, Grenada, and St. Vincent and the Grenadines.

SAINT LUCIA

Visitors combining a visit to Saint Lucia with a visit to Martinique, Dominica, or Guadeloupe may opt for the L'Express des Iles fast ferry, a modern, high-speed catamaran that calls in Castries four days a week. The trip between Saint Lucia and Fort de France, Martinique, takes 1½ hours; Roseau, Dominica, 3½ hours; and Point à Pitre, Guadeloupe, 5½ hours.

Water taxis are available to shuttle passengers between Soufrière and Marigot Bay or Castries. When cruise ships are in port in Castries, a water taxi shuttles back and forth between Pointe Seraphine on the north side of the harbor and La Place Carenage on the south side of the harbor for $2 per person each way.

Bus

BARBADOS

Bus service is efficient and inexpensive. Public buses are blue with a yellow stripe; yellow buses with a blue stripe are privately owned and operated; and private "Zed-R" vans (so called for their ZR license plate designation) are white with a maroon stripe and also privately owned and operated. All buses travel frequently along Highway 1 (between Bridgetown and Speightstown) and Highway 7 (along the south coast), as well as inland routes. The fare is Bds$3.50 for any one destination; exact change in local currency is appreciated. Buses run about every 20 minutes until midnight. Small signs on roadside poles that say "To City" or "Out of City," meaning the direction relative to Bridgetown, mark the bus stops. Flag down the bus with your hand, even if you're standing at the stop. Bridgetown terminals are at Fairchild Street for buses to the south and east and at Lower Green for buses to Speightstown via the west coast.

SAINT LUCIA

Privately owned and operated minivans constitute Saint Lucia's bus system, an inexpensive and efficient means of transportation used primarily by local people. Minivan routes cover the entire island and run from early morning until approximately 10 pm. You may find this method of getting around most useful for short distances—between Castries and the Rodney Bay area, for example; longer hauls can be uncomfortable. The fare between Castries and Gablewoods Mall is EC$1.25; Castries and Rodney Bay, EC$2; Castries and Gros Islet, EC$2.25; Castries and Vieux Fort (a trip that takes more than two hours), EC$10; Castries and Soufrière (a bone-crushing journey that takes even longer), EC$10. Minivans follow designated routes (signs are displayed on the front window) and have green number plates beginning with the letter *M*; ask at your hotel for the appropriate route number for your destination. Wait at a marked bus stop or hail a passing minivan from the roadside. In Castries, minivans depart from the corner of Micoud and Bridge streets, behind the markets.

In addition to the driver, each minivan usually has a conductor, a young man whose job it is to collect fares, open and close the door, and generally take charge of the passenger area. If you're sure of where you're going, simply knock twice on the metal window frame to signal that you want to get off at the next stop. Otherwise, just let the conductor or driver know where you're going, and he'll stop at the appropriate place.

Car

BARBADOS

Barbados has busy roads, many of which are quite damaged. Traffic can be heavy on the highways, particularly around Bridgetown. Be sure to keep a map handy, as the road system in the countryside can be very confusing—although the friendly Bajans are always happy to help you find your way. Apps such as Waze are also accurate and widely used in Barbados. Drive on the left, British-style. Bajans flash their lights often, either to let you out at an intersection, or to simply say "Hello" if they recognize you. Be especially careful negotiating roundabouts (traffic circles). The speed limit is 30 mph (50 kph) in the country, 20 mph (30 kph) in town. Bridgetown actually has rush hours: 7 to 9 am and 4 to 6 pm. Park only in

approved parking areas; downtown parking costs Bds75¢ to Bds$1 per hour.

CAR RENTALS

Most car-rental agencies require renters to be between 21 and either 70 or 75 years of age and have a valid driver's license and major credit card. Dozens of agencies rent cars, jeeps, or minimokes (small, open-sided vehicles). Rates range from about $75 per day for a minimoke to $100 or more per day for a four-wheel-drive vehicle and $150 or more for a luxury car (you can get a better deal if you book for a week or more) in high season. Most firms also offer discounted three-day rates, and many require at least a two-day rental in high season. The rental generally includes insurance, pickup and delivery service, maps, 24-hour emergency service, and unlimited mileage.

A local driver's permit, which costs $5 (valid for two months), is obtained through the rental agency.

SAINT LUCIA

Roads in Saint Lucia are winding and mountainous, except north of Castries, making driving a challenge for timid or apprehensive drivers and exhausting for everyone else. Between Castries and Rodney Bay, traffic jams are not uncommon, particularly during

Getting Here and Around

rush hours. You drive on the left, British-style. Seat belts are required, and speed limits (32 mph/51 kmh in urban areas) are enforced, especially in and around Castries.

CAR RENTALS

To rent a car you must be at least 25 years old and provide a valid driver's license and a credit card. If you don't have an international driver's license, you must buy a temporary Saint Lucia driving permit at the car-rental office for $20 (EC$54), which is valid for three months. Car-rental rates are usually quoted in U.S. dollars and start at $50 per day or $300 per week.

 Cruise

BARBADOS

Up to eight ships at a time can dock at Bridgetown's Deep Water Harbour, on the northwest side of Carlisle Bay. The cruise-ship terminal has duty-free shops, handicraft vendors, a post office, a telephone station, a tourist information desk, and a taxi stand. To get to downtown Bridgetown, follow the shoreline to The Careenage. It's a 15-minute walk or a $10 taxi ride.

Taxis await ships at the pier. Drivers accept U.S. dollars and appreciate a 10% tip. Taxis are unmetered and operate at an hourly rate of $35 to $40 per carload (up to three passengers) plus a 10% tip. Most drivers will cheerfully narrate an island tour.

SAINT LUCIA

Most cruise ships dock at the capital city of Castries, on the island's northwest coast, at either of two docking areas: Pointe Seraphine, a port of entry and duty-free shopping complex, or Port Castries (Place Carenage), a commercial wharf across the harbor. Ferry service connects the two piers. Smaller vessels occasionally call at Soufrière, on the island's southwest coast. Ships calling at Soufrière must anchor offshore and bring passengers ashore via tender. Tourist information booths are at Pointe Seraphine and at Place Carenage. Downtown Castries is within walking distance of the pier, and the produce market and adjacent crafts and vendors' markets are the main attractions. Soufrière is a sleepy West Indian town, but it's worth a short walk around the central square to view the French Colonial architecture; many of the island's spectacular natural sights are in or near Soufrière.

Taxis are available at the docks in Castries. Although they are unmetered, the standard fares are posted at the entrance to Pointe Seraphine. Taxi drivers are well informed and can give you a full tour—often an excellent one—thanks to government-sponsored training programs. From the Castries area, full-day island tours for up to four people cost $40 to $75 per person, depending on the route and whether entrance fees and lunch are included; full-day sightseeing trips to Soufrière cost around $140 for up to four people. If you plan your own day, expect to pay the driver at least $40 per hour plus a 10% tip. Whatever your destination, negotiate the price with the driver before you depart—and be sure that you both understand whether the rate is quoted in EC or U.S. dollars.

🚘 Taxi

BARBADOS
Taxis operate 24 hours a day. They aren't metered but rates are fixed by the government. Taxis carry up to three passengers, and the fare may be shared. Sample one-way fares from Bridgetown are $20 to Holetown, $25 to Speightstown, $20 to St. Lawrence Gap, and $30 to Bathsheba. Always ask the driver to quote the price before you get in, and be sure that you both understand whether it's quoted in Bds or U.S. dollars. Drivers can also be hired for an hourly rate of about $35–$40 for up to three people. There are also local taxi apps such as PickUp.

SAINT LUCIA
Fully licensed taxis have number plates beginning with *TX*. They are unmetered, although fares are fairly standard. Sample fares for up to four passengers are: Castries to Rodney Bay, $25; Rodney Bay to Cap Estate, $12; Castries to Cap Estate, $25; Castries to Marigot Bay, $30; Castries to Anse La Raye, $40; Castries to Soufrière, $80–$100; and Castries to Vieux Fort, $80. Always ask the driver to quote the price before you get in, and be sure that you both understand whether it's quoted in EC or U.S. dollars. Drivers are generally careful, knowledgeable, and courteous. Drivers can also be hired for an hourly rate of about $40 per hour for up to three people.

Essentials

Activities

BARBADOS

There's always something to do in Barbados, and that's the appeal to most visitors. White-sand beaches await your arrival whether you choose to stay among the luxury resorts on the west coast or on the more affordable south coast.

Exceptional golf courses lure a lot of players to the island, but the private courses—notably Royal Westmoreland and Sandy Lane—aren't for anyone with a light wallet.

The island's restaurant scene is impressive; you can choose from street-party barbecue to international cuisine that rivals the finest dining on the planet.

Getting out on the water is the favored activity, whether that's snorkeling or cruising on a catamaran, deep-sea fishing or surfing at Bathsheba Soup Bowl.

SAINT LUCIA

The island's beaches are certainly inviting—but Saint Lucia is a volcanic island, so you won't find long stretches of fine white sand. Reduit Beach, in the north, is considered the island's best beach with more than a mile of golden sand.

Saint Lucia offers excellent diving, particularly along its southwest coast near Soufrière. Dive Saint Lucia, in Rodney Bay, is a state-of-the-art facility that offers dive trips, equipment, and instruction. Dive shops located at Anse Chastanet, an upscale resort near the Pitons, and Ti Kaye, farther north at Anse Cochon, specialize in beach-access diving.

A day sail on a catamaran is one of the best ways to see the island and perhaps the best way to travel from Castries to Soufrière, or vice versa. And deep-sea fishing is also first-rate.

Saint Lucia's crown jewel is its well-preserved rain forest, which is best explored on a guided hike.

Climbing one of the Pitons is a rewarding experience for adventurers, but you must hire a guide.

Dining

BARBADOS

Barbados prides itself on its many wonderful restaurants, many of which can compete with top-notch dining experiences anywhere in the world. On the west coast, excellent restaurants are concentrated in St. James Parish along Highway 1, particularly in and around Holetown. Restaurants on 1st Street and 2nd Street in

Holetown, for example, offer a variety of cuisines and prices that range from inexpensive to plan ahead! On the south coast, there are a number of dining choices lining both sides of the street from oceanfront restaurants and microbreweries to food truck parks.

SAINT LUCIA

The bulk of Saint Lucia's restaurants—both casual and classy—are concentrated in Rodney Bay Village, although you'll find excellent dining in the Vigie area of Castries and in pretty Marigot Bay. In Soufrière, the best dining is in small hotels and inns, which always welcome nonguests for both lunch and dinner. The barbecue street party at Gros Islet is a must.

MEALS AND MEAL TIMES

Resort breakfasts are frequently lavish buffets that offer tropical fruits and fruit juices, cereal, fresh rolls and pastries, hot dishes (such as codfish, corned-beef hash, and potatoes), and prepared-to-order eggs, pancakes, and French toast. Lunch could be a sit-down meal at a beachfront café or a picnic at a secluded cove. But dinner is the highlight, often combining the expertise of internationally trained chefs with local know-how and ingredients. In Barbados, many all-inclusive

resorts also serve "afternoon tea" with sandwiches and light bites, a nod to the island's British ties.

Of course, you'll want to take advantage of the weekend evening street parties in both Barbados (Oistins) and Saint Lucia (Gros Islet and Anse La Raye), where you can buy and try local food barbecued right before your eyes and accompanied by music and conviviality—a wonderful experience for the whole family.

Expect breakfast to be served from 7:30 am to 10 am; lunch from noon to 2 pm or so; and dinner from 7 pm to about 10 pm. Some restaurants have specific mealtimes; others serve continuously all day long.

Unless otherwise noted, the restaurants listed in this guide are open daily for lunch and dinner.

PAYING

Major credit cards (American Express, MasterCard, and Visa) are accepted in most Caribbean restaurants. We note in reviews when credit cards are not accepted. Price charts for restaurants are included in each island's Planner.

RESERVATIONS AND DRESS

It's always a good idea to make a reservation if you can. In some small or pricey

Essentials

restaurants, it's required. For very popular restaurants, book as far ahead as you can (often 30 days) and reconfirm as soon as you arrive. Large parties should always call ahead to check the reservations policy. Very few, if any, restaurants require men to wear a jacket or a jacket and tie. Shorts and T-shirts at dinner and beach attire or bare feet anytime are universally frowned upon in restaurants throughout the Caribbean.

WINES, BEERS, AND SPIRITS

Mount Gay, Cockspur, and Doorley's are the most popular local rum brands in Barbados, "the birthplace of rum"; Bounty and Chairman's Reserve, in Saint Lucia. Some distilleries are open to the public for tours, tastings, and duty-free shopping.

Both islands also have their own breweries—Banks in Barbados and Piton in Saint Lucia. Both are light, refreshing beers—perfect for hot summer afternoons at the beach. Barbados also has a micro brewery called DreadHop Brewing, which serves a wide selection of craft beers made in-house. They distribute bottled beer to a number of local restaurants and hotels.

Those who prefer a nonalcoholic drink will love the fresh fruit punch, a lime squash, or a bottle of Ting—a carbonated grapefruit drink from Jamaica that's often available in Barbados and Saint Lucia. For something unusual and purely local, try *mauby*, a strong, dark, rather bitter beverage made from the bark of a tree; ginger beer; sea moss, a reputed aphrodisiac made from a combination of seaweed, sweetener, milk, and spices. In Barbados, fresh coconut water is available on the side of the road on Sunday, often sold by coconut vendors who, for $1 or so, will nip off the top of the coconut with sharp machetes so you can drink the coconut water inside. "Sno cones"—sweet, flavored syrup poured over a cup of finely crushed ice—are often found near beaches in Barbados.

 Electricity

BARBADOS

The electric current throughout Barbados is 110 volts, 50 cycles (U.S. standard).

SAINT LUCIA

The electric current on Saint Lucia is 220 volts, 50 cycles, with a square, three-pin plug (U.K. standard). Dual-voltage computer and phone chargers or other appliances require a plug adapter, which you can often borrow from the hotel. For North American appliances that are not dual-voltage, you'll also need a transformer to convert the voltage. More and more hotels and resorts have added 110-volt outlets for general use but sometimes only for electric razors. Many hotels and resorts also provide iPod docking stations.

✚ Health

Tap water in both Barbados and Saint Lucia is generally safe to drink, although bottled water is always available if you prefer. ■TIP➔ **Bring a reusable water bottle with you as it can be refilled at most restaurants and bars for free.**

The major health risk in the Caribbean is sunburn or sunstroke. Protect your skin, wear a hat, drink lots of water, and reapply sunscreen throughout the day.

Swimming on the windward (Atlantic Ocean) side of either island is unsafe—even for experienced swimmers. Tricky currents, powerful waves, strong undertows, and rocky bottoms can be extremely dangerous—and lifeguards are nonexistent.

Watch out for black, spiny sea urchins that live on the rocky sea floor in both shallow and deep waters. Stepping on one is guaranteed to be painful for quite some time, as the urchin releases its spikes into the offending body. To remove a spike, simply pull it out and apply an antiseptic. To remove an embedded spike, first apply some warm oil (preferably olive oil) to soften and dilate the skin and then remove the spike with a sterile needle.

Dengue fever is one of the common viral diseases transmitted to humans by the bite of mosquitoes, and the Caribbean—including the islands of Barbados and Saint Lucia—is one of the regions of the world that is considered a "risk area" by the CDC. No vaccine is available to prevent dengue fever, but travelers are advised to protect against mosquito bites by using insect repellent and protective clothing when in swampy or forested areas. ■TIP➔ **Citronella oil is a nontoxic alternative to bug repellent.**

The worst insect problem may well be the tiny "no-see-ums" (sand flies) that appear after a rain, near swampy ground, and around sunset. If you're hiking through the rain forest in Saint Lucia, wear long pants and a shirt with long sleeves—just in case.

On the west coast of Barbados in particular, beware of the manchineel tree, which grows

Essentials

near the beach, looks like a beautiful shade tree, and has fruit that looks like little green apples—but are poisonous—and bark and leaves that can burn the skin if you touch them; even the droplets of water that might reach your skin can burn you if you seek protection under the tree during a shower.

HIV is a problem throughout the Caribbean, and visitors to the region should take appropriate precautions to prevent contracting the virus.

Do not fly within 24 hours of scuba diving.

COVID-19

COVID-19 brought all travel to a virtual standstill in the first half of 2020, and interruptions to travel have continued into 2021. Although the illness is mild in most people, some experience severe and even life-threatening complications. Once travel started up again, albeit slowly and cautiously, travelers were asked to be particularly careful about hygiene and to avoid any unnecessary travel, especially if they are sick.

Older adults, especially those over 65, have a greater chance of having severe complications from COVID-19. The same is true for people with weaker immune systems

or those living with some types of medical conditions, including diabetes, asthma, heart disease, cancer, HIV/AIDS, kidney disease, and liver disease. Starting two weeks before a trip, anyone planning to travel should be on the lookout for some of the following symptoms: cough, fever, chills, trouble breathing, muscle pain, sore throat, new loss of smell or taste. If you experience any of these symptoms, you should not travel at all.

And to protect yourself during travel, do your best to avoid contact with people showing symptoms. Wash your hands often with soap and water. Limit your time in public places, and, when you are out and about, wear a face mask that covers your nose and mouth. Indeed, a mask may be required in some places, such as on an airplane or in a confined space like a theater, where you share the space with a lot of people.

You may wish to bring extra supplies, such as disinfecting wipes, hand sanitizer (12-ounce bottles were allowed in carry-on luggage at this writing), and a first-aid kit with a thermometer.

Given how abruptly travel was curtailed in March 2020, it is wise to consider protecting yourself by purchasing a travel insurance policy that will reimburse you for any cancellation costs related to COVID-19. Not all travel insurance policies protect against pandemic-related cancellations, so always read the fine print.

Hours of Operation

BARBADOS

Banks are open Monday through Thursday 8–3, Friday 8–5 (some branches in supermarkets are open Saturday morning 9–noon). At the airport, the Barbados National Bank is open from 8 am until the last plane leaves or arrives, seven days a week (including holidays). Most stores in Bridgetown are open weekdays from 8:30 or 9 to 4:30 or 5, Saturday from 8:30 to 1 or 2. Stores in shopping malls outside Bridgetown may stay open later. Some supermarkets are open daily 8–6 or later.
■ TIP➔ **The island practically shuts down on Sunday.**

SAINT LUCIA

Banks are open Monday through Thursday 8–2, Friday 8–5; a few branches in Rodney Bay are also open Saturday 9–noon. Most stores are open weekdays 8:30–4:30, Saturday 8–12:30; stores in shopping malls are open Monday through Saturday 9–7; Pointe

Seraphine and Place Carenage shops are open weekdays 9–5, Saturday 9–2. Some hotel gift shops may be open on Sunday.

Internet

BARBADOS

Most hotels and resorts provide free Wi-Fi and one or more Internet terminals for guest use. Most cafés, restaurants, and even beach bars, offer free Wi-Fi as well.

SAINT LUCIA

Most hotels and resorts in Saint Lucia offer Wi-Fi and Internet terminals, often at no charge to guests. Wi-Fi hotspots are located in several bars and restaurants and at Marina Village at Marigot Bay.

🛌 Lodging

BARBADOS

Great resorts run the gamut—from unpretentious to knock-your-socks-off—in size, intimacy, amenities, and price. Many are well suited to families. Most visitors stay either in luxurious beachfront enclaves on the fashionable west coast—in St. James and St. Peter parishes, north of Bridgetown—or on the action-packed south coast with easy access to small, independent restaurants, bars,

Essentials

and nightclubs in and around St. Lawrence Gap. A few inns on the remote southeast and east coasts offer spectacular ocean views and tranquillity, but those on the east coast don't have swimming beaches nearby.

Families and long-term visitors may choose from a variety of condos—from busy time-share resorts to more sedate holiday complexes. Villas and villa complexes range from luxurious to simple.

In keeping with the smoke-free policy enforced throughout Barbados, smoking is restricted to open outdoor areas such as the beach. It is not permitted in hotels (neither rooms nor public areas) or in restaurants.

Prices in Barbados may be twice as high in season (December 15–April 15) as during the quieter months, although special promotions and vacation packages are often available throughout the year. Most hotels include no meals in their rates; some include breakfast, many offer a meal plan, others require you to purchase the meal plan in the high season, and a few offer all-inclusive packages.

SAINT LUCIA

Nearly all resorts and small inns are tucked into lush surroundings on secluded coves, unspoiled beaches, or forested hillsides in three locations along the calm Caribbean (western) coast: in the greater Castries area between Marigot Bay, a few miles south of the city, and Labrelotte Bay in the north; in and around Rodney Bay and north to Cap Estate; and in and around Soufrière on the southwest coast near the Pitons. There's only one pair of resorts in Vieux Fort, near Hewanorra. The advantage of being in the north is that you have access to a wider range of restaurants and nightlife; in the south you may be limited to hotel dining rooms—albeit some of the best—and a few other dining options in and around Soufrière.

Most people choose to stay in one of Saint Lucia's many beach resorts, the majority of which are upscale and fairly pricey. Several resorts offer an all-inclusive option, including three Sandals resorts and two Sunswept resorts (The Body Holiday and Rendezvous), St. James's Club Morgan Bay Resort & Spa, East Winds Inn, Coconut Bay Beach Resort & Spa and Serenity at Coconut Bay, and Royalton St. Lucia Resort & Spa.

If you want something more intimate and perhaps less expensive, Saint Lucia has dozens of small, locally owned inns and hotels that may or may not be directly on the beach.

Luxury villa communities and independent private villas are a good alternative for families. Many of these are in the north in or near Cap Estate.

📍 Mail

BARBADOS
An airmail letter from Barbados to the United States or Canada costs Bds$2.80 for a half ounce, Bds$3.80 for one ounce; an airmail postcard costs Bds$2.80. When sending mail to Barbados, be sure to include the parish name in the address and postal codes. The General Post Office in Cheapside, Bridgetown, is open weekdays 7:30–5; branches in each parish are open weekdays 8–3; the Sherbourne Conference Center branch is open weekdays 8:15–4:30 during conferences.

SAINT LUCIA
The General Post Office is on Bridge Street in Castries and is open weekdays 8:30–4:30; all towns and villages have branches. Post offices are open weekdays 8:30–4:30. Postage for airmail letters to the United States, Canada, and the United Kingdom is EC$1.50 per ½ ounce; postcards are EC80¢.

💲 Money

BARBADOS
The Barbados dollar is pegged to the U.S. dollar at the rate of Bds$1.98 to $1. U.S. paper currency (not coins) is widely accepted, although you are likely to get your change in local currency. Major credit cards and traveler's checks are also widely accepted. ATMs are available 24 hours a day throughout the island and dispense local currency. All prices quoted in this book are in U.S. dollars unless indicated as Bds$.

SAINT LUCIA
The official currency in Saint Lucia is the Eastern Caribbean dollar (EC$) at the exchange rate of EC$2.67 to $1. U.S. paper currency (not coins) is accepted nearly everywhere—although you are likely to get your change in local currency. Major credit cards and traveler's checks are also widely accepted. ATMs dispense local currency. All prices quoted in this book are in U.S. dollars unless indicated as EC$.

🌐 Passports

To enter either Barbados or Saint Lucia, all visitors must produce a valid passport and have a return or ongoing ticket.

Essentials

➕ Safety

Although crime isn't a significant problem in either Barbados or Saint Lucia, take the same precautions that you would at home—lock your door, secure your valuables, and don't carry too much money or flaunt expensive jewelry on the street or beach.

Do not visit beaches at night, and please be cognizant of catcalling when walking around as it's an issue throughout the Caribbean.

Refrain from any illegal drug use, as both islands have strict laws against this.

💲 Taxes and Service Charges

BARBADOS

A 7.75% government tax is added to all hotel bills. A 7.5% V.A.T. (value-added tax) is imposed on restaurant meals, admissions to attractions, and merchandise sales (other than those that are duty-free). Prices are often tax-inclusive; if not, the V.A.T. will be added to your bill. A 10% service charge is often added to hotel bills and restaurant checks.

SAINT LUCIA

A V.A.T. of 10% is added to all hotel and restaurant bills. Most restaurants and some hotels also add a service charge of 10% in lieu of tipping.

📞 Telephones

BARBADOS

The area code for Barbados is 246. Local calls from private phones are free; some hotels charge a small fee. For directory assistance, dial 411. Prepaid phone cards, which can be used throughout Barbados, are sold at shops and transportation centers.

Most U.S. cell phones will work in Barbados, though roaming charges can be expensive. Buying a local SIM card for your own unlocked phone may be less expensive if you're planning an extended stay or expect to make a lot of local calls. Top-off services are available throughout the island.

SAINT LUCIA

The area code for Saint Lucia is 758. Some hotels charge a small fee (usually about EC$1) for local calls. Many retail outlets sell phone cards to use for either local or international calls.

Most U.S. cell phones will work in Saint Lucia, though

roaming charges can be expensive. Buying a local SIM card for your own unlocked phone may be a less expensive alternative if you're planning an extended stay or expect to make a lot of local calls. Top-off services are available at several locations throughout the island.

📍 Time

Barbados and Saint Lucia are both in the Atlantic Standard Time zone, which is one hour later than Eastern Standard Time and four hours earlier than GMT. As is true throughout the Caribbean, neither island observes daylight saving time, so Atlantic Standard Time is the same time as Eastern Daylight Time during that period (March through October).

💲 Tipping

If no service charge is added to your bill, tip waiters 10%–15%. Tip porters and bellhops $1 per bag and hotel cleaners $2 per night, although many of the all-inclusive resorts have a no-tipping policy. Taxi drivers and tour guides also appreciate a 10% tip.

📅 When to Go

High season in Barbados and Saint Lucia runs from mid-December through mid-April. If you visit in mid-May or June, prices may be 20% to 50% less, particularly in Barbados. The period from mid-August through late November is typically the least busy time in both Barbados and Saint Lucia; however, some hotels on Barbados close for several weeks in September and/or October (the slowest months in the off-season) for annual maintenance and staff vacations. Some restaurants close during that time, too.

Temperatures are fairly consistent throughout the year in Barbados and Saint Lucia. The "rainy season" (June–November), which coincides with the Atlantic hurricane season, feels hotter because there's more humidity. Hurricanes are rare in Barbados, as they usually pass well to the north, but drenching tropical rainstorms are not unusual in the fall.

Great Itineraries: Saint Lucia

Each of these fills one day in Saint Lucia. Together they span the area's most quintessential experiences, from hiking in the rain forest or sailing down the island's west coast to snorkel to shopping in Castries.

A Day in the South. Saint Lucia's most interesting natural attractions are in the south—specifically, in and around Soufrière. From Rodney Bay or Castries, take a sailing trip down the west coast and admire the eye-popping views of the iconic Pitons as you approach Soufrière Harbor. Tour the sulfurous La Soufrière "drive-in volcano," the spectacular Diamond Botanical Garden with its mineral-encrusted waterfall, and the historic Morne Coubaril agricultural estate (which also has a zipline ride). Enjoy a Creole lunch at Fond Doux Estate, where you can also walk along the garden pathways and learn how to turn cacao beans into delicious St. Lucian chocolate.

A Day in the Rain Forest. One of the island's most amazing natural attractions is its vast rain forest. There are two ways to enjoy it—from above or below. Kids may prefer a thrilling zipline trip through the forest canopy, while others may prefer the more sedate aerial tram that takes a slow, two-hour tour through the forest;

both of these attractions are in the Castries Waterworks Rain Forest east of Rodney Bay. Those looking for a more down-to-earth experience may want to take a guided hike in the Edmund Forest Reserve in the central part of the island, but you're expected to hire a guide from the Forest and Lands Department.

A Day of Shopping in Castries. Saint Lucia's capital has one of the most extensive market complexes in the Caribbean with more than 300 vendors. You'll find row upon row of tropical fruits and vegetables in the orange-roofed produce market, where vendors also sell spices, vanilla, wood carvings, and locally bottled sauces at bargain prices. Next door and across the street, you'll find huge indoor markets with souvenirs ranging from really cheesy to handcrafted beauties. For duty-free shopping, try Place Carenage or Point Seraphine.

A Day at Pigeon Island. Take a taxi, minibus, or rental car to Pigeon Island National Park—a historic site and natural playground at the island's northwestern tip. You'll find ruins of 18th-century batteries and garrisons scattered around the 44-acre grounds, along with a multimedia display of the island's ecology and history in the museum and two small beaches. Bring a picnic or buy refreshments at the snack bar.

A Day at Rodney Bay Village. The daytime focal point of Rodney Bay Village is Reduit Beach, a broad swath of golden sand considered the island's finest beach. Just offshore, kids (and adults) love the open-water, inflatable Splash Island Water Park. In the evening, the village becomes "restaurant central," everything from quick snacks to fine dining. Stick around for the nightlife, where several bars and clubs have live bands. And if you didn't stop by the Bay Walk Mall (with its hundreds of shops) during the day, you may want to try your luck in the evening—it has the island's only casino. On Friday, check out the local fish fry at Gros Islet village. It's a huge street party with DJs, freshly grilled fish, and flowing drinks.

A Day on St. Lucia's West Coast Road. While getting to Soufrière by boat is both fun and expeditious, traveling between Castries and the South along the winding, mountainous West Coast Road provides a grand overview of St. Lucia's natural beauty. About 15 minutes south of Castries, stop at Marigot Bay to view its pretty harbor (great photo ops) and have lunch or a snack. Continuing past banana fields, the winding road threads up the mountains, through hairpin turns in the rain forest, and past spectacular views out to sea. You'll pass through the fishing towns of Anse-la-Raye and Canaries before seeing in the distance the iconic Pitons and the picturesque town of Soufrière. It's about a 90-minute (nonstop) drive each way and best done by a taxi driver, who isn't intimidated by the road and doesn't mind the return trip.

Great Itineraries: Barbados

Each of these fills one day in Barbados. Together they span the area's most quintessential experiences, from catamaran cruises with snorkeling and swimming with turtles to spending the day on the island's South Coast that ends with Friday night's Oistins Fish Fry.

Barbados from Bottom to Top. You must visit Harrison's Cave—a unique natural wonder in the Caribbean. The underground tram ride through the cave will thrill the whole family. Afterward, pop over to Hamilton's Pottery (located across the street from the caves) to pick up some beautiful, locally made gifts. Stop at Lemon Arbour for a delicious local lunch. Sundowners at La Cabane are a perfect end to the day.

A Day in the Wild, Wild East. From Speightstown, head east to Farley Hill and the Barbados Wildlife Reserve before continuing on to St. Nicholas Abbey, a family-owned micro–rum distillery. Nearby, the scenic overlook at Cherry Tree Hill provides a spectacular view of the whole Atlantic coast. The ride along the coastal road, which hugs the Atlantic Ocean, is particularly scenic and you might even glimpse some daredevil surfers at Bathsheba Soup

Bowl! Stop for lunch—perhaps a Bajan buffet—at the Round House. Take a long, relaxing walk and search for seashells along Cattlewash Beach before heading back through the center of the island. From south-coast hotels, do the trip in reverse. If you are staying on the South, end your day with a drink and dinner at Castaways Bar and Grill.

A Day at Sea along the West Coast. Catamaran party boats— *Tiami* and *Cool Runnings*— depart from Bridgetown, near the cruise-ship terminal, for a full day of sailing, snorkeling, and swimming with turtles; it's a unique and fascinating experience for the whole family. Lunch and drinks are included. Alternatively, explore wrecks and reefs 100 to 150 feet underwater without getting wet on an Atlantis Submarine cruise. Day trips on the submarine are fascinating, but the evening cruise utilizes the sub's bright spotlights to illuminate interesting sea creatures that only appear at night. End the day with a walk along the South Coast boardwalk, followed by dinner at Salt Cafe.

A Day Exploring Barbados's Historic Capital. In Bridgetown, head for the Parliament Buildings, which are in the center of this bustling city that's full of shops, offices, and people. Take a tour, if you wish, and then use the pedestrian-only Chamberlain Bridge to cross The Careenage, a waterway where, in years past, schooners were "careened" for maintenance. You may also wish to visit Nidze Israel Synagogue, whose congregation dates to the 1620s; it's open to the public year-round. Or just stroll along the Esplanade adjacent to the Careenage (and the bridges for which Bridgetown was named), take a seat, and "people watch" in the lovely, and shaded, Independence Square. Escape the afternoon heat at the Barbados Museum in the Historic Garrison District, a UNESCO World Heritage site. End your day with lunch and day at the beach at Copacabana Beach Club.

A Day (and Evening) on the South Coast. Escape the hot sun at Coco Hill Forest, a 53-acre rain forest tucked away in the center of the island, where you can enjoy "Forest bathing" by immersing yourself in nature. Guided walks are also available. On your way home, stop at Gun Hill Signal Station for a panoramic view of the whole southern half of the island. If it's Friday night, head down to the Oistins Fish Fry—a street party where you can buy an inexpensive meal of barbecued fish or chicken, sides, cold drinks, music, and see lots of people—locals and visitors alike.

A Day (and Evening) on the West Coast. Enjoy a coffee and shopping at Limegrove Lifestyle Centre, then make your way to any one of the beautiful beaches on the West Coast—also known as the "Platinum coast." Water-sports equipment, beach chairs, and refreshments are available at most beaches, including Payne's Bay, Mullins, and Speightstown. At night, head for 1st and 2nd streets in Holetown. Pick any restaurant—they're all good—and end the day at The Mews or Red Door Lounge.

Contacts

Air

AIRLINES American Airlines.
☎ *246/428–4170, 800/744–0006 in Barbados, 800/433–7300 in U.S.* ⊕ *www.aa.com.*
Caribbean Airlines. ☎ *800/744–2225 in the Caribbean, 800/920–4225 in U.S.* ⊕ *www.caribbean-airlines.com.* **Grenadine Air Alliance.** ☎ *246/228–5544* ⊕ *www.grenadine-air.com.* **JetBlue.** ☎ *877/596–2413 in Barbados, 800/538–2583 in U.S.* ⊕ *www.jetblue.com.* **LIAT.** ☎ *246/434–5428 in Barbados, 888/844–5428 in the Caribbean, 268/480–5601 in U.S. (toll call)* ⊕ *www.liat.com.*

BARBADOS AIRPORT Grantley Adams International Airport (BGI). ☎ *246/536–1300* ⊕ *www.gaia.bb.*

SAINT LUCIA AIRPORTS George F. L. Charles Airport (SLU). ☎ *758/457–6149* ⊕ *www.georgeflcharlesairport.com.* **Hewanorra International Airport (UVF).** ☎ *758/457–6160* ⊕ *www.hewanorrainternationalairport.com.* **St. Lucia Helicopters.** ✉ *Sunny Acres, George F. L. Charles Airport, Vigie* ☎ *758/453–6950* ⊕ *www.stluciahelicopters.com.*

Boat and Ferry

SAINT LUCIA FERRY CONTACTS Feel Good Water Taxi & Tours. ✉ *14 Victoria St., Soufrière* ☎ *758/721–2174* ⊕ *www.feelgoodwatertaxiandtours.com.* **Israel King Water Taxi & Tours.** ✉ *Rodney Bay Marina, Rodney Bay* ☎ *758/717–3301* ⊕ *www.israelkingwater-taxi.com.* **L'Express des Iles.** ✉ *Castries Ferry Terminal* ☎ *758/456–5000* ⊕ *coxcoltd.com/lexpress-des-iles/.* **Solomon Water Taxi & Tours.** ✉ *Boulevard St., Soufrière* ☎ *758/725–8681* ⊕ *www.solomon-saintlucia.com.*

Car

BARBADOS CAR-RENTAL CONTACTS Coconut Car Rentals. ✉ *Dayrell's Rd., Rockley* ☎ *246/262–1115.* **Courtesy Rent-A-Car.** ✉ *Grantley Adams International Airport* ☎ *246/431–4160* ⊕ *www.courtesyrentalsbb.com.* **Drive-a-Matic Car Rentals.** ✉ *CWTS Complex, Lower Estate, Warrens* ☎ *246/434–8440, 800/581–8773* ⊕ *www.carhire.tv.*

SAINT LUCIA CAR-RENTAL CONTACTS Avis. ⊠ *Hewanorra International Airport, Vieux Fort* ☎ *758/454–6325, 758/452–2046 George F. L. Charles Airport* ⊕ *www.avis.com.* **Cool Breeze Jeep/Car Rental.** ☎ *758/459–7729* ⊕ *www.cool-breezecarrental.com.* **Cost Less Rent-a-Car.** ⊠ *Harmony Suites, Rodney Bay* ☎ *758/450–3416, 908/818–8506 in U.S.* ⊕ *www.costless-rentacar.com.* **Courtesy Car Rentals.** ☎ *758/452–8140, 315/519–7684 in U.S.* ⊕ *www.courtesycarrentals.com.* **Hertz.** ⊠ *Hewanorra International Airport, Vieux Fort* ☎ *758/454–9636* ⊕ *www.hertz.com.*

➕ Health

MEDICAL ASSISTANCE COMPANIES AirMed International. ☎ *800/356–2161, 205/443–4840* ⊕ *www.airmed.com.* **International SOS.** ☎ *+44/02087628008* ⊕ *www.internationalsos.com.*

MEDICAL-ONLY INSURERS International Medical Group. ☎ *866/2630669, 317/655–4500* ⊕ *www.imglobal.com.*

📍 Telephones

BARBADOS MOBILE PHONES Digicel. ⊠ *Williams Tower, Williams Industries Complex, 2nd fl.* ☎ *246/467–7000* ⊕ *www.digicelbarbados.com.* **FLOW.** ⊠ *Windsor Lodge, Government Hill, Bridgetown* ☎ *800/804–2994* ⊕ *discoverflow.co/barbados.*

SAINT LUCIA MOBILE PHONES Digicel. ☎ *758/728–3400* ⊕ *www.digicelgroup.com/lc/en.html.* **FLOW.** ☎ *800/804–2994* ⊕ *discoverflow.co/saint-lucia.*

📍 Visitor Information

BARBADOS TOURISM AUTHORITY Barbados Tourism Marketing, Inc. ⊠ *1 Barbados Pl., Warrens* ☎ *246/535–3700, 212/551–4350 in U.S.* ⊕ *www.visitbarbados.org.*

SAINT LUCIA TOURIST BOARD Saint Lucia Tourism Authority. ☎ *212/867–2950, 800/456–3984 in U.S., 758/458–7101* ⊕ *www.stlucia.org.*

On the Calendar

February

Holetown Festival, Barbados. The event commemorates the arrival of the first European settlers in 1627. ⊕ *www. holetownfestivalbarbados.org*

April

Barbados Reggae Festival. The island's biggest music festival celebrates with a week of live performances by local and international bands. ⊕ *thebarbadosreggaefestival.com*

St. Lucia Golf Open. This amateur tournament is held annually at the Sandals St. Lucia Golf & Country Club at Cap Estate.

May

Gospelfest, Barbados. This annual event features performances by gospel headliners from around the world. ⊕ *barbadosgospelfest.com*

June

Carnival, Saint Lucia. Held in Castries beginning in late June, the celebration culminates in two days of music, dancing, and parading in mid-July.

Crop Over, Barbados. This summer festival begins in June and ends on Kadooment Day (a national holiday) in August to mark the end of the sugarcane harvest; it's how Bajans do Carnival. ⊕ *www.barbadoscropoverfestival.com*

October

St. Lucia Billfishing Tournament. Anglers from far and wide attend this annual event. ⊕ *www.stlucia.org*

Creole Heritage Month, Saint Lucia. This month-long celebration culminates in Jounen Kwéyol Entenasyonnal (International Creole Day)—featuring Creole food, music, games, and folklore performances in Castries and other locales—on the last Sunday of the month.

November

Barbados Food & Rum Festival. In mid-November, the annual event attracts international chefs, wine experts, and local rum ambassadors. ⊕ *www.visitbarbados.org/food-and-rum-festival*

December

Atlantic Rally for Cruisers, Saint Lucia. The finish of the world's largest ocean-crossing race is marked by a week of festivities at Rodney Bay. ⊕ *www.worldcruising.com/arc/arcitinerary.aspx*

Chapter 3

BARBADOS

Updated by
Malou Morgan

👁 Sights   🍴 Restaurants   🛏 Hotels   🛍 Shopping   🍸 Nightlife

★★★★★   ★★★★★   ★★★★★   ★★★★★   ★★★★★

WELCOME TO BARBADOS

TOP REASONS TO GO

★ **Great Resorts:** They run the gamut—from unpretentious to ultraluxe.

★ **Great Golf:** Tee off at some of the best championship courses in the Caribbean.

★ **Restaurants Galore:** Great food ranges from street-party barbecue to world-class dining.

★ **Wide Range of Activities:** Land and water sports, historic sites, tropical gardens, and nightlife … there's always plenty to do.

★ **Welcoming Locals:** Bajans are friendly, welcoming, helpful, and hospitable. You'll like them; they'll like you.

1 Bridgetown and The Garrison. The bustling capital has a compact shopping area and a waterfront esplanade where you can dine and people watch.

2 South Coast. Broad, breezy beaches with powdery white, palm-dotted sands and reef-protected, crystal-clear waters.

3 St. Lawrence Gap. This section of the south coast has beachfront hotels and many places to shop, eat, and drink.

4 Oistins and the Surrounding South Point Area. The village of Oistins, just east of St. Lawrence Gap, is known for its Friday night Fish Fry. The island's southernmost points are marked by lighthouses and broad beaches.

5 Crane and the Southeast. Magnificent beaches and stunning views mark this remote, mainly residential area, where the Caribbean Sea meets the Atlantic Ocean.

6 Holetown and Vicinity. The center of the Platinum Coast area with luxurious resorts and mansions.

7 Speightstown. The north's commercial center has shops, informal restaurants, and many restored 19th-century buildings.

8 East Coast. There is no swimming, but the pounding Atlantic surf is a sight to behold, and there are some cozy inns.

9 Central Interior. The interior has botanical gardens, far-reaching views, and a rather amazing cave to explore.

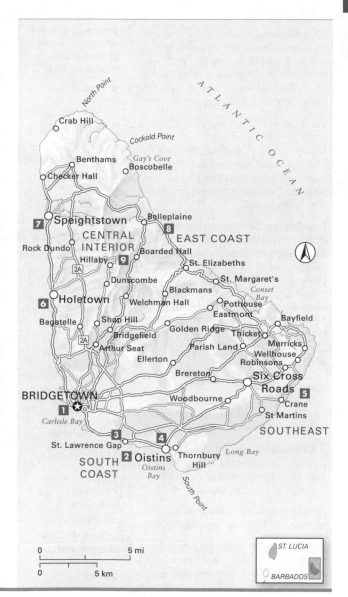

ATLANTIC OCEAN

North Point

Crab Hill

Cockold Point

Benthams
Checker Hall
Gay's Cove
Boscobelle

7 Speightstown
Belleplaine
8 EAST COAST

CENTRAL
INTERIOR

Rock Dundo
Boarded Hall
St. Elizabeths
2A
9
St. Margaret's
Conset Bay
Dunscombe
Blackmans
6 Holetown
Welchman Hall
Pothouse
Bagatelle
Eastmont
Bayfield
Shop Hill
Golden Ridge
Thicket
2A
Bridgefield
Parish Land
Merricks
Arthur Seat
Wellhouse
Ellerton
Robinsons
Brereton
Six Cross
Roads
5
BRIDGETOWN
Woodbourne
1
Crane
Carlisle Bay
St Martins
3
4
SOUTHEAST
St. Lawrence Gap
2 Oistins
Thornbury Hill
Long Bay
SOUTH
COAST
Oistins Bay
South Point

0   5 mi

0   5 km

ST. LUCIA

BARBADOS

ISLAND SNAPSHOT

WHEN TO GO

High Season: Mid-December through mid-April is the most popular time to visit as there's great weather and low humidity. Good hotels are often booked far in advance though, and some hotels require a meal plan during high season.

Value Season: From late April to July and again from November to mid-December, hotel prices drop 20% to 50% from high-season prices. Scattered showers are possible, but so are sun-kissed days and comfortable nights with fewer crowds.

Low Season: From August to late October, temperatures can become oppressively hot and the weather muggy, with a risk of tropical storms. Many upscale hotels close during September and October for annual renovations. Those remaining open offer deep discounts and do not usually require a meal plan.

WAYS TO SAVE

Head south. Compared to the west coast, the south coast (south of Bridgetown) has more affordable options for lodging, restaurants, and nightlife.

Take buses. Buses are an inexpensive way to explore Barbados, especially between Bridgetown and stops along the west and south coasts.

Hit the beach. All of the island's beaches are free and open to the public.

Eat like a local. Fare found in rum shops, roadside vans, and food trucks is delicious and very reasonably priced.

AT A GLANCE

■ **Currency:** Barbados dollar; pegged to the U.S. dollar at Bds$1.98 to US$1

■ **Money:** ATMs common; credit cards and U.S. dollars (no coins) are widely accepted

■ **Language:** English

■ **Country Code:** ☎ 1 246

■ **Emergencies:** ☎ 211

■ **Driving:** On the left

■ **Electricity:** 110v/50 cycles; plugs are U.S. standard two- and three-prong

■ **Time:** Same as New York during daylight saving time; one hour ahead otherwise

■ **Documents:** Visit up to six months with a valid passport and return ticket

■ **Major Mobile Companies:** Digicel, Flow (Cable & Wireless)

■ **Barbados Tourism Authority:** ⊕ www.visitbarbados.org

Isolated in the Atlantic Ocean, 100 miles (161 km) due east of Saint Lucia, Barbados stands apart from its neighbors in the Lesser Antilles archipelago, the chain of islands that stretches in a graceful arc from the Virgin Islands to Trinidad. It's a sophisticated tropical island with a rich history, lodgings to suit every taste and pocketbook, and plenty to pique your interest both day and night.

The island's name, which means "bearded one," was given to it by the Portuguese who encountered a large number of bearded fig trees when they visited some centuries ago. An unusual name isn't the only thing that separates this island from others in the region. In terms of location, Barbados is completely surrounded by the Atlantic Ocean and is not touched by the Caribbean Sea at all. In terms of geology, instead of being the peak of a volcanic mountain range, Barbados is the top of a single, relatively flat protuberance of coral and limestone.

Many Bajans (*Bay*-juns, derived from the phonetic British pronunciation of Barbadian) live and work in and around Bridgetown, the capital city, which is situated on the southwest coast of the pear-shape island and is, along with its surrounding Garrison, a UNESCO World Heritage Site. In this region, broad sandy beaches, craggy cliffs, and numerous coves make up the coastline; the interior is consumed by forested hills and gullies and acre upon acre of sugarcane.

In contrast to the turbulent colonial past experienced by neighboring islands, which included repeated conflicts between France and Britain for dominance and control, British rule in Barbados carried on uninterrupted for 340 years, with the first settlement established in 1627. That's not to say, of course, that there weren't significant struggles in Barbados, as elsewhere in the Caribbean, between the British landowners and their African-born enslaved people and indentured servants.

Although Barbados achieved universal voting rights in 1943 and opted for full independence from the United Kingdom in 1966,

British influence remains strong today in terms of local manners, attitudes, sports, customs, and politics. It's all tempered, of course, by the characteristically warm nature of the Bajan people. What's more, African and North American influences here have resulted in a truly Caribbean cocktail of arts, culture, language, and identity.

Visitor amenities are concentrated on the west coast, in St. James and St. Peter parishes (appropriately dubbed the Platinum Coast), and the south coast, in Christ Church Parish. Along the west coast—toward historic Holetown, site of the first British settlement, and north to the quaint "city" of Speightstown—are luxury beachfront resorts, luxurious private villas, and fine restaurants—all enveloped by lush gardens and tropical foliage. The trendier, more commercial south coast offers competitively priced hotels and beach resorts, and its St. Lawrence Gap area is jam-packed with restaurants and nightlife. The relatively wide-open spaces along the southeast coast are proving ripe for development, with some wonderful inns and hotels already taking advantage of the intoxicating ocean vistas. For their own vacations, though, Bajans escape to the rugged east coast, where the Atlantic surf pounds the dramatic shoreline with unrelenting force.

Barbadians are a warm, friendly, and hospitable people who are genuinely proud of their country and culture. Although tourism is the island's number one industry, the island has a sophisticated business community and stable government; so life here doesn't skip a beat once vacationers head home or cruise passengers return to their ship. That said, your heart may skip a beat when you think about your wonderful time on Barbados.

MAJOR REGIONS

The terrain changes dramatically from each of the island's 11 parishes to the next, and so does the pace. **Bridgetown,** the capital, is a small but busy Caribbean city in St. Michael Parish. Just south of Bridgetown is the **Garrison Historic District,** which became a UNESCO World Heritage Site in 2011.

On the lively **South Coast,** the daytime hustle and bustle produce a palpable energy that continues well into the night at restaurants and nightspots. Stretching along Highway 7 from The Garrison are the bustling commercial areas of **Hastings, Rockley,** and **Worthing.** This area, including **St. Lawrence Gap,** is chockablock with condos, high- and low-rise hotels, and beach parks. It also has many places to eat, drink, shop, and party. **Oistins,** just east of St. Lawrence Gap, is one of the island's four major towns (along

Crop Over, one of the Caribbean's most popular celebrations, takes place in Barbados May through August.

with Bridgetown, Holetown, and Speightstown) and the only "town" on the south coast. It's known for its Friday night Fish Fry. **Crane** marks the beginning of the island's southeast coast, which extends as far as Ragged Point.

The **West Coast** extends from just north of Bridgetown, through St. James Parish and the city of **Holetown,** to **Speightstown** in St. Peter Parish. Gentle Caribbean waves lap the coastline, and leafy mahogany trees shade its stunning coves and sandy beaches. Elegant homes and luxury hotels face much of the waterfront property in this area, dubbed Barbados's "Platinum Coast," which is a contrast to the small villages and vast sugar plantations found throughout the **Central Interior** that reflect the island's history.

On the dramatic **East Coast,** the crashing Atlantic surf has eroded the shoreline, forming steep cliffs and exposing prehistoric rocks that look like giant mushrooms. **Bathsheba and Cattlewash** in St. Joseph Parish are favorite seacoast destinations for local folks on weekends and holidays. Farther north in St. Andrew Parish, **Farley Hill** is about halfway between the tiny fishing towns along the island's northwestern coast and the sweeping views out over the Atlantic. Part of the St. Nicholas Abbey plantation, **Cherry Tree Hill** was named for the large number of cherry trees that once stood here.

Planning

Getting Here and Around

The terrain changes dramatically from each of the island's 11 parishes to the next, and so does the pace. Bridgetown, the capital, is a small Caribbean city. West-coast resorts and private estates ooze luxury, whereas the small village rum shops and churches found throughout central Barbados reflect the island's history. The relentless Atlantic surf shaped the cliffs of the dramatic east coast, and the northeast is called the Scotland District because of its hilly landscape and broad vistas. Along the lively south coast, the daytime hustle and bustle produce a palpable energy that continues well into the night at countless restaurants, dance clubs, and nightspots.

AIR

Several airlines fly nonstop to Barbados, or you may have to connect in Miami. Grantley Adams International Airport (BGI) is in Christ Church Parish on the south coast; the airport is about 15 minutes from hotels situated along the south coast, 45 minutes from the west coast, and 30 minutes from Bridgetown.

Ground transportation is available immediately outside the customs area. Airport taxis aren't metered, but fares are regulated. A chart shows pricing to various areas in the island, but be sure to establish the fare before getting into the taxi and confirm whether the price quoted is in U.S. or Barbadian dollars. You can also pick up your rental car at the airport.

CAR

You may want to rent a car if you are staying in an isolated area, although bus service is good—especially between Bridgetown and stops along the west and south coasts. Taxis are on call 24 hours a day and may suffice for visitors staying anywhere on the island. There are also a number of local taxi apps such as PickUp. ⇨ *For more information on car travel in Barbados and car rentals, see Car Travel in Travel Smart.*

If you're staying on the remote southeast or east coasts, you may want to rent a car for your entire stay. In more populated areas, where taxis and public transportation are readily available, you might rent a car for a day or two of exploring on your own. Rates start at about $100 per day during the high season.

Essentials

BEACHES

Geologically, Barbados is a coral-and-limestone island (not volcanic) with few rivers and, as a result, beautiful beaches. The southern and western coastlines tend to have calmer stretches, with clear waters that are perfect for swimming and snorkeling. The east and north coasts are more dramatic, with cliffs and large waves; perfect for surfing, but dangerous for swimming.

Across the island, when the surf is too high and swimming becomes dangerous, a red flag will be hoisted on the beach. A yellow flag—or a red flag at half-staff—means swim with caution. Topless sunbathing is not allowed anywhere in Barbados.

HEALTH AND SAFETY

Dengue, chikungunya, and zika have all been reported throughout the Caribbean. We recommend that you protect yourself from these mosquito-borne illnesses by keeping your skin covered and/or wearing mosquito repellent. The mosquitoes that transmit these viruses are as active by day as they are by night.

Crime isn't a major problem in Barbados, but take normal pre-cautions. Lock your room, and don't leave valuables—particularly passports, tickets, and wallets—in plain sight or unattended on the beach. Use your hotel safe. For personal safety, avoid walking on the beach or on unlighted streets at night. Lock your rental car, and don't pick up hitchhikers. Using or trafficking in illegal drugs is strictly prohibited in Barbados. Any offense is punishable by a hefty fine, imprisonment, or both.

HOTELS

Great resorts run the gamut—from unpretentious to knock-your-socks-off—in terms of size, intimacy, amenities, and price. Many are well suited to families. People stay either in luxurious enclaves on the fashionable west coast—north of Bridgetown—or on the action-packed south coast with easy access to small, independ-ent restaurants, bars, and nightclubs. On the west coast, the beachfront resorts in St. Peter and St. James parishes are mostly luxurious, self-contained enclaves. Highway 1, a two-lane road with considerable traffic, runs past these resorts, which can make strolling to a nearby bar or restaurant a bit difficult. Along the south coast in Christ Church Parish, many hotels are clustered near the busy strip known as St. Lawrence Gap, convenient to small restaurants, bars, and nightclubs. A few hotels and private villas on the remote southeast and east coasts offer oceanfront views and get-away-from-it-all tranquillity.

Some wonderful, cozy inns are located in the east and southeast regions of the island.

In keeping with the smoke-free policy enforced throughout Barbados, smoking is restricted to open outdoor areas such as the beach. It is not permitted in hotels (neither rooms nor public areas such as the pool) or in restaurants.

Prices in Barbados may betwice as high in season (December 15–April 15) than in the quieter months. Most hotels include no meals in their rates, but some include breakfast; most offer optional meal plans. A few may require you to purchase a meal plan in the high season. Several offer all-inclusive packages.

Hotel reviews have been shortened. For full information, visit Fodors.com.

Families and long-term visitors may choose from a wide variety of condos (everything from busy time-share resorts to more sedate vacation complexes). Villas and villa complexes can be luxurious, simple, or something in between. There are also a wide range of booking platforms available, including Airbnb.

Local real-estate agencies will arrange vacation rentals of privately owned villas and condos along the west coast in St. James and St. Peter. All villas and condos are fully furnished and equipped, including appropriate staff depending on the size of the villa or unit—which can range from one to eight bedrooms; the staff usually works six days a week. Most villas have TVs and other entertainment devices; all properties have telephones and Internet access. International telephone calls are usually blocked; plan on using your own mobile phone or a phone card. Vehicles generally are not included in the rates, but rental cars can be arranged for and delivered to the villa upon request. Linens and basic supplies (such as bath soap, toilet tissue, and dishwashing detergent) are normally included.

Units with one to six bedrooms and as many baths run $200 to $2,500 per night in summer and double that in winter. Rates include utilities and government taxes. The only additional cost is for groceries, staff gratuities, and extraordinary or optional requests. A security deposit is required upon booking and refunded seven days after departure less any damages or unpaid miscellaneous charges.

Apartments are available for vacation rentals in buildings or complexes that can have as few as three or four units or as many as 30 to 40 units—or even more. Prices range from $30 to $300 per night.

VILLA RENTAL CONTACTS Altman Real Estate. ✉ Hwy. 1, Derricks, Durants ☎ 246/432–0840, 866/360–5292 in U.S. ⊕ www.altmanbarbados.com. **Blue Sky Luxury.** ✉ Newton House, Hwy. 1B, Little Battaleys ☎ 246/622–4466, 866/404–9600 in U.S. ⊕ www.blueskyluxury.com. **Island Villas.** ✉ Trents Bldg., Holetown ☎ 246/432–4627, 866/978–8499 in U.S. ⊕ www.island-villas.com.

What It Costs in U.S. Dollars

	$	$$	$$$	$$$$
RESTAURANTS				
	under $13	$13–$20	$21–$30	over $30
HOTELS				
	under $275	$275–$375	$376–$475	over $475

RESTAURANTS

First-class restaurants and hotel dining rooms serve quite sophisticated cuisine—often prepared by chefs with international experience and rivaling the dishes served in the world's best restaurants. Most menus include seafood: dolphin—the fish, not the mammal, and also called dorado or mahi-mahi—kingfish, snapper, and flying fish prepared every way imaginable. Flying fish is so popular that it has officially become a national symbol. Shellfish also abounds, as do steak, pork, chicken, and local black-belly lamb.

Local specialty dishes include *buljol* (a cold salad of pickled codfish, tomatoes, onions, sweet peppers, and celery) and *conkies* (cornmeal, coconut, pumpkin, raisins, sweet potatoes, and spices, mixed together, wrapped in a banana leaf, and steamed). *Breadfruit cou cou*, often served with steamed flying fish, is a mixture of breadfruit and okra, usually topped with a spicy Creole sauce made from tomatoes, onions, and sweet peppers. Bajan-style pepperpot is a hearty stew of oxtail, beef, and other meats in a rich, spicy gravy and simmered overnight.

For lunch, restaurants often offer a traditional Bajan buffet of fried fish, baked chicken, salads, macaroni pie (macaroni and cheese), and a selection of steamed or stewed provisions (local root vegetables). Be cautious with the West Indian condiments—like the sun, they're hotter than you think. Typical Bajan drinks—in addition to Banks Beer and Mount Gay and Cockspur rum—are *falernum* (a liqueur concocted of rum, sugar, lime juice, and almond essence) and *mauby* (a nonalcoholic drink made by boiling bitter bark and spices, straining the mixture, and sweetening it). You're sure to enjoy the fresh fruit, sorrel, and rum punch, as well.

What to Wear: The dress code for dinner in Barbados is conservative, casually elegant, and, occasionally, formal—a jacket and tie for gentlemen and a cocktail dress for ladies only in the fanciest restaurants and hotel dining rooms, particularly during the winter holiday season. Jeans, shorts, and T-shirts (either sleeveless or with slogans) are always frowned upon at dinner. Beach attire is appropriate only at the beach.

NIGHTLIFE

When the sun goes down, the people come out to "lime" (which can mean anything from a casual chat to a full-blown "jump-up" or street party). Performances by world-renowned stars and regional groups are major events; and tickets can be hard to come by—but give it a try. Most resorts have nightly entertainment in season, and nightclubs often have live bands for listening and dancing. The busiest bars and dance clubs rage until 3 am. On Saturday night some clubs—especially those with live music—charge a cover of $15 or more.

Barbados supports the rum industry with more than 1,600 "rum shops," simple bars where (mostly) men congregate to discuss the world or life in general, drink rum, eat a cutter (sandwich), and play dominoes. In more sophisticated establishments you can find upscale rum cocktails made with the island's renowned local rum brands—and no shortage of Barbados's own Banks Beer or craft brews.

One of the most long-lasting souvenirs to bring home from Barbados is a piece of authentic Caribbean art. The colorful flowers, quaint villages, mesmerizing seascapes, and fascinating cultural experiences and activities that are endemic to the region and familiar to visitors have been translated by local artists onto canvas and into photographs, sculpture, and other mediums. Gift shops and even some restaurants display local artwork for sale, but the broadest array of artwork will be found in a gallery. Typical crafts include pottery, shell and glass art, wood carvings, handmade dolls, watercolors, and other artwork (both originals and prints).

Although many of the private homes, great houses, and museums in Barbados are filled with priceless antiques, you'll find few for sale—mainly British antiques and some local pieces, particularly mahogany furniture. Look especially for planters' chairs and the classic Barbadian rocking chair, as well as old prints and paintings.

Duty-free luxury goods—china, crystal, cameras, porcelain, leather items, electronics, jewelry, perfume, and clothing—are found in Bridgetown's Broad Street department stores and their branches, at the high-end Limegrove Lifestyle Centre in Holetown, at the Bridgetown Cruise Terminal (for passengers only), and in the departure lounge at Grantley Adams International Airport. Prices are often 30% to 40% less than full retail. To buy goods at duty-free prices, you must produce your passport, immigration form, or driver's license, along with departure information (such as flight number and date) at the time of purchase—or you can have your purchases delivered free to the airport or harbor for pickup. Duty-free alcohol, tobacco products, and some electronic equipment *must* be delivered to you at the airport or harbor.

If you've chosen self-catering lodgings, are looking for snacks, or just want to explore a local grocery store, you'll find large, modern supermarkets at Sunset Crest in Holetown on the west coast; in Oistins, at Sargeant's Village (Sheraton Mall), and in Worthing on the south coast; and at Warrens (Highway 2, north of Bridgetown) in St. Michael. Don't be shocked by the prices: Barbados imports most food. Local, more affordable options include Cheapside Market (located in Bridgetown) and roadside vendors. Local meat can be purchased from Carmita's, and fish can be bought at the Bridgetown and Oistins fish markets.

TOURS

Taxi drivers will give you a personalized tour of Barbados for about $35 to $40 per hour for up to three people. Or you can choose an overland mountain-bike journey, a 4x4 safari expedition, or a full-day bus excursion. The prices vary according to the mode of travel and the number and kind of attractions included. Ask guest services at your hotel to help you make arrangements.

Eco Adventures

GUIDED TOURS | This tour company proudly declares that they offers tours by Bajans. The 5½ hour Freedom Footprints tour explains the real story of Barbados and takes guests to interesting historical places like the Newton Slave Burial Ground, the only known burial ground in the Western Hemisphere for the enslaved on a plantation, the free villages of Bourne's Land and Sweet Bottom, and the Barbados museum. A full traditional Bajan lunch is included. ⊕ *www.ecoadventuresbarbados.com.*

Island Safari

TOUR—SPORTS | **FAMILY** | Discover all the popular attractions and scenic locations via a 4x4 jeep—including some gullies, forests, and remote areas that are inaccessible by conventional cars and buses. A full-day tour (5½ hours) includes snacks or lunch. You can also arrange your own private safari (three to six hours). ⊠ *CWTS Complex, Salters Rd., Lower Estate* ☎ *246/429–5337* ⊕ *www. islandsafari.bb* 🖃 *From $98*.

SunTours Barbados

TOUR—SPORTS | FAMILY | Whether you want to take a full-day island tour, concentrate on historic sites, focus on photography, or go as you please, SunTours is happy to accommodate your interests. Options range from a half-day tour of Bridgetown and The Garrison to a full-day island tour (including lunch and entrance fees)—or you can pay by the hour for a personalized adventure for up to four people. Vehicles vary depending on the group; the fleet includes comfortable passenger cars and SUVs, luxury cars and limos, minivans (with or without a wheelchair lift), and large tour buses. ⊠ *CWTS Complex, Hwy. 4B, Lower Estate* ☎ *246/434– 8430* 🖃 *From $35*.

WEDDINGS

There are no minimum residency requirements to get married; however, you both need to obtain a marriage license, in person, from the Ministry of Home Affairs (☎ *246/621–0227*). All fees must be paid in cash. Fees vary greatly; it's best to get in touch with a local wedding planner or your hotel for specifics. If either party is divorced or widowed, appropriate paperwork must be presented to obtain the license.

WHEN TO GO

Barbados is busiest in the high season, which extends from December 15 through April 15. Off-season hotel rates can be half of those required during the busy period. During the high season, too, a few hotels may require you to buy a meal plan, which is usually not required in the low season. As noted in the listings, some hotels close in September and October, the slowest months of the off-season, for annual renovations. Some restaurants may close for brief periods within that time frame as well.

Bridgetown and The Garrison

This bustling capital city, inscribed in 2011—along with the Garrison Historic Site—onto the UNESCO World Heritage List, is a duty-free port with a compact shopping area. The principal thoroughfare is Broad Street, which leads west from National Heroes Square. Downtown Bridgetown is easily walkable, whether you're interested in visiting historical sites, duty-free shopping, or simply having lunch and people-watching along The Careenage.

GETTING HERE AND AROUND

Several hotels offer a free shuttle service that takes guests to and from downtown Bridgetown (Monday through Saturday during business hours), and it's a short walk or quick taxi ride from the cruise sShip terminal. For sites and experiences located beyond the city center, you'll need to drive or take a taxi or bus.

Sights

The busy capital city is a duty-free port with a compact shopping area. The principal thoroughfare is Broad Street, which leads west from National Heroes Square. Both Bridgetown and its Garrison Historic District became a UNESCO World Heritage Site in 2011. Starting in 1705 with St. Ann's Fort and established in 1780 as the military headquarters of the British forces station in Barbados, the area is now home to the Barbados Defence Force and Coast Guard. Several important historic buildings surround or are nearby Garrison Savannah, a broad grassy field that features a horse-racing track.

Barbados Military Cemetery

CEMETERY | The cemetery, also referred to as Gravesend or Garrison Military Cemetery, is near the shore behind historic St. Ann's Fort. First used in 1780, when the area was pretty much marshland, the dead were placed in shallow graves or simply left on top of the ground where, within a few short days, many were absorbed into the swamp. In the early 20th century, a number of the remaining graves were dug up to provide room for oil storage tanks; salvaged headstones were placed on a cenotaph, erected in 1920–24. A "Cross of Sacrifice" was erected in 1982 to honor all the military dead; a second cenotaph, erected in 2003, honors the Barbadian merchant seamen who died in World War II. ⊠ *Needham's Point, Carlisle Bay, Garrison* ⊕ *Behind Hilton Barbados Resort* ☎ *246/536–2021* ⊠ *Free.*

★ Barbados Museum & Historical Society

LIBRARY | FAMILY | The galleries of this museum, established in 1933 and located in Barbados's UNESCO World Heritage Site, are housed in a 19th-century military prison building. More than 5,000 artifacts—dating from prehistoric times through the 21st century—tell the story of the people of Barbados, revealing the island's rich history, culture, and heritage. The on-site Shilstone Memorial Library is home to rare West Indian materials, archival documents, photographs, hard-to-find books, and maps dating from the 17th century. The entry fee varies; call ahead to confirm. ⊠ *St. Ann's Garrison, Hwy. 7, Garrison* ☎ *246/538–0201.*

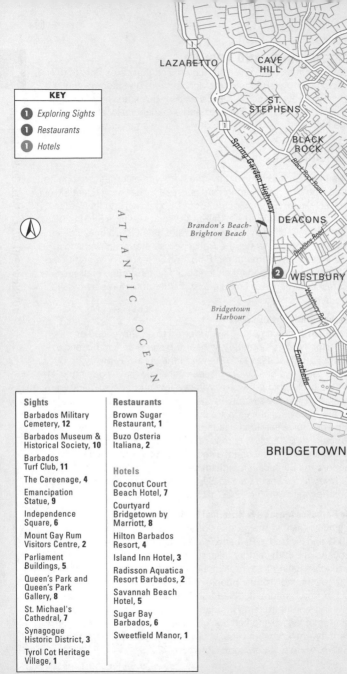

KEY

1 *Exploring Sights*

1 *Restaurants*

1 *Hotels*

LAZARETTO

CAVE HILL

ST. STEPHENS

BLACK ROCK

Spring Garden Highway

Black Rock Road

DEACONS

Deacons Road

Brandon's Beach-
Brighton Beach

A T L A N T I C   O C E A N

2 WESTBURY

Westbury Rd.

Bridgetown
Harbour

Fontabelle

Tudor St.

BRIDGETOWN

4

Sights

Barbados Military
Cemetery, **12**

Barbados Museum &
Historical Society, **10**

Barbados
Turf Club, **11**

The Careenage, **4**

Emancipation
Statue, **9**

Independence
Square, **6**

Mount Gay Rum
Visitors Centre, **2**

Parliament
Buildings, **5**

Queen's Park and
Queen's Park
Gallery, **8**

St. Michael's
Cathedral, **7**

Synagogue
Historic District, **3**

Tyrol Cot Heritage
Village, **1**

Restaurants

Brown Sugar
Restaurant, **1**

Buzo Osteria
Italiana, **2**

Hotels

Coconut Court
Beach Hotel, **7**

Courtyard
Bridgetown by
Marriott, **8**

Hilton Barbados
Resort, **4**

Island Inn Hotel, **3**

Radisson Aquatica
Resort Barbados, **2**

Savannah Beach
Hotel, **5**

Sugar Bay
Barbados, **6**

Sweetfield Manor, **1**

Bridgetown and The Garrison

GREEN HILL

WHITE HALL

GRAZETTES

①

WATERFORD

NEILS

TUDOR BRIDGE

EAGLE HALL

BUSH HALL

BANK HALL

BELMONT

TICHBOURNE

My Lords Hill

IVY

⑨

WEYMOUTH

②
③
⑤ ⑦ ⑧
⑥

BELLEVILLE

Government Hill

Pine Hill Rd.

Pine East West Blvd.

THE PINE

Gallymore Rock Rd.

WILDEY

BAYVILLE

BRITTONS HILL

⑥

Pebbles Beach

Beckles Road

Carlisle Bay

①②
③
④ ⑫

①
⑩

DALKEITH

⑪

Dayrells Rd.

RENDEZVOUS

Golf Club Road

⑤
⑥ ⑦

⑧②

HASTINGS

Hastings Rd.

ROCKLEY

0   1/2 mi

0   1/2 km

Accra Beach (Rockley Beach)

⑦

St. Lawrence Gap

White Hall Main Rd.

Errol Barrow Highway

Bank Hall Rd.

Bank Hall Cross Rd.

Belleville Road

Brittons Cross Rd.

Brittons New Rd.

Bay St.

Garrison Rd.

Dalkeith Rd.

Rendezvous Road

Barbados Turf Club

SPORTS—SIGHT | FAMILY | Horse racing is a big part of Bajan culture, and "going to the races" is an event for everyone. The races are administered by the Barbados Turf Club. Races take place on alternate Saturdays throughout the year at the Garrison Savannah, a 6-furlong grass oval in Christ Church, about 3 miles (5 km) south of Bridgetown. There is also occasional night racing. Important events include the Sandy Lane Barbados Gold Cup, held in late February or early March, and the Boxing Day Races on December 26. You can watch for free on the grounds, or pay for tickets, which vary in price according to where you sit—the dress-to-the-nines boxes, the members lounge, or the grandstands (grabbing a seat up close on the grounds with a picnic is also an option). Regardless of where you sit, you can't help but get caught up in the energy and excitement of the events. ⊠ *The Garrison Savannah, Garrison* ☎ *246/626–3980* ⊕ *www.barbadosturfclub.org* ⊠ *Entrance to grounds $10.*

The Careenage

HISTORIC SITE | In the early days, Bridgetown's natural harbor was where schooners were turned on their sides (careened) to be scraped of barnacles and repainted. Today, The Careenage serves as a marina for pleasure yachts and excursion boats, as well as a gathering place for locals and tourists alike. A boardwalk skirts the north side of The Careenage; on the south side, a lovely esplanade has pathways and benches for pedestrians and a statue of Errol Barrow, the first prime minister of Barbados. The Chamberlain Bridge and the Charles Duncan O'Neal Bridge span The Careenage. ⊠ *Bridgetown.*

Emancipation Statue

PUBLIC ART | This powerful statue of a slave—whose raised hands, with broken chains hanging from each wrist, evoke both contempt and victory—is commonly referred to as the Bussa Statue. Bussa was the man who, in 1816, led the first slave rebellion on Barbados. The work of Barbadian sculptor Karl Brodhagen, the statue was erected in 1985 to commemorate the emancipation of the slaves in 1834. ⊠ *St. Barnabas Roundabout, Haggatt Hall* ✛ *At intersection of ABC Hwy. and Hwy. 5.*

Independence Square

PLAZA | Located on the waterfront, this lovely, shaded spot is a great place to relax and take in the sights and sounds of Bridgetown, while you enjoy the view of the parliament buildings and National Heroes Square across the water. Note the statue of the island's first prime minister, the late Errol Walton Barrow, affectionately known as the "Father of Independence." ■**TIP→ Don't miss**

The Sandy Lane Gold Cup is held annually at the Barbados Turf Club.

the Independence Arch on the Chamberlain Bridge right next door.
⊠ *Fairchild St., Bridgetown.*

Mount Gay Rum Visitors Centre

WINERY/DISTILLERY | On this popular tour, you learn the colorful story behind the world's oldest rum—made in Barbados since 1703. Although the modern distillery is in St. Lucy Parish, in the far north, tour guides here explain the rum-making process. Equipment, both historic and modern, is on display, and rows and rows of barrels are stored in this location. Tours conclude with a tasting and the opportunity to buy duty-free rum and gifts—and even have lunch or cocktails (no children on cocktail tour), depending on the day. The lunch or cocktail tour includes transportation.
⊠ *Exmouth Gap, Brandons, Spring Garden Hwy., Bridgetown* ☎ *246/227–8864* ⊕ *www.mountgayrum.com* 🎟 *$20, $70 with cocktails, $75 with lunch* 🕑 *Closed Sun.*

Parliament Buildings

GOVERNMENT BUILDING | **FAMILY** | Overlooking National Heroes Square in the center of town, these Victorian buildings were constructed around 1870 to house the British Commonwealth's third-oldest parliament (after Britain itself and Bermuda). A series of stained-glass windows in the East Wing depicts British monarchs from James I to Victoria. The National Heroes Gallery & Museum of Parliament is in the West Wing. ⊠ *National Heroes Sq., Trafalgar St., Bridgetown* ☎ *246/310–5400* ⊕ *www.barbadosparliament.com* 🎟 *Museum $5* 🕑 *Closed Tues. and Sun.*

Where de Rum Come From

For more than 300 years (from 1655 through Black Tot Day, July 31, 1970), a daily "tot" of rum (2 ounces) was duly administered to each sailor in the British Navy as a health ration. At times rum has also played a less appetizing—but equally important—role. When Admiral Horatio Nelson died in 1805 aboard ship during the Battle of Trafalgar, his body was preserved in a cask of his favorite rum until he could be properly buried.

Most Caribbean islands have a locally made rum, but Barbados is truly "where de rum come from." Mount Gay, the world's oldest rum distillery, has continuously operated on Barbados since 1703, according to the original deed for the Mount Gay Estate, which itemized two stone windmills, a boiling house, seven copper pots, and a still house. The presence of rum-making equipment on the plantation at the time suggests that the previous owners were actually producing rum in Barbados long before 1703.

Today much of the island's interior is still planted with sugarcane and several historic sugar plantations are open to the public. But, to really fathom rum, you need to delve a little deeper than the bottom of a glass of rum punch. Mount Gay offers an interesting 45-minute tour of its main plant—followed by a tasting—where visitors learn about the rum-making process, hear rum-inspired anecdotes, and have an opportunity to buy the rum at duty-free prices.

Queen's Park and Queen's Park Gallery

ARTS VENUE | FAMILY | This national park is the site of beautiful gardens, a children's playground, a sports/events field, and one of the island's two immense baobab trees. Brought to Barbados from Guinea, West Africa, around 1738, this tree has a girth of more than 60 feet. Queen's Park House, built in 1783 and the historic home of the British troop commander, now houses the Daphne Joseph Hackett Theatre, which hosts special events and exhibits, and the Queen's Park Gallery, which features work by both emerging and established artists. ⊠ *Queen's Park, Constitution Rd., Bridgetown* ☎ *246/427–2345* ⊕ *www.ncf.bb/queens-park-gallery* ☜ *Free* ⊙ *Gallery closed Sun. and Mon.*

St. Michael's Cathedral

RELIGIOUS SITE | Although no one has proven it, George Washington is said to have worshipped here in 1751 during his only trip outside the United States. By then, the original structure was already nearly a century old. Destroyed or damaged twice by hurricanes,

Bridgetown is the capital and commercial center of Barbados.

the cathedral was rebuilt in 1789 and again in 1831. Officially called "Cathedral Church of Saint Michael and All Angels," it currently seats 1,600 people and boasts the largest pipe organ in the Caribbean. ⊠ *St. Michael's Row, Bridgetown* ✛ *East of National Heroes Sq.* ☎ *246/427–0790* ⊕ *saintmichaelscathedral.bb.*

★ Synagogue Historic District

CEMETERY | FAMILY | Providing for the spiritual needs of one of the oldest Jewish congregations in the western hemisphere, the Nidhe Israel Synagogue was formed by Sephardic Jews who arrived in 1628 from Brazil and introduced sugarcane to Barbados. The adjoining cemetery has tombstones dating from the 1630s. The original house of worship, built in 1654, was destroyed in an 1831 hurricane, rebuilt in 1833, and restored in 1986 with the assistance of the Barbados National Trust. The adjacent museum, opened in 2009 in a restored coral-stone building from 1750, documents the story of the Barbados Jewish community. A significant project in 2017 updated the grounds and restored artisans' workshops and other buildings on the newly designated Synagogue Historic Site. You can arrange an insightful, private tour of both the grounds and the museum. Friday-night services are held in winter months, but the building is open to the public year-round. Shorts are not acceptable during services but may be worn at other times. ⊠ *Synagogue La., Bridgetown* ☎ *246/436–6869* ⊕ *synagoguehistoricdistrict.com* ✉ *Synagogue free, museum $13* ⊙ *Closed weekends.*

Tyrol Cot Heritage Village

HOUSE | This coral-stone cottage just south of Bridgetown, constructed in 1854, is preserved as an example of period architecture. In 1929, it became the home of Sir Grantley Adams, the first premier of Barbados and the namesake of the island's international airport. Part of the Barbados National Trust, the cottage is filled with antiques and memorabilia that belonged to the late Sir Grantley and Lady Adams. Refreshments are available at the "rum shop." ⊠ *Codrington Hill, Bridgetown* ☎ *246/424–2074* ⊕ *www. barbadosnationaltrust.org* 🖼 *$5* ⊘ *Closed weekends.*

Beaches

Brandon's Beach–Brighton Beach

BEACH—SIGHT | **FAMILY** | Just north of downtown Bridgetown and within walking distance of the cruise ship terminal, the sea at this southernmost pair of west coast beaches is as calm as a lake. This is also one of the island's longest sandy stretches: you can easily walk from here all the way up to Batts Rock Beach. On hot days, particularly on weekends and holidays, you'll find locals taking a quick dip. Beach chairs and umbrellas are available for rent. **Amenities:** food and drink; lifeguard; parking (no fee); showers; toilets. **Best for:** swimming; walking. ⊠ *Spring Garden Hwy., Bridgetown.*

★ Pebbles Beach

BEACH—SIGHT | **FAMILY** | On the southern side of Carlisle Bay, just south of Bridgetown, this broad half circle of white sand is one of the island's best family-friendly beaches—and it can become crowded on weekends and holidays. The southern end of the beach wraps around the Hilton Barbados; the northern end is adjacent to the Radisson Aquatica Resort Barbados. Umbrellas and beach chairs are available to rent. Bring snorkel gear and swim out to see one of the shipwrecks. Arrive early in the morning (before 7 am) to watch race horses from Garrison Savannah taking a swim. **Amenities:** food and drink; parking; showers; toilets; water sports. **Best for:** snorkeling; swimming; walking. ⊠ *Aquatic Gap, Garrison* ⊹ *South of Bridgetown.*

🍴 Restaurants

★ Brown Sugar Restaurant

$$$ | **CARIBBEAN** | **FAMILY** | Set back from the road in a traditional Bajan home, the lattice-trimmed dining patios here are filled with ferns, flowers, and water features. Brown Sugar is a popular lunch spot for local businesspeople, who come for the nearly 30 delicious local and creole dishes spread out at the all-you-can-eat, four-course Planter's Buffet. **Known for:** Bajan buffet luncheon; kids under 5 eat free (under 10 are half price); steel pan entertainment at Sunday buffet. ⑤ *Average main: $30* ⊠ *Aquatic Gap, Garrison* ⊹ *Off Bay St.* ☎ *246/426–7684* ⊕ *www.brownsugarbarbados. net* ⊗ *No lunch Sat.*

Buzo Osteria Italiana

$$$$ | **ITALIAN** | **FAMILY** | Specialties at this lively, modern, air-conditioned restaurant include fresh pasta, thin-crust pizzas, colorful salads, and decadent desserts. Enjoy an aperitif, martini, or their specialty sorrel cocktail at the chic bar. **Known for:** consistently good service; variety of pizza toppings; extensive wine list. ⑤ *Average main: $40* ⊠ *The Pavillion, Hastings Main Rd., Worthing* ☎ *246/629–2896* ⊕ *buzorestaurant.com.*

Barbados's Fast-Food Chain 🍽

Chefette, a locally owned, family-run, fast-food chain, has 17 outlets throughout the island, primarily in Bridgetown, along the west and south coasts, and at the airport. Try the chicken breast sandwiches (barbecued, "broasted," or "krunched") and rotis (turnovers filled with meat and/or vegetables). Every month, the restaurant features different specials: favorites include "Wing Dings" (chicken wings) and "Tenders" (strips of chicken breast). Bajans love their chicken! All outlets have salads and veggie choices, nearly all sell pizza, and a couple have "BBQ Barns." Most have playgrounds and drive-through service.

Hotels

There are no hotels within Bridgetown, but hotels in the Garrison neighborhood are close enough if you want to be near to the capital.

Coconut Court Beach Hotel

$ | **HOTEL** | **FAMILY** | This family-run, modest but recently renovated hotel is popular among families, who love the activities room for kids, the kitchenettes, and the convenient beachfront location. **Pros:** safe swimming and snorkeling at the beautiful beach; free airport transfers and Bridgetown shopping shuttle; easy walk to The Garrison, South Coast Boardwalk, restaurants, shops. **Cons:** close to the road, so noise can be an issue; restricted views of the beach in "west wing" rooms; guests without kids might find it too busy. ⑤ *Rooms from: $252* ⊠ *Main Rd., Hastings* ☎ *246/427–1655, 888/506–0448 in U.S.* ⊕ *www.coconut-court. com* ⌖ *112 rooms* ⦿ *Free breakfast.*

Courtyard Bridgetown by Marriott

$$$ | **HOTEL** | Comfortable, contemporary, and convenient, this hotel is pleasant and the rooms are well appointed. **Pros:** excellent customer service; especially suited to business travelers (lobby is great for remote work); modern, attractive accommodations. **Cons:** walk to beach; comparatively little "Caribbean resort" atmosphere; limited on-site dining options. ⑤ *Rooms from: $401* ⊠ *Hwy. 7, Hastings Main Rd., Garrison* ✛ *Set back a block from road* ☎ *246/625–0000* ⊕ *www.marriott.com* ⤳ *118 rooms* ⑩ *No meals*.

Hilton Barbados Resort

$$$$ | **HOTEL** | **FAMILY** | Beautifully situated on the sandy Needham's Point peninsula, all 350 units in this high-rise resort hotel have private balconies overlooking either the ocean or Carlisle Bay; 77 rooms on executive floors offer a private lounge and concierge services. **Pros:** great location near town and on a beautiful beach; lots of services and amenities; accessible rooms available. **Cons:** service and communication should be better; huge group/convention hotel; lacks island ambience. ⑤ *Rooms from: $480* ⊠ *Aquatic Gap, Needham's Point, Garrison* ☎ *246/426–0200* ⊕ *www.hilton-barbadosresort.com* ⤳ *350 rooms* ⑩ *No meals*.

Island Inn Hotel

$$$ | **HOTEL** | Constructed in 1804 as a rum storage facility for the British Regiment, this quaint, all-inclusive boutique hotel—less than a mile from Bridgetown and steps away from beautiful Pebbles Beach on Carlisle Bay—appeals to singles, couples, and families. **Pros:** friendly, accommodating, attractive atmosphere; smartly decorated rooms; excellent all-inclusive value. **Cons:** small pool; rooms near the front may be noisier and don't have a patio; near but not directly on the beach. ⑤ *Rooms from: $435* ⊠ *Aquatic Gap, Garrison* ☎ *246/436–6393* ⊕ *www.islandinnbarbados.com* ⤳ *24 rooms* ⑩ *All-inclusive*.

Radisson Aquatica Resort Barbados

$$$ | **HOTEL** | Rooms in this high-rise hotel overlooking pretty Carlisle Bay, just south of Bridgetown, are modern and sleek with espresso-color furniture, sparkling white linens, desk with ergonomic chair, comfortable sitting chair and ottoman, 42-inch flat-screen TV, and the latest in-room technology. **Pros:** excellent beach; beautiful sunsets from ocean-facing rooms; convenient location. **Cons:** pool area could use more umbrellas; noisy air-conditioning, no room refrigerator; skip the restaurant and opt for neighboring Brown Sugar or the Hilton. ⑤ *Rooms from: $430* ⊠ *Aquatic Gap, Garrison* ☎ *246/426–4000, 800/333–3333 in U.S.* ⊕ *www.radisson.com/barbados* ⤳ *124 rooms* ⑩ *No meals*.

Savannah Beach Hotel

$ | **HOTEL** | **FAMILY** | Appealing to those who don't require fancy surroundings or organized entertainment, the Savannah is convenient for walks to The Garrison Historic Area, the Barbados Museum, and the racetrack—and minutes from Bridgetown by car or taxi. **Pros:** inviting pool; convenient to Bridgetown and nearby sites; complimentary cribs/infant beds. **Cons:** beach is somewhat rocky; few activities for kids other than the beach; nothing fancy. ⑤ *Rooms from: $239 ⊠ Hastings Main Rd., Hastings ☎ 246/434–3800 ⊕ www.savannahbarbados.com ⊶ 92 rooms ⦿ Free breakfast.*

Sugar Bay Barbados

$$$$ | **ALL-INCLUSIVE** | **FAMILY** | Tropical gardens and a dramatic water feature mask the proximity of the main road to this large, all-inclusive beachfront resort near the Garrison Historic Area. **Pros:** great swimming and snorkeling beach and close to Garrison sights; friendly, accommodating staff; sustainable practices. **Cons:** one pool is small and larger pool is often full of kids; limited access to specialty restaurants without a surcharge; dining and entertainment area gets congested. ⑤ *Rooms from: $500 ⊠ Hastings Main Rd., Hastings ☎ 246/622–1101 ⊕ www.sugarbaybarbados.com ⊶ 138 rooms ⦿ All-inclusive.*

★ Sweetfield Manor

$$ | **B&B/INN** | Perched on a ridge about a mile from downtown Bridgetown, this restored plantation house (circa 1900) was once the residence of the Dutch ambassador and is now a delightful bed-and-breakfast. **Pros:** peaceful enclave, primarily for adults; inviting pool and gardens; delicious gourmet breakfast. **Cons:** long walk (or short car ride) to beach; rental car advised; not recommended for young children. ⑤ *Rooms from: $300 ⊠ Brittons New Rd., Bridgetown ☎ 246/429–8356 ⊕ sweetfieldmanor.com ⊶ 10 rooms ⦿ Free breakfast.*

Nightlife

While Bridgetown has a couple of popular nightspots, Baxter's Road, just south of the city center, is sometimes called "The Street That Never Sleeps." Night owls head there any night of the week for after-hours fun and food. The strip of rum shops begins to hit its stride at 11 pm, but locals usually show up around 3 am. Street vendors sell freshly made "Baxter's Road" fried chicken and other snacks all night long, but Enid's is the place to see and be seen.

The Boatyard

BARS/PUBS | FAMILY | There's never a dull moment at this popular beachside bar—day or night. From happy hour until the wee hours, you can enjoy refreshing cocktails, beautiful sunsets, and lively music. There are also several offerings for children, including a rope swing into the sea and a trampoline in the water. ⊠ *Bay St., south of town, Carlisle Bay, Bridgetown* ☎ *246/436–2622* ⊕ *www. theboatyard.com.*

★ Copacabana Beach Club

GATHERING PLACES | FAMILY | This lively, family-friendly club—complete with beach chairs, bars, good food, and shower facilities—is on a beautiful, calm beach with excellent snorkeling spots. Lounge under an umbrella on the sand, cocktail in hand, or enjoy fresh fish tacos while watching a sports match on an indoor screen. This is also a venue for concerts and outdoor movie screenings during the Barbados Independent Film Festival. Day passes include use of amenities and act as credit that guests can redeem at the bar and restaurant. ⊠ *Bay St., Bridgetown* ☎ *246/622–1910* ⊕ *www.copacabanabb.com* ☑ *$20 Day Pass, which includes beach chair, shared umbrella, and $40 food and beverage credit.*

Harbour Lights

THEMED ENTERTAINMENT | This open-air, beachfront club claims to be the "home of the party animal." Wednesday, Friday, and Sunday nights (during high season) are the hottest, with dancing under the stars to reggae and soca music. On Monday and Wednesday evening, there's a family-friendly "cultural" dinner show on the beach, along with three live bands and a Bajan barbecue dinner, with drinks. ⊠ *Marine Villa, Bay St., Bridgetown* ⊹ *South of town, Carlisle Bay* ☎ *246/436–7225* ⊕ *www.harbourlightsbarbados.com.*

Shopping

Bridgetown's **Broad Street** is the primary downtown shopping area. **The Colonnade Mall,** in the historic Colonnade Building on Broad Street, has about 40 shops that sell everything from Piaget watches to postcards; across the street, **Mall 34** has more than 20 shops where you can buy duty-free goods, souvenirs, and snacks. At the **cruise ship terminal** shopping arcade, passengers can buy both duty-free goods and Barbadian-made crafts at more than 30 boutiques and a dozen vendor carts and stalls. Allow time before boarding your plane to shop in the **airport departure lounge,** which has a dozen or more shops that sell duty-free alcohol, souvenirs, clothing, and more.

A free Bridgetown shopping shuttle serves hotels on the south and west coasts, so guests can visit downtown shops, see the sights, and perhaps have lunch. The shuttle operates Monday through Saturday, departing from the hotels at 9:30 and 11 am and returning from Bridgetown at 1:30 and 3 pm. Reserve your seat with your hotel concierge a day ahead.

DEPARTMENT STORES
Cave Shepherd
DEPARTMENT STORES | The main store on Broad Street sells an array of clothing for men, women, and children; make-up and perfume; jewelry; and souvenirs and luxury goods at duty-free prices. Branches are at Holetown's Sunset Crest mall on the west coast and at the Vista shopping complex in Worthing and Sheraton Mall in Sargeants on the south coast; the airport departure lounge and cruise ship terminal each have a boutique. ⊠ *10–14 Broad St., Bridgetown* ☎ *246/629–4400* ⊕ *www.mycaveshepherd.com.*

DUTY-FREE GOODS
Diamonds International Barbados
DUTY-FREE | This duty free shop carries fine watches and jewelry fashioned in Italian gold, Caribbean silver, diamonds, and other gems. They also carry Cartier, Breitling, Bulgari, and Crown of Light. The main shop is on Broad Street, with branches at the Limegrove Lifestyle Centre and the cruise ship terminal. ⊠ *Lower Broad St., Bridgetown* ☎ *246/430–2412* ⊕ *www.diamondsinternationalbarbados.com.*

Little Switzerland
DUTY-FREE | This minichain's shop, where you can find perfume, jewelry, cameras, audio equipment, Swarovski and Waterford crystal, and Wedgwood china, is at The Colonnade Mall in Bridgetown. ⊠ *The Colonnade Mall, Broad St., Bridgetown* ☎ *246/431–0030* ⊕ *www.littleswitzerland.com.*

HANDICRAFTS
Brighton Farmers Market
OUTDOOR/FLEA/GREEN MARKETS | **FAMILY** | Every Saturday morning, hundreds of people (both expat and local) make their way to Brighton Farmers Market to explore the great selection of food items and crafts from a wide range of Barbadian producers and artisans. This is a family-friendly event, hosted on the grounds of Brighton plantation and farm between 6 am and 10 am. There is a playground and live music. ⊠ *Brighton Plantation, Brighton.*

South Coast

Hastings, Rockley, and Worthing are bustling commercial areas, one after the other, that stretch along Highway 7 from The Garrison Historic Area to St. Lawrence Gap along the south coast. You'll find a variety of hotels, restaurants, shops, and other businesses here, as well as the mile-long South Coast Boardwalk that's perfect for a morning run or an evening stroll; a public golf course (in Rockley); and beach after beach after beach.

Sights

DreadHop Brewing

WINERY/DISTILLERY | FAMILY | This family-owned and-managed micro-brewery burst onto the scene in 2013, much to the delight of beer enthusiasts bored with the regular local beers. DreadHop brewery offers nine varieties of beer on tap, from a double IPA to stout and summer ale. The breezy, lively tap room is a favorite among locals, families, and visiting brew enthusiasts, who enjoy a few pints over the weekend or at one of the popular weekly quiz nights. Bar food such as samosas, burgers, loaded fries, and roti are available. Pets are welcome but must remain outside. ⊠ *Brewery La., Gibbons Industrial Park, Gibbons, Oistins* ☎ *246/622–1225* ⊕ *www.caribbeanbrewhouse.com* ⊗ *Closed Sun.*

Harry Bayley Observatory

OBSERVATORY | FAMILY | Equipped with a 16-inch Meade telescope with the latest robotic controls and digital cameras and a new Lunt 80 mm solar telescope, this observatory lets you view the moon, stars, planets, comets, and other astronomical objects that aren't otherwise be visible from mainland North America or Europe. The Friday-evening programs (8–10 pm, weather permitting), which start with an informative presentation, are run by volunteers; call ahead to make sure it's open. The observatory has been the headquarters of the Barbados Astronomical Society since 1963. ⊠ *Observatory Rd., Clapham* ⊹ *Off Hwy. 6* ☎ *246/622–2000, 246/622–2000* ⊕ *www.hbo.bb* 🖾 *$13* ⊗ *Closed Sat.–Thurs.*

Beaches

A young, energetic crowd favors the south-coast beaches, which are broad and breezy, blessed with powdery white sand, and dotted with tall palms. The reef-protected areas with crystal-clear water are safe for swimming and snorkeling. The surf is medium to high, and the waves get bigger and the winds stronger (wind-surfers take note) the farther southeast you go.

Accra Beach (*Rockley Beach*)
BEACH—SIGHT | FAMILY | This
popular beach, adjacent to the
Accra Beach Hotel, has a broad
swath of white sand with
gentle surf and a lifeguard,
plenty of nearby restaurants for
refreshments, a playground,
and beach stalls for renting
chairs and equipment for snorkeling and other water sports.
The South Coast Boardwalk,
great for walking or running,
begins here and follows the
waterfront west—past private
homes, restaurants, and
bars—for about a mile (1½ km)
to Needham's Point. **Amenities:**
food and drink; lifeguards;
parking (no fee); water sports.
Best for: snorkeling; swimming;
walking. ⊠ *Hwy. 7, Rockley.*

The Dreaded Manchineel 👁

Large, leafy manchineel
trees grow along many of
the west-coast beaches.
Although they look like
perfect shade trees, just
touching a leaf or the bark
can cause nasty blisters.
And don't seek refuge
under the tree during a
rain shower, as even drips
from its leaves can affect
sensitive skin. The fruit of
the tree, which looks like
a tiny green apple, is toxic.
Most of the manchineels
are marked with signs or
with red bands painted on
the trunk. Why not just
cut them all down? Their
root systems are extremely
important for preventing
beach erosion.

🍴 Restaurants

★ Champers

$$$$ | CARIBBEAN | FAMILY | Chiryl Newman's snazzy seaside res-
taurant is in an old Bajan home just off the main road in Rockley.
The cliff-top setting overlooking the eastern end of Accra Beach
offers daytime diners—about 75% local businesspeople—a
panoramic view of the sea and a relaxing Caribbean atmosphere
in the evening. **Known for:** upscale, consistently good Caribbean
food; waterfront terrace or air-conditioned dining; on-site art
gallery. ⑤ *Average main: $35* ⊠ *Skeetes Hill, Rockley* ↔ *Off Hwy. 7*
☎ *246/434–3463* ⊕ *www.champersbarbados.com* ⊗ *No lunch Sat.*

Just Grillin'

$$ | CARIBBEAN | FAMILY | Locals and visitors alike gather at this
no-frills, fast-casual restaurant for affordable, relatively healthy,
and delicious local food. Simple dishes like grilled catch of the
day and grilled steak deliver the goods, but the barbecued ribs,
jerk chicken, and Caesar salad are excellent. **Known for:** affordable meals for the whole family; good portions; another location
in Holetown. ⑤ *Average main: $15* ⊠ *Quayside Centre, Rockley*
☎ *246/435–6469* ⊕ *www.justgrillinbarbados.com* ⊗ *Closed Sun.*

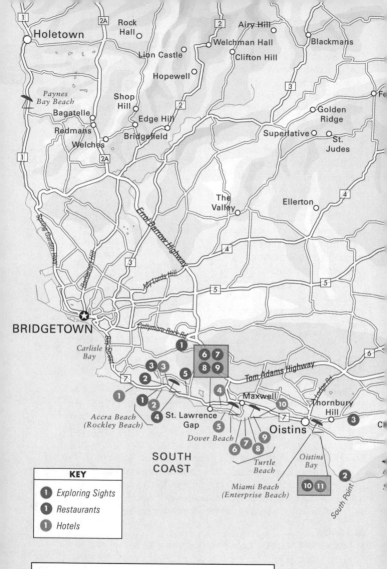

KEY

- 1 *Exploring Sights*
- 1 *Restaurants*
- 1 *Hotels*

South Coast, St. Lawrence Gap,
Oistins and the Surrounding
South Point Area,
and Crane and the Southeast

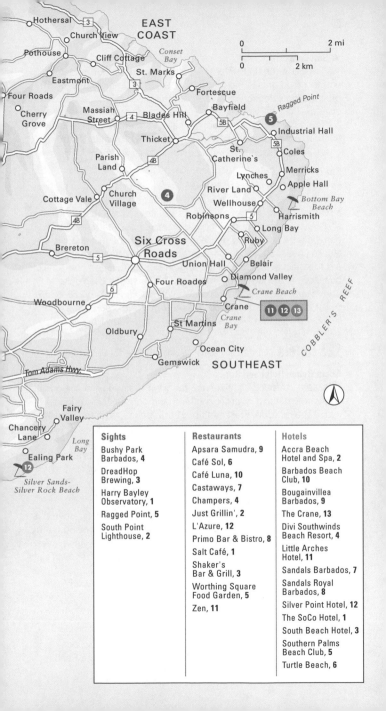

EAST COAST

Hothersal
Church View
Pothouse
Cliff Cottage
Eastmont
St. Marks
Conset Bay
Four Roads
Cherry Grove
Massiah Street
Blades Hill
Fortescue
Bayfield
Ragged Point
5
Industrial Hall
Thicket
St. Catherine's
Coles
Parish Land
Lynches
Merricks
Apple Hall
4
Church Village
River Land
Wellhouse
Bottom Bay Beach
Cottage Vale
Robinsons
Harrismith
Brereton
Six Cross Roads
Long Bay
Ruby
Union Hall
Belair
Four Roades
Diamond Valley
Crane Beach
Woodbourne
Crane
11 **12** **13**
Oldbury
St Martins
Crane Bay
Ocean City
Gemswick
SOUTHEAST
Tom Adams Hwy.
Fairy Valley
Chancery Lane
Long Bay
Ealing Park
12
Silver Sands–Silver Rock Beach

0   2 mi
0   2 km

COBBLER'S REEF

Sights

Bushy Park Barbados, **4**
DreadHop Brewing, **3**
Harry Bayley Observatory, **1**
Ragged Point, **5**
South Point Lighthouse, **2**

Restaurants

Apsara Samudra, **9**
Café Sol, **6**
Café Luna, **10**
Castaways, **7**
Champers, **4**
Just Grillin', **2**
L'Azure, **12**
Primo Bar & Bistro, **8**
Salt Café, **1**
Shaker's Bar & Grill, **3**
Worthing Square Food Garden, **5**
Zen, **11**

Hotels

Accra Beach Hotel and Spa, **2**
Barbados Beach Club, **10**
Bougainvillea Barbados, **9**
The Crane, **13**
Divi Southwinds Beach Resort, **4**
Little Arches Hotel, **11**
Sandals Barbados, **7**
Sandals Royal Barbados, **8**
Silver Point Hotel, **12**
The SoCo Hotel, **1**
South Beach Hotel, **3**
Southern Palms Beach Club, **5**
Turtle Beach, **6**

★ Salt Cafe

$$$ | **INTERNATIONAL** | **FAMILY** | If you're in the mood for modern comfort food, this is the place for you. Chef Simon and his team offer a wide selection of Asian-, Southern-, and Caribbean-inspired dishes—from barracuda baos, plantain tostadas, and fried pig ears to delicious deserts such as salted caramel brownie. **Known for:** fried pig ears; fresh fish; salted-caramel brownies. ⑤ *Average main: $25* ⊠ *Hastings Main Rd., Hastings* ☎ *246/537–7258.*

Shaker's Bar & Grill

$$ | **CARIBBEANCARIBBEAN** | **FAMILY** | Locals and visitors alike gather at this no-frills hangout for drinks—perhaps a Banks beer or two, a margarita, a pitcher of sangria, or whatever wets their whistle—and delicious local food. Simple dishes like beer-battered flying fish, grilled catch of the day, barbecued chicken, grilled steak, or a solid cheeseburger deliver the goods, but the barbecued ribs are the main event. **Known for:** finger-lickin' barbecued ribs; small, busy, convivial "rum shop" on a quiet side street; cash only. ⑤ *Average main: $17* ⊠ *Browne's Gap, Rockley* ☎ *246/228–8855* ⊕ *www.shakersbarbados.com/visit.html* ▭ *No credit cards* ⊗ *Closed Sun. and Mon. and mid-Aug.–mid-Sept. No lunch.*

 ## Hotels

Accra Beach Hotel and Spa

$ | **RESORT** | **FAMILY** | A full-service resort in the middle of the busy south coast, Accra is large, modern, and competitively priced—with a great beach. **Pros:** can't beat that beach; walk to shopping, restaurants, and nightspots; reasonable prices. **Cons:** "island view" rooms facing the street have an unattractive view and can be noisy; rooms need some TLC; customer service needs attention. ⑤ *Rooms from: $252* ⊠ *Hwy. 7, Rockley* ☎ *246/435–8920* ⊕ *www.accrabeachhotel.com* ⇆ *221 rooms* ⒪ *No meals.*

The SoCo Hotel

$$$$ | **HOTEL** | Sophisticated travelers, particularly couples, love this ultramodern, adults-only boutique hotel strategically poised on the beachfront in Hastings. **Pros:** all rooms have an ocean view; lovely beach with long boardwalk; convenient location. **Cons:** showers only, no tubs; mixed reviews on the food; morning road noise can be distracting. ⑤ *Rooms from: $700* ⊠ *Hastings Main Rd., Hastings* ☎ *246/537–7626* ⊕ *www.thesocohotel.com* ⇆ *24 rooms* ⒪ *All-inclusive.*

South Beach Hotel

$$ | **HOTEL** | **FAMILY** | You enter the sleek lobby of this cool condo-style hotel, across the street from spectacular Accra Beach, via a footbridge across a double-wide lap pool that runs the length of the property. **Pros:** near shopping, restaurants, and nightlife; Accra Beach is great for families; washer/dryer on every floor. **Cons:** beach is across the street; pool, while beautiful, is a shallow lap pool; more Miami Beach than Caribbean style. Ⓢ *Rooms from: $312* ✉ *Main Rd., Hwy. 7, Rockley* ⊕ *At Accra Beach* ☎ *246/435–8561, 888/964–0030 in U.S.* ⊕ *www.south-beachbarbados.com* 🛏 *49 suites* ❍ *Free breakfast.*

Nightlife

Bubba's Sports Bar

BARS/PUBS | FAMILY | During the day, this is a family-friendly restaurant. At night, merrymakers and sports lovers find live action on three 10-foot video screens and nearly two-dozen TVs, along with bar food and local Banks beer on tap. ✉ *Rockley Main Rd., Worthing* ☎ *246/435–8731* ⊕ *www.bubbassportsbar.net* ☞ *Closed Mon. and Tues.*

🛍 Shopping

In Rockley, Christ Church, **Quayside Shopping Center** houses a small group of boutiques, restaurants, and services.

Best of Barbados

CRAFTS | Best of Barbados showcases the works of artist Jill Walker, who founded the shops (along with her architect husband) in 1975. Their daughter is now in charge. Products range from her frameable prints, housewares, and textiles to arts and crafts in both native style and modern designs. Everything is made or designed on Barbados. Branch shops are at Chattel House Village in Holetown, at Southern Palms Resort in St. Lawrence Gap, at the cruise ship terminal, and in the airport departure lounge. ✉ *Quayside Centre, Main Rd., Rockley* ☎ *246/622–1761* ⊕ *www.best-of-barbados.com.*

St. Lawrence Gap

St. Lawrence Gap, a busy section of the island's South Coast, has several beachfront hotels and resorts and many places to eat, drink, shop, and party.

Beaches

Dover Beach

BEACH—SIGHT | **FAMILY** | All along the St. Lawrence Gap waterfront, Dover is one of the most popular beaches on the south coast. The sea is fairly calm, with small to medium waves, and the white-sand beach is broad and brilliant. The resorts of Divi Southwinds and Ocean Two, as well as several restaurants, are nearby. There's a small boardwalk, a promenade with a food court, water sports and beach chair rentals, and a playground. **Amenities**: food and drink; parking (no fee); toilets; water sports. **Best for**: snorkeling; swimming. ⊠ *Hwy. 7, Dover.*

Turtle Beach

BEACH—SIGHT | **FAMILY** | Stretching from Turtle Beach Resort and Sandals Barbados at the eastern end of St. Lawrence Gap to Bougainvillea Beach Resort on Maxwell Coast Road, this broad strand of powdery white sand is great for sunbathing, strolling, and—with low to medium surf—swimming and bodyboarding. This beach is a favorite nesting place for turtles, hence its name; if you're lucky, you may see hundreds of tiny hatchlings emerge from the sand and make their way to the sea. ■**TIP→ There's public access and parking on Maxwell Coast Road, near the Bougainvillea Beach Resort.** **Amenities**: food and drink; parking (no fee). **Best for**: swimming; walking. ⊠ *St. Lawrence Gap, Maxwell.*

 Restaurants

Apsara Samudra

$$$$ | **INDIAN** | This romantic Indian and Thai restaurant has a large outdoor terrace overlooking the ocean. You can dine under the stars, or escape to one of the air-conditioned rooms upstairs. **Known for:** romantic setting overlooking the sea; authentic North Indian and Thai dishes; gluten-free, vegan, and vegetarian options. ⑤ *Average main: $40* ⊠ *Waverely House, St. Lawrence Gap* ☎ *246/420–5454.*

Café Sol

$$ | **MEXICAN** | **FAMILY** | Have a hankerin' for Tex-Mex food? Enjoy nachos, tacos, burritos, empanadas, fajitas, and tostadas in

Nightspots Aplenty

On the south coast, St. Lawrence Gap and Worthing Square are popular nightlife destinations. Both have a number of bars and restaurants that host bands and special events throughout the year. Mojos is a notable favorite for live music, especially on Reggae Wednesdays. On the west coast, the restaurants and clubs on 1st and 2nd streets always have a crowd of partygoers. Along with a half dozen or so restaurants that offer fare ranging from ribs and pizza to elegant cuisine, a handful of nightspots and night "experiences" have cropped up recently, such as La Cabane. After-dinner drinks at the Mews or Red Door Lounge are popular any night, but on Sunday evenings, locals and tourists alike head to One Love Bar for the karaoke and to Ragamuffin's restaurant, next door, for the after-dinner drag show.

this Mexican bar and grill at the western entrance to busy St. Lawrence Gap. **Known for:** busy, boisterous, and fun; good service despite the crowded space; good, filling Mexican specialties—plus "gringo" favorites. ⑤ *Average main: $20* ⊠ *St. Lawrence Gap, Dover* ☎ *246/420–7655* ⊕ *www.cafesolbarbados.com* ⊘ *No lunch Mon.*

Castaways

$$$ | CARIBBEAN | Enjoy the breathtaking views overlooking St. Lawrence Bay—you may see sea turtles bobbing around in the shallow surf during the day—paired with a diverse menu and cocktail list. The reasonably priced menu caters to various diets and restrictions, featuring local dishes with fresh fish, as well as international dishes. **Known for:** perfect spot for sunset cocktails; early dinner locale before a night out in The Gap; Saturday lunch. ⑤ *Average main: $30* ⊠ *St. Lawrence Gap, Dover* ☎ *246/420–7587* ⊕ *www.castawaysbb.com* ⊘ *No lunch Sun.–Fri.*

Primo Bar & Bistro

$$$$ | MEDITERRANEAN | Renovated in 2020, this sleek, open-plan, Mediterranean bistro offers waterfront dining at its best. Book ahead for a table with a view—and plan to arrive in time for cocktails at sundown, which generally occurs at about 6 pm. **Known for:** waterside location; open-air dining; cocktail hours with great sunsets. ⑤ *Average main: $35* ⊠ *St. Lawrence Gap, Dover* ☎ *246/573–7777* ⊕ *www.primobarandbistro.com* ⊘ *Closed Mon.*

Hotels

Barbados Beach Club

$$$ | RESORT | FAMILY | Designed with families in mind, this four-story, all-inclusive hotel (with elevators) sits on a beautiful stretch of south-coast beach, and for the price of your room, you can enjoy activities ranging from beach volleyball or miniature golf to nature walks. **Pros:** great beach; promotional deals add value; wonderful for kids. **Cons:** buzz of activity not for everyone; meals at set times, not all day; food varies daily but is rather uninspired. ⑤ *Rooms from: $400* ✉ *Maxwell Coast Rd., Maxwell* ☎ *246/428–9900* ⊕ *www.barbadosbeachclub.com* ⮑ *110 rooms* ¶⊚¶ *All-inclusive.*

Bougainvillea Barbados

$$$ | RESORT | FAMILY | Attractive seaside town houses, each with a separate entrance, wrap around the pool or face the beachfront; the suites, decorated in appealing Caribbean pastels, are huge compared with hotel suites elsewhere in this price range and have full kitchens. **Pros:** great for families but also appeals to couples and honeymooners; tennis court and air-conditioned fitness center; three pools, one with a swim-up bar, and lots of water sports. **Cons:** rooms are on four levels with no elevator; sea can be a little rough for swimming; seven-night minimum stay in high season. ⑤ *Rooms from: $410* ✉ *Maxwell Coast Rd., Maxwell* ☎ *246/628–0990, 800/495–1858 in U.S.* ⊕ *www.bougainvillearesort.com* ⮑ *100 suites* ¶⊚¶ *No meals.*

Divi Southwinds Beach Resort

$ | RESORT | FAMILY | This all-suites resort is situated on 20 acres of lawn and gardens bisected by action-packed St. Lawrence Gap. The property south of "The Gap" wraps around a stunning half mile of Dover Beach, where 16 beach villas provide an intimate setting steps from the sand. **Pros:** beautiful beach plus three pools; close to shopping, restaurants, and nightspots; kids' club. **Cons:** water sports cost extra; some rooms aching for renovations; service needs improvement. ⑤ *Rooms from: $225* ✉ *St. Lawrence Main Rd., Hwy. 7, Dover* ☎ *246/428–7181, 800/367–3484* ⊕ *www.divisouthwinds.com* ⮑ *133 rooms* ¶⊚¶ *No meals.*

Sandals Barbados

$$$$ | RESORT | Romance is definitely in the air at this truly magnificent (couples-only) Sandals property, which surrounds an 8-acre garden and lagoon—the longest and largest in Barbados. **Pros:** great beach and beautiful garden; myriad activities, including unlimited scuba diving, windsurfing, and sailing; visit, dine, and play at Sandals Royal Barbados next door. **Cons:** fabulously

Turtle Time

Along most of the beaches on Barbados, mother hawksbill turtles dig a pit in the sand, lay 100 or more eggs, cover the nest with sand, and then return to the sea. The eggs, which look just like Ping-Pong balls, are usually deposited between May and November and take about 60 days to hatch. If you happen to be strolling along the beach at the time they emerge, you'll see a mass of newborn turtles scrambling out of the sand and making a dash (at turtle speed, of course) for the sea. Although the journey takes only a few minutes, this can be a very dangerous time for the tiny turtles. They are easy prey for gulls and large crabs. The folks involved in the Barbados Sea Turtle Project (☎ 246/230–0142) at the University of the West Indies are working hard to protect and conserve the marine turtle populations in Barbados through educational workshops, tagging programs, and other research efforts.

expensive, so look for frequent promotional offers; with so much to do, it's easy to forget there's a whole island to explore; lacks Bajan authenticity. ⑤ *Rooms from: $811* ⊠ *St. Lawrence Gap, Maxwell* ⊹ *At Maxwell Coast Rd.* ☎ *246/620–3600, 888/726–3257* ⊕ *www.sandals.com/barbados* ⇱ *280 rooms* ⦵ *All-inclusive.*

Sandals Royal Barbados

$$$$ | ALL-INCLUSIVE | Sandal's second resort on the island, opened in December 2017 adjacent to sister resort Sandals Barbados, features all concierge- and butler-level suites with all the implied pampering. **Pros:** suites are ultraluxurious, ultraromantic … ultra-ultra; with 17 possible dining options, you'll never go hungry; complimentary airport shuttle service. **Cons:** with so much to do on-site, you may not experience the island itself; spa services cost extra; getting a taxi is always an issue at Sandals, as you're urged to use their own tour service. ⑤ *Rooms from: $950* ⊠ *Maxwell Coast Rd., Maxwell* ☎ *246/620–3600, 888/726–3257 in U.S.* ⊕ *www.sandals.com/royal-barbados* ⇱ *222 suites* ⦵ *All-inclusive.*

Southern Palms Beach Club

$$ | RESORT | FAMILY | This resort is pretty in pink, you might say, with its (pink) plantation-style main building opening onto an inviting pool area and 1,000 feet of white sandy beach. **Pros:** friendly and accommodating staff; hotel food and entertainment are very good, and other options are nearby; great location with nice beach. **Cons:** rooms are large and clean but bathrooms are dated; beach vendors can be a nuisance (not the hotel's fault); property is dated. ⑤ *Rooms from: $325* ⊠ *St. Lawrence Gap,*

Dover ☎ 246/428–7171 ⊕ www.southernpalms.net ⊷ 92 rooms ⦿ No meals.

Turtle Beach

$$$$ | RESORT | FAMILY | Families flock to this resort, part of the Marriott portfolio, because it offers large, bright suites and enough all-included activities for everyone. **Pros:** good choice for families; daily rounds of golf at Barbados Golf Club included; lots of complimentary water sports. **Cons:** refrigerators are stocked only in one-bedroom suites; pools are small relative to the number of kids in them; buffet meals are a little tired. ⑤ *Rooms from: $624* ✉ *St. Lawrence Gap, Dover ⊹ At Maxwell Coast Rd. ☎ 246/428–7131, 855/687–6453 in U.S. ⊕ www.turtlebeachresortbarbados. com ⊷ 161 suites ⦿ All-inclusive.*

Nightlife

St. Lawrence Gap, the narrow waterfront byway with restaurants, bars, and hotels one right after another, is where the action is on the south coast.

McBride's Pub

BARS/PUBS | McBride's is, as you might have guessed, a popular Irish pub with Irish beer on tap, pub grub from the kitchen, and karaoke or traditional Irish, reggae, rock, Latin, or techno music every night. Happy hour(s), also nightly, run from midnight to 2 am. ✉ *St. Lawrence Gap, Dover ☎ 246/436–6352.*

The Old Jamm Inn

MUSIC CLUBS | "Booze, beats, and burgers" are the attractions at this music venue in St. Lawrence Gap. Listen, dance, and enjoy live performances by local performers and/or DJs who spin tunes in all styles. Add a juicy burger, Bajan fish cakes, or jerk pork—and rum drinks are always two-for-one. It's a party every night! ✉ *St. Lawrence Gap, Dover ☎ 246/428–3919.*

Shopping

At **Chattel House Village,** a cluster of boutiques in St. Lawrence Gap, you can buy locally made crafts and other souvenirs.

My Collection Barbados

SPECIALTY STORES | This locally owned enterprise has locations on the south and west coasts. It sells a wide range of local products such as jewelry, hand-printed accessories, bags, food items, and other gifts. ✉ *Hastings ☎ 246/261–8876 ⊕ www.mycollectionbarbados.com.*

Oistins and the Surrounding South Point Area

Oistins, an active fishing village just east of St. Lawrence Gap, is one of the island's four major towns (along with Bridgetown, Holetown, and Speightstown) and the only "town" on the south coast. Oistins is well-known for its Friday night Fish Fry. In Enterprise, a short distance east of town, there's a popular beach and delightful inn.

The southernmost point of Barbados is marked by one of the island's four historic lighthouses. Primarily a residential area, the broad beaches at Silver Sands and Silver Rock are a favorite gathering place of windsurfers and kitesurfers.

Sights

South Point Lighthouse

LIGHTHOUSE | This is the oldest of four lighthouses on Barbados. Assembled on the island in 1852, after being displayed at London's Great Exhibition the previous year, the landmark lighthouse is just east of Miami (Enterprise) Beach near the southernmost point of land on Barbados. The 89-foot tower, with its distinguishing red and white horizontal stripes, is closed to the public—but visitors may freely walk about the site, take photos, and enjoy the magnificent ocean view. ⊠ *South Point, Lighthouse Dr., Atlantic Shores.*

Beaches

★ Miami Beach (*Enterprise Beach*)

BEACH—SIGHT | This lovely spot on the coast road, just east of Oistins, is a slice of pure white sand with shallow and calm water on one side, deeper water with small waves on the other, and cliffs on either side. Located in a mainly upscale residential area, the beach is mostly deserted except for weekends when folks who live nearby come for a swim. You'll find a palm-shaded parking area, snack carts, and chair rentals. It's also a hop, skip, and jump from Little Arches Hotel. **Amenities:** food and drink; parking (no fee). **Best for:** solitude; swimming. ⊠ *Enterprise Beach Rd., Enterprise.*

Silver Sands–Silver Rock Beach

BEACH—SIGHT | **FAMILY** | Nestled between South Point, the southernmost tip of the island, and Inch Marlow Point, the Silver Point

Hotel overlooks this long, broad strand of beautiful white sand that always has a strong breeze. That makes this beach the best in Barbados for intermediate and advanced windsurfers and, more recently, kiteboarders. There's a small playground and shaded picnic tables. **Amenities:** parking (no fee); water sports. **Best for:** solitude; swimming; walking; windsurfing. ⊠ *Off Hwy. 7, Silver Sands*.

Restaurants

Café Luna

$$$$ | **ECLECTIC** | With a sweeping view of pretty Miami (Enterprise) Beach, the alfresco dining deck on top of the Mediterranean-style Little Arches Hotel is spectacular at lunchtime and magical in the moonlight. At dinner, the expertise of executive chef and owner Mark "Moo" de Gruchy is displayed through his classic Bajan fish stew, as well as contemporary and gluten-free "Pan-Tropical" dishes. **Known for:** romantic cocktails and dining under the stars; mouthwatering dishes; focus on sustainable, locally produced ingredients. Ⓢ *Average main: $32* ⊠ *Little Arches Hotel, Enterprise Beach Rd., Oistins* ☎ *246/428–6172* ⊕ *www.cafelunabarbados. com.*

🛏 Hotels

Little Arches Hotel

$$ | **HOTEL** | Just east of the fishing village of Oistins, this classy boutique hotel has a distinctly Mediterranean atmosphere and a perfect vantage point overlooking the sea. **Pros:** stylish accommodations; complimentary full breakfasts with weeklong stay; across from Miami Beach. **Cons:** fairly remote residential area; road traffic is sometimes distracting; small pool. Ⓢ *Rooms from: $340* ⊠ *Enterprise Beach Rd., Oistins* ☎ *246/420–4689* ⊕ *www. littlearches.com* ➷ *10 rooms* ⊙ *No meals.*

Silver Point Hotel

$$ | **HOTEL** | **FAMILY** | This remote, gated community of modern condos at Silver Sands–Silver Rock Beach is operated as a trendy boutique hotel that appeals to singles, couples, and families—but especially to windsurfers and kitesurfers. **Pros:** stylish suites; perfect location for windsurfers and kitesurfers; gated community. **Cons:** far from anything but the beach, so a rental car is recommended; sea can be rough for swimming; no entertainment other than the beach. Ⓢ *Rooms from: $275* ⊠ *Silver Point, Silver Sands* ☎ *246/420–4416* ⊕ *www.silverpointhotel.com* ➷ *58 suites* ⊙ *No meals.*

The Oistins Fish Fry is held every Friday night in the south-coast fishing village.

Nightlife

★ Oistins Fish Fry

THEMED ENTERTAINMENT | FAMILY | This is the place to be on Friday evening, when this south-coast fishing village becomes a lively and convivial outdoor street party suitable for the whole family. Barbecued chicken and a variety of fish, along with all the traditional sides, are served fresh from the grill and consumed at roadside picnic tables. Servings are huge, and prices are inexpensive—about $10–$15 per plate. Recommendations include lionfish, plantain, and breadfruit. Drinks, music, and dancing add to the fun. To avoid the crowds, come any day but Friday for lunch or dinner. ⊠ *Oistins Main Rd., Oistins.*

Crane and the Southeast

Crane marks the beginning of the island's southeast coast, which extends as far as Ragged Point. The coastline is marked by an expansive villa resort, another in the development stage, pretty bays, and a couple of the island's most magnificent beaches. The inland area is mostly residential—along with miles of canefields, a historic greathouse, and an occasional oil well.

Sights

Bushy Park Barbados

SPORTS VENUE | **FAMILY** | Bushy Park in Saint Philip parish is a 2.2 kilometer, FIA Grade Three motorsports course that hosts professional auto racing events, including the annual Global Rally Cross Championship. Visitors can test their skills in a variety of race cars, from go-karts to Suzuki Swift Sport race cars. The track is open to the public on days when races are not scheduled. ⊠ *Gaskin* ☎ *246/537–1360* ⊕ *www.bushyparkbarbados.com* ⊡ *From $35 for go-karts, from $180 for driving experiences.*

Ragged Point

LIGHTHOUSE | This is the location of East Coast Light, one of four strategically placed lighthouses on the island. Although civilization in the form of new homes is encroaching on this once-remote spot, the view of the entire Atlantic coastline is still spectacular— and the cool ocean breeze is refreshing on a hot day. ⊠ *Marley Vale* ⊡ *Free.*

Beaches

★ Bottom Bay Beach

BEACH—SIGHT | **FAMILY** | Popular for fashion and travel-industry photo shoots, Bottom Bay is the quintessential Caribbean beach. Secluded, surrounded by a coral cliff, studded with a stand of palms, and blessed with an endless ocean view, this dreamy enclave is near the southeasternmost point of the island. The Atlantic Ocean waves can be too strong for swimming, but it's the picture-perfect place for a picnic lunch on the shore. Park at the top of the cliff and follow the steps down to the beach. Note: because of the seclusion, it's not advisable for women to go to this beach alone; going with a group is much safer. **Amenities:** none. **Best for:** solitude; swimming; walking. ⊠ *Hwy. 5, Apple Hall.*

★ Crane Beach

BEACH—SIGHT | **FAMILY** | This exquisite crescent of pink sand on the southeast coast was named not for the elegant, long-legged wading bird but for the crane used to haul and load cargo when this area served as a busy port. Crane Beach usually has a steady breeze and lightly rolling surf that varies in color from aqua to turquoise to lapis and is great for bodysurfing. Access to the beach is either down 98 steps or via a cliffside, glass-walled elevator on The Crane resort property. **Amenities:** food and drink; lifeguards; parking (no fee); toilets. **Best for:** swimming; walking. ⊠ *Crane.*

🍴 Restaurants

★ L'Azure

$$$$ | **CARIBBEAN** | Perched on an oceanfront cliff overlooking Crane Beach, L'Azure is an informal breakfast and luncheon spot by day that becomes elegant after dark. Enjoy seafood chowder or a light salad or sandwich while absorbing the breathtaking panoramic view of the beach and sea beyond. **Known for:** lovely setting whether day or evening; classy cuisine and service; Sunday gospel brunch. ⑤ *Average main: $32* ⊠ *The Crane Resort, Crane* 🕾 *246/423–6220* ⊕ *www.thecrane.com* ⊗ *No dinner Sat.–Mon. or Wed.*

★ Worthing Square Food Garden

$ | **INTERNATIONAL** | **FAMILY** | This food-truck park is a great spot to sample a wide variety of dishes for lunch or dinner. Venezuelan arepas, Italian pizzas, Jamaican jerk pork, Trinidadian roti, and Bajan classics are among the many options here. **Known for:** casual atmosphere; affordable international and Caribbean cuisine; family friendly. ⑤ *Average main: $10* ⊠ *Worthing, Worthing* ⊹ *Behind Cave Shepherd and gas station* 🕾 *246/832–6060* ⊟ *No credit cards.*

Zen

$$$$ | **ASIAN** | Thai and Japanese specialties reign supreme in a magnificent setting overlooking Crane Beach. The centerpiece of the sophisticated, Asian-inspired decor is a 12-seat sushi bar, where chefs prepare exotic fare before your eyes. **Known for:** Thai or Japanese prix-fixe tasting menu—or à la carte dining; traditional Japanese-style tatami room; modern, Asian-inspired decor. ⑤ *Average main: $32* ⊠ *The Crane Resort, Crane* 🕾 *246/423–6220* ⊕ *www.thecrane.com* ⊗ *No lunch. Closed Mon. and Tues.*

🛏 Hotels

★ The Crane

$$$$ | **RESORT** | **FAMILY** | Hugging a seaside bluff on the southeast coast, The Crane incorporates the island's oldest hotel in continuous operation; the original coral-stone hotel building (1887) is the centerpiece of a luxurious, 40-acre villa complex that includes private residences, numerous pools, restaurants, bars, and even a little village. **Pros:** enchanting view, beach, and pools; complimentary kids' club; fabulous suites and five great restaurants. **Cons:** remote location; rental car recommended; villas are considerably more expensive and more modern than historic hotel rooms. ⑤ *Rooms from: $550* ⊠ *Crane* 🕾 *246/423–6220, 866/978–5942 in U.S.* ⊕ *www.thecrane.com* ⇄ *252 rooms* ⊗ *No meals.*

Errol Barrow, National Hero

Errol Barrow (1920–87), trained in Britain as a lawyer and economist, led his native Barbados to independence in 1966, and became the island nation's first prime minister. During his initial tenure, which lasted through 1976, Barrow expanded the tourist industry, reduced the island's dependence on sugar, introduced national health insurance and social security, and extended free education to the community college level. Barrow was reelected prime minister in 1986 but collapsed and died at his home a year later. He is honored as a national hero and the "Father of Independence," and his birthday—January 21—is celebrated as a national holiday. On that day in 2007, a 9-foot-tall statue of Errol Barrow was erected on the esplanade along The Careenage, picturesquely sited between the city's two bridges and facing Parliament.

Nightlife

Dis Ole House Kitchen and Beer Garden

BREWPUBS/BEER GARDENS | FAMILY | This is a quaint, unexpected spot for great food, live music, brunch, and delicious cocktails. Enjoy juicy ribs with a beer (or a full flight) in the tropical back garden, which has been designed with coziness in mind. It's cash only! ⊠ Long Bay, Sunbury ☎ 246/571–0502.

Holetown and Vicinity

Holetown, in St. James Parish, marks the center of the Platinum Coast—so called for the vast number of luxurious resorts and mansions that face the sea. Holetown is also where Captain John Powell and the crew of the British ship Olive Blossom landed on May 14, 1625, to claim the island for King James I (who had died of a stroke seven weeks earlier).

Sights

Folkestone Marine Park and Museum

BEACH—SIGHT | FAMILY | Facilities at this family-oriented marine park include a playground, basketball court, picnic area, and a beach with lifeguards. There's also an underwater snorkeling trail (equipment rental, $10 for the day) around Dottins Reef, just off the beach in the 2.2-mile (3½-km) protected marine reserve.

Nonswimmers can opt for a glass-bottom boat tour. The ship *Stavronikita*, deliberately sunk in 120 feet of water about a half mile from shore, is home to myriad fish and a popular dive site. ⊠ *Hwy. 1, Church Point, Holetown* ☎ *246/422–2314* 🖼 *Museum exhibits $1.*

Beaches

Paynes Bay Beach

BEACH—SIGHT | The stretch of beach just south of Sandy Lane is lined with luxury hotels—Tamarind, The House, and Treasure Beach among them. It's a very pretty area, with plenty of beach to go around, calm water, and good snorkeling. Public access is available at several locations along Highway 1, though parking is limited. **Amenities:** food and drink. **Best for:** snorkeling; sunset; swimming; walking. ⊠ *Hwy. 1.*

🍴 Restaurants

★ La Cabane

$$$$ | **MEDITERRANEAN** | **FAMILY** | The chef and his brigade whip up a Mediterranean inspired, organic, farm to table menu at this relaxed, beachfront spot that's popular with locals and visitors. Mains such as roasted pork or whole fish are paired with seasonal vegetables and delicious hand-cut fries. **Known for:** delightful beachfront atmosphere; farm to table menu; shoes are optional. ⑤ *Average main: $40* ⊠ *Batts Rock Beach* ☎ *246/256–2131* ⊕ *www.lacabanebarbados.com.*

★ The Cliff Bistro

$$$$ | **INTERNATIONAL** | **FAMILY** | The seaside views here are dramatic, but the atmosphere is informal and fun. Lunch options include sandwiches, burgers, fish-and-chips, soups, and salads. **Known for:** excellent bistro-style cuisine; delicious pastries at brunch; beautiful ocean vistas. ⑤ *Average main: $40* ⊠ *Hwy. 1, Derricks* ☎ *246/432–0797* ⊕ *thecliffbeachclub.com.*

★ Lone Star

$$$$ | **MODERN EUROPEAN** | **FAMILY** | At the tiny but chic Lone Star Hotel, a short drive north of Holetown, the finest local ingredients are turned into gastronomic delights. Lunchtime brings tasty salads, sandwiches, and wood-fired pizzas, served in the oceanfront bar; after sunset, the casual daytime atmosphere turns trendy. **Known for:** lovely setting overlooking the sea; breakfast on the boardwalk; sunset cocktails in the lounge. ⑤ *Average main: $45* ⊠ *Lone Star Hotel, Hwy. 1, Mount Standfast* ☎ *246/629–0599* ⊕ *www.thelonestar.com.*

Holetown, Speightstown, and Vicinity

0   1 mi
0   1 km

Sights

Folkestone Marine Park and Museum, **1**

Restaurants

The Cliff Bistro, **8**
The Fish Pot, **1**
Fisherman's Pub, **2**
La Cabane, **9**
Lone Star, **4**
The Mews, **6**
Ragamuffins Bar & Restaurant, **5**
Sea Shed, **3**
The Tides, **7**

Hotels

The Club, Barbados Resort & Spa, **11**
Cobblers Cove, **4**
Colony Club, **7**
Coral Reef Club, **8**
Crystal Cove Hotel, **16**
Fairmont Royal Pavilion, **6**
The House, **15**
Little Good Harbour, **1**
Lone Star Hotel, **5**
Mango Bay, **10**
Port Ferdinand, **2**
Port St Charles, **3**
The Sandpiper Hotel, **9**
Sandy Lane Hotel and Golf Club, **12**
Tamarind, **13**
Treasure Beach, **14**
Waves Hotel and Spa, **17**

KEY

1 *Exploring Sights*
1 *Restaurants*
1 *Hotels*

Holetown Landing

On May 14, 1625, British Captain John Powell anchored his ship off the west coast of Barbados and claimed the island on behalf of King James I. He named his landfall Jamestown. Nearly two years later, on February 17, 1627, Captain Henry Powell landed in Jamestown with a party of 80 settlers and 10 slaves. They used a small channel, or "hole," near the settlement to offload and clean ships, so Jamestown soon became known as Holetown. Today Holetown is a vibrant town with shopping centers, restaurants, night-spots, and, of course, hotels and resorts. It is also the site of the annual Holetown Festi-val—a week of parades, crafts, music, and partying—held in mid-February each year to commemorate the first settle-ment. The celebration begins at the Holetown Monument in the center of town.

The Mews

$$$$ | **INTERNATIONAL** | Once the private home of actress Minnie Driver's dad, the front room is now an inviting bar; an interior courtyard is an intimate, open-air dining area; and the second floor is a maze of small dining rooms and balconies. But it's the food—classic, bistro, or tapas—that draws the visitors. **Known for:** eclectic menu; unique atmosphere; becomes a cozy bar and party spot after dinner. ⑤ *Average main: $35* ⊠ *2nd St., Holetown* ☎ *246/432–1122* ⊕ *www.themewsbarbados.com.*

Ragamuffins Bar & Restaurant

$$$ | **CARIBBEAN** | At this tiny, funky, lively, and informal spot, you can dine inside in an authentic chattel house or outside on the porch. Although the restaurant focuses on fun, the chef specializ-es in the freshest seafood, perfectly broiled T-bone steaks, West Indian curries, and vegetarian dishes such as Bajan stir-fried vege-tables with noodles. **Known for:** good food, good music, and good fun; unpretentious, friendly, welcoming atmosphere; Sunday-night Drag Show, a must. ⑤ *Average main: $22* ⊠ *1st St., Holetown* ☎ *246/432–1295* ⊕ *www.ragamuffinsbarbados.com* ☉ *No lunch.*

★ Sea Shed

$$$$ | **INTERNATIONAL** | **FAMILY** | This trendy, bustling restaurant is a favorite west-coast dining spot of local professionals, families, and visitors. Mediterranean and Caribbean flavors enliven inventive thin-crust pizzas and tasty salads; the dinner menu also includes fresh seafood and vegetarian selections. **Known for:** lively, bustling atmosphere; casual chic dining on the beach; family-friendly, kids

can play on the beach. $ *Average main: $40* ✉ *Mullins Beach, Mullins* ☎ *246/572–5111* ⊕ *www.seashedbarbados.com.*

★ The Tides

$$$$ | MODERN EUROPEAN | Perhaps the most intriguing feature of this stunning setting—besides the sound of waves crashing onto the shore just feet away—is the row of huge tree trunks growing right through the dining room. The food is equally dramatic as a contemporary twist is given to fresh seafood, fillet of beef, rack of lamb, and other top-of-the-line main courses by adding inspired sauces and delicate vegetables and garnishes. **Known for:** long considered one of the island's best restaurants; vegetarian and children's menus; the cozy lounge and on-site art gallery. $ *Average main: $45* ✉ *Balmore House, Hwy. 1, Holetown* ☎ *246/432–8356* ⊕ *www.tidesbarbados.com* ☉ *No lunch Mon. or Sat. No dinner Mon.*

 Hotels

The Club, Barbados Resort & Spa

$$$$ | RESORT | This is one of the island's few adults-only (age 16 and up) all-inclusive resorts and the only one on the west coast; only spa and salon services and room service cost extra. **Pros:** intimate adults-only atmosphere; walk to beaches; waterskiing included. **Cons:** beach erodes to almost nothing after fall storms, but the sandy beach deck is a good substitute; not fully accessible to people with disabilities; three-night stay required in high season. $ *Rooms from: $890* ✉ *Hwy. 1, Vauxhall, Holetown* ☎ *246/432–7840, 866/830–1617* ⊕ *www.theclubbarbados.com* ⇥ *158 rooms* ❚⊘❚ *All-inclusive.*

★ Colony Club

$$$$ | RESORT | The signature hotel of seven Elegant Hotel properties on Barbados is certainly elegant, but with a quiet, friendly, understated style primarily targeted to adults. **Pros:** swim-up rooms and bar; Bait-to-Plate fishing trip with the chef; complimentary motorized and nonmotorized water sports. **Cons:** pricey but often has good promotional offers; kid-friendly activities only during summer and holidays; beach comes and goes, depending on storms. $ *Rooms from: $1040* ✉ *Hwy. 1, Porters* ☎ *246/422–2335, 855/805–6646* ⊕ *eleganthotels.com/colony-club* ⇥ *96 rooms* ❚⊘❚ *Free breakfast.*

★ Coral Reef Club

$$$$ | RESORT | This upscale resort, with pristine coral-stone cottages scattered over 12 acres of flower-filled gardens, offers elegance in a welcoming, informal atmosphere. **Pros:** delightful appearance and atmosphere; beautiful suites with huge verandahs; delicious dining. **Cons:** few room TVs; narrow beach sometimes disappears, depending on fall weather; no kids mid-January through February. ⑤ *Rooms from: $915* ✉ *Hwy. 1, Porters* ☎ *246/422–2372* ⊕ *www. coralreefbarbados.com* ⊘ *Closed mid-May–mid-July and Sept.* ⤷ *88 rooms* ⦿ *Free breakfast.*

Crystal Cove Hotel

$$$$ | **RESORT** | **FAMILY** | This seaside colony of attached duplex cottages, whitewashed and trimmed in perky pastels, appeals to both couples and families. **Pros:** kids club with activities all day and babysitting service at night; exchange dining program with sister resorts on the west coast; all water sports, including waterskiing and banana boat or tube rides, are complimentary. **Cons:** few activities immediately outside the resort, although it's not far from Bridgetown; lots of stairs make it difficult for physically challenged visitors; quality and variety of culinary offerings could use improvement. ⑤ *Rooms from: $1130* ✉ *Hwy. 1, Appleby* ☎ *246/419–2800, 855/258–0902 in U.S.* ⊕ *eleganthotels.com/ crystal-cove* ⤷ *88 rooms* ⦿ *All-inclusive.*

Fairmont Royal Pavilion

$$$$ | **RESORT** | **FAMILY** | Every unit in this luxurious resort has immediate access to 11 acres of tropical gardens and an uninterrupted sea view from a broad balcony or patio. **Pros:** top-notch service— everyone remembers your name; excellent dining; swimming with turtles included. **Cons:** dining—and everything else—is expensive; small bathrooms; breakfast buffet needs inspiration. ⑤ *Rooms from: $1120* ✉ *Hwy. 1, Porters* ☎ *246/422–5555, 866/540–4485* ⊕ *www.fairmont.com/barbados* ⊘ *Closed Oct.–mid-Nov.* ⤷ *73 rooms* ⦿ *Free breakfast.*

★ The House

$$$$ | **HOTEL** | Privacy, luxury, and service are hallmarks of this intimate, adults-only sanctuary adjacent to sister resort Tamarind. **Pros:** pure relaxation in stylish surroundings; privacy assured; complimentary half-hour massage. **Cons:** small pool and narrow beach; unable to walk anywhere; not enough sunbeds in pool area. ⑤ *Rooms from: $1185* ✉ *Hwy. 1, Paynes Bay* ☎ *246/432–5525, 855/220–8459 in U.S.* ⊕ *www.eleganthotels/the-house.com* ⤷ *34 rooms* ⦿ *Free breakfast.*

Lone Star Hotel

$$$$ | **HOTEL** | **FAMILY** | A 1940s-era service station just north of Holetown was transformed into a sleek beachfront boutique hotel that—fortunately or unfortunately—has since been discovered by celebrities. **Pros:** on a beautiful beach, great for walking; close to Holetown and west coast activities; family friendly. **Cons:** no

Cuban Monument

On October 6, 1976, Cubana Airlines Flight 455, a DC-8 aircraft en route to Cuba from Barbados, was brought down by a terrorist bombing attack, killing all 73 people on board. The aircraft crashed into the sea off Paynes Bay on the west coast of Barbados. Four anti-Castro Cuban exiles were arrested for the crime. Two were sentenced to 20-year prison terms; one was acquitted; the fourth was held for eight years awaiting sentencing and later fled. A pyramid-shape granite monument dedicated to the victims was installed along Highway 1 in Paynes Bay at the approximate location where the wreckage was brought ashore; the monument was unveiled during a 1998 visit by Cuban president Fidel Castro.

activities except for the beach; no pool; close to road, so early morning traffic can be noisy. ⑤ *Rooms from: $705* ⊠ *Hwy. 1, Mount Standfast* ☎ *246/629–0600* ⊕ *www.thelonestar.com* ⌑ *6 rooms* ⑩ *No meals.*

Mango Bay
$$$$ | **RESORT** | **FAMILY** | This beachfront resort in the heart of Holetown is within walking distance of shops, restaurants, nightspots, historic sites, and the public bus to Bridgetown and Speightstown. **Pros:** the Holetown location; food is good, but there's only one restaurant; accommodating staff. **Cons:** small pool; vendors on the beach can be annoying; noise can be an issue for rooms facing the bar area or that back up to the street. ⑤ *Rooms from: $680* ⊠ *2nd St., Holetown* ☎ *246/626–1384* ⊕ *www.mangobaybarbados.com* ⌑ *76 rooms* ⑩ *All-inclusive.*

★ The Sandpiper Hotel
$$$$ | **RESORT** | **FAMILY** | An intimate vibe and (practically) private beach keep guests coming back to this family-oriented hideaway, with accommodations spread throughout 7 acres of gardens. **Pros:** private and sophisticated; dining, spa, and tennis privileges at nearby Coral Reef Club; Tree Top suites are fabulous—but pricey. **Cons:** beach is small, typical of west coast beaches; book far in advance, as hotel is small and popular (75% repeat guests); few room TVs. ⑤ *Rooms from: $915* ⊠ *Hwy. 1, Folkestone, Holetown* ☎ *246/422–2251* ⊕ *www.sandpiperbarbados.com* ⌑ *50 rooms* ⑩ *Free breakfast.*

★ Sandy Lane Hotel and Golf Club
$$$$ | **RESORT** | **FAMILY** | Few places in the Caribbean compare to Sandy Lane's luxurious facilities and ultrapampering service—or to

its astronomical prices. **Pros:** cream of the crop; excellent dining and amazing spa; great golf. **Cons:** over-the-top for most mortals; although you don't need to dress up to walk through the lobby, you'll feel that you should; though lovely, beach can feel crowded. ⓢ *Rooms from: $1800* ✉ *Hwy. 1, Paynes Bay, Holetown* ✛ *1½ miles (2 km) south of town* ☎ *246/444–2000, 866/444–4080 in U.S.* ⊕ *www.sandylane.com* 🏌️ *Two 18-hole championship courses, one 9-hole course* 🛏️ *113 rooms* ❢⃝❙ *Free breakfast.*

Tamarind

$$$$ | RESORT | FAMILY | This sleek Mediterranean-style resort, which sprawls along 750 feet of prime west-coast beachfront south of Holetown, is large enough to cater to active families and sophisticated couples, including honeymooners. **Pros:** very big resort, yet layout affords privacy; right on superb Paynes Bay beach; lots of complimentary water sports, including waterskiing and banana boat rides. **Cons:** some rooms could use a little TLC; uninspired buffet breakfast; rooms on the road side of the property prone to traffic noise. ⓢ *Rooms from: $855* ✉ *Hwy. 1, Paynes Bay* ☎ *246/432–1332, 855/326–5189 in U.S.* ⊕ *eleganthotels.com/tamarind* 🛏️ *104 rooms* ❢⃝❙ *Free breakfast.*

Treasure Beach

$$$$ | HOTEL | Quiet, upscale, and intimate, this adults-only boutique hotel a couple of miles south of Holetown was gutted and completely refurbished in late 2017. **Pros:** cozy retreat; complimentary art gallery tour; complimentary Chef's Table dinner with a five-night stay. **Cons:** narrow beach; offshore turtle swimming attracts boatloads of tourists; no kids allowed. ⓢ *Rooms from: $939* ✉ *Hwy. 1, Paynes Bay* ☎ *246/419–4200, 888/996–9947 in U.S.* ⊕ *eleganthotels.com/treasure-beach* 🛏️ *35 rooms* ❢⃝❙ *Free breakfast.*

Waves Hotel and Spa

$$$$ | ALL-INCLUSIVE | The main part of this hotel—lobby, most guest rooms, restaurant, snack bar, bar and lounge, and a pool—is perched on a cliff overlooking a sandy beach, while adults-only guest rooms are across the road, along with the spa, a specialty restaurant, and a second pool. **Pros:** relaxed atmosphere for both couples and families; friendly, accommodating staff; motorized water sports (and instruction) are included. **Cons:** adults-only rooms are across the street from the beach; no connecting rooms for families with kids; pools are small. ⓢ *Rooms from: $650* ✉ *Hwy. 1, Prospect Bay* ☎ *246/424–7571, 855/465–8886 in U.S.* ⊕ *eleganthotels.com/waves* 🛏️ *70 rooms* ❢⃝❙ *All-inclusive.*

🍸 Nightlife

Holetown's restaurants and clubs on 1st and 2nd streets are giving "The Gap" a run for its money. Along with a half dozen or so restaurants that offer fare ranging from ribs or pizza to elegant cuisine, a handful of nightspots and night "experiences" have cropped up recently.

Drift Ocean Terrace Lounge

CAFES—NIGHTLIFE | Sophisticated in style and seductive in setting, this is a romantic place to enjoy some champagne, a tropical cocktail, or a glass of wine before heading out to party in Holetown. ⊠ *Hwy. 1, Holetown* ☎ *246/432–2808* ⊕ *www.driftinbarbados. com.*

Red Door Lounge

PIANO BARS/LOUNGES | Cocktails, DJs, and live music—this local hot spot is the place to be on Thursday, Friday, and Saturday nights after 9. ⊠ *Mango Bay Hotel, 2nd St., Holetown* ☎ *246/620–3761* ⊕ *reddoorbarbados.com.*

West Bar

BARS/PUBS | Restaurant by day, trendy outdoor bar in the Limegrove Lifestyle Centre courtyard by night, this is a good place to meet friends for a drink and chill. Expect good vibes, good dancing, and a good party atmosphere on Friday and Saturday nights starting at 10 pm. ⊠ *Limegrove Lifestyle Centre, Holetown* ☎ *246/571–7300* ⊕ *www.westbarbarbados.com.*

👜 Shopping

Holetown has the upscale **Limegrove Lifestyle Centre,** a stylish shopping mall with high-end designer boutiques, as well as **Chattel House Village,** small shops in colorful cottages with local products, fashions, beachwear, and souvenirs. Also in Holetown, **Sunset Crest Mall** has two branches of the Cave Shepherd department store, a bank, a pharmacy, and several small shops; at **West Coast Mall,** you can buy duty-free goods, island wear, and groceries.

★ Earthworks Pottery

CRAFTS | At his family-owned-and-operated pottery workshop, items range from dishes and knickknacks to complete dinner services and one-of-a-kind art pieces. The characteristically blue or green—and, more recently, peach and brown—pottery decorates hotel rooms and is sold in gift shops throughout the island, but the biggest selection (including "seconds") is here, where you also can watch the potters at work. And they'll carefully pack your purchase for traveling, or ship it home for you. ⊠ *2 Edgehill*

Port St. Charles Marina in Speightstown, the island's "second city"

Heights ✛ *Southeast of Holetown via Hwy. 2A* ☎ *246/425–0223* ⊕ *www.earthworks-pottery.com* ◷ *Closed Sun.*

★ On the Wall Art Gallery

ART GALLERIES | Artist and gallery owner Vanita Comissiong offers an array of original paintings by Barbadian artists, along with handmade arts and crafts and jewelry products. Additional galleries are located at Limegrove Lifestyle Centre in Holetown and in a dedicated space at Champers restaurant in Rockley on the south coast. ⊠ *Earthworks Pottery, 2 Edgehill Heights, Edge Hill* ✛ *Southeast of Holetown via Hwy. 2A* ☎ *246/234–9145* ⊕ *www. onthewallartgallery.com* ◷ *Closed Sun.*

Speightstown

The west coast extends from just north of Bridgetown, through St. James Parish, to Speightstown in St. Peter Parish. Speightstown, the north's commercial center and once a thriving port city, now relies on its local shops and informal restaurants. Many of Speightstown's 19th-century buildings, with traditional overhanging balconies, have been restored. The island's northernmost reaches, St. Peter and St. Lucy parishes, have a varied topography and are lovely to explore.

 Beaches

Gentle Caribbean waves lap the west coast, and leafy mahogany trees shade its stunning coves and sandy beaches. The water is perfect for swimming and water sports. An almost unbroken chain of beaches runs between Bridgetown and Speightstown. Elegant homes and luxury hotels face much of the beachfront property in this area, dubbed Barbados's "Platinum Coast."

West-coast beaches are considerably smaller and narrower than those on the south coast. Also, prolonged stormy weather in September and October may cause sand erosion, temporarily making the beach even narrower. Even so, west-coast beaches are seldom crowded. Vendors stroll by with handmade baskets, hats, dolls, jewelry, even original watercolors; owners of private boats offer waterskiing, parasailing, and snorkeling excursions. Hotels and beachside restaurants welcome nonguests for terrace lunches (wear a cover-up), and you can buy picnic items at supermarkets in Holetown.

Mullins Beach

BEACH—SIGHT | FAMILY | At this popular beach just south of Speightstown, the water is safe for swimming and snorkeling. There's easy parking on the main road, and refreshments are available at nearby restaurants. A beach vendor rents chairs and umbrellas. **Amenities:** food and drink. **Best for:** sunset; swimming; walking. ⊠ *Hwy. 1B, Mullins.*

🍴 Restaurants

The Fish Pot

$$$$ | CARIBBEAN | Bright and cheery by day and relaxed and cozy by night, The Fish Pot offers a tasty dining experience in a setting that's classier than its name might suggest. Just north of Speightstown and the little fishing village of Six Men's Bay, this attractive restaurant serves internationally inspired, modern Caribbean cuisine. Gaze seaward through windows framed with pale-green louvered shutters while you dine. **Known for:** modern Caribbean cuisine; laid-back ambience; seaside locale. $ *Average main: $35* ⊠ *Little Good Harbour Hotel, Hwy. 1B* ☎ *246/439–3000* ⊕ *www. littlegoodharbourbarbados.com.*

Fisherman's Pub

$ | CARIBBEAN | FAMILY | As local as local gets, this open-air, waterfront beach bar (a former rum shop) is built on stilts a stone's throw from the Speightstown fish market. For years, fishermen and other locals have come here for the inexpensive, authentic

Bajan lunch buffet. **Known for:** truly local food in a truly local (family owned) environment; fill up for a few bucks; right on the waterfront. ⑤ *Average main: $12* ⊠ *Queen's St., Speightstown* ☏ *246/422–2703* ⊘ *Closed Sun. Apr.–Oct.*

 Hotels

★ Cobblers Cove

$$$$ | RESORT | Flanked by tropical gardens on one side and the sea on the other, this English country–style resort has 10 two-story cottages, each with four elegant suites that include a bedroom, a comfy sitting room with sofa bed, a small library, and a wall of louvered shutters that open wide to a patio. **Pros:** peaceful and quiet; complimentary excursion to swim with the turtles; amazing penthouse suites. **Cons:** small beach; no room TVs; only bedrooms and some sitting rooms have air-conditioning. ⑤ *Rooms from: $658* ⊠ *Road View, Hwy. 1B, Speightstown* ☏ *246/422–2291* ⊕ *www.cobblerscove.com* ↴ *42 suites* ⑩ *Free breakfast.*

Little Good Harbour

$$$ | HOTEL | FAMILY | A cluster of spacious self-catering cottages, built in updated chattel-house style with gingerbread balconies, overlooks a narrow strip of beach north of Speightstown—just beyond the fishing community of Six Men's Bay. This little enclave, with one-, two-, and three-bedroom (mostly) duplex suites, is a perfect choice for self-sufficient travelers who don't need the hand-holding that resorts provide and who relish the chance to experience a delightful slice of Bajan village life. **Pros:** spacious units with fully equipped kitchens; laid-back atmosphere; good choice for families. **Cons:** tiny beach across a busy road; air-conditioning in bedrooms only; remote location. ⑤ *Rooms from: $450* ⊠ *Hwy. 1B* ☏ *246/439–3000* ⊕ *www.littlegoodharbourbarbados. com* ⊘ *Closed Sept.* ↴ *20 suites* ⑩ *No meals.*

Port Ferdinand

$$$$ | RENTAL | FAMILY | At this luxurious lifestyle resort surrounding a human-made waterway, residents can dock their megayachts at the back door and rest their heads in breathtaking one-, two-, and three-bedroom units with high-end furnishings, wall-to-wall windows that take in the view, full kitchens, en suite bathrooms, and lots of space for either relaxing or entertaining. **Pros:** indoor and outdoor kids activities; spacious units with designer furnishings; elevator access from lobby to upper floors and dock level. **Cons:** a boater's dream; kids need to be well-behaved given the high-end furnishings and dock access; more like condo living than a resort experience. ⑤ *Rooms from: $735* ⊠ *Hwy. 1B, Retreat, Six Men's*

Bay, Heywoods ☎ *246/272–2000, 855/346–8662 in U.S.* ⊕ *www. portferdinand.com* ⌘ *46 suites* ⑩*I No meals* ▭ *No credit cards.*

Port St. Charles

$$$$ | RENTAL | FAMILY | A luxury residential marina development near historic Speightstown, Port St. Charles is a great choice for boating enthusiasts who either arrive on their own yacht or plan to charter one during their stay. **Pros:** a boater's dream; well-appointed units with beautiful views; free water taxi around the property. **Cons:** far removed from many activities and restaurants; minimum 14-night stay for some units in high season; the number of units available for short-term stays varies. ⑤ *Rooms from: $535* ⊠ *Hwy. 1B, Heywoods* ☎ *246/419–1000* ⊕ *www.portstcharles.com* ⌘ *156 suites* ⑩*I No meals.*

⬤ Shopping

Gallery of Caribbean Art

ART GALLERIES | This gallery is committed to promoting Caribbean art from Haiti and Cuba in the north to Curaçao and Guyana in the south—and, particularly, the works of Barbadian artists. ⊠ *Northern Business Centre, Queen's St., Speightstown* ☎ *246/419–0858* ⊕ *www.artgallerycaribbean.com* ⊗ *Closed Sun.*

★ Hamilton's Pottery

CRAFTS | FAMILY | Hamilton Wiltshire uses red Barbadian clay to create beautiful pieces such as table ware, mugs, and pots using environmentally friendly glazes; custom pieces can be ordered. Known affectionately as "Hammi," Hamilton himself is charming and very welcoming to those who visit his studio. ■**TIP**➔ **Call ahead to ensure that Hamilton is in the studio.** ⊠ *Sturges, Lot 4, Welchman Hall* ⊕ *After you pass entrance to Harrison's Cave follow road to left. Take next left turn, drive along dirt track until you come to pottery on your right-hand side* ☎ *246/242–7176.*

East Coast

On the east coast, the crashing Atlantic surf has eroded the shoreline, forming steep cliffs and exposing prehistoric rocks that look like giant mushrooms. Bathsheba and Cattlewash are favorite seacoast destinations for local folks on weekends and holidays. In the central interior, narrow roads weave through tiny villages and along and between the ridges. The landscape is covered with tropical vegetation and is rife with fascinating caves and gullies. Between the sweeping views out over the Atlantic and the tiny fishing towns along the northwestern coast are forest and farm, moor and mountain. Most guides include a loop through the far north on a daylong tour of the east coast—it's a beautiful drive.

Sights

★ Andromeda Botanic Gardens

GARDEN | FAMILY | More than 600 beautiful and unusual plant specimens from around the world are cultivated in 6 acres of gardens nestled among streams, ponds, and rocky outcroppings overlooking the sea above the Bathsheba coastline near Tent Bay. The gardens were created in 1954 with flowering plants collected by the late horticulturist Iris Bannochie (1914–88). They're now administered by the Barbados National Trust. The Gallery Shop features local art, photography, and crafts. The Garden Café serves sandwiches, salads from the gardens, desserts, and drinks. Entrance fees include unlimited return visits within 3 weeks. ⊠ *Bathsheba* ☎ *246/433–9384* ⊕ *www.andromedabarbados.com* ⊠ *$15*.

★ Animal Flower Cave

CAVE | FAMILY | Small sea anemones, or sea worms, resemble flowers when they open their tiny tentacles. They live in small pools in this sea cave at the island's very northern tip. The cave itself, discovered in 1750, has a coral floor that ranges from 126,000 to 500,000 years old, according to geological estimates. Coral steps lead through an opening in the "roof" into the cave. Bring your bathing suit. Depending on that day's sea swells, you can swim in the naturally formed pool—and the view of breaking waves from inside the cave is magnificent. Steep stairs, uneven surfaces, and rocks make this an unwise choice for anyone with walking difficulties. The Restaurant, perched at the top of the cliff, opens daily for lunch. The property has a playground, as well as lots of pet goats and sheep wandering around. ■**TIP**➔ **The far north is an alternative route to the east coast, and this is a great place to stop for an adventure and refreshments.** ⊠ *North Point, Conneltown* ☎ *246/439–8797* ⊕ *www.animalflowercave.com* ⊠ *$13*.

★ Barbados Wildlife Reserve

NATURE PRESERVE | FAMILY | This reserve at the top of Farley Hill is the habitat of herons, innumerable land turtles, screeching peacocks, shy deer, elusive green monkeys, brilliantly colored parrots (in a large walk-in aviary), snakes, and a caiman. Except for the snakes and the caiman, the animals run or fly freely—so step carefully and keep your hands to yourself. Feeding times (10 am and 2 pm) are your best chances to glimpse green monkeys. ■**TIP**➔ **Admission to the reserve also includes admission to nearby Grenade Hall Signal Station (a 19th-century lookout tower) and Forest.**

Cricket is the national pastime (and passion) of many Bajans.

✉ *Hwy. 2* ✛ *Across from Farley Hill National Park* ☎ *246/422–8826* ⊕ *www.barbadoswildlifereserve.com* 💲 *$15.*

Barclays Park

CITY PARK | **FAMILY** | Straddling the Ermy Bourne Highway on the east coast, just north of Bathsheba, this 50-acre public park was gifted to Barbados by Barclays Bank (now First Caribbean International Bank) after independence was declared in 1966. Pack a picnic lunch, run around, and enjoy the gorgeous ocean view. ✉ *Ermy Bourne Hwy., Cattlewash.*

Chalky Mount

LOCAL INTEREST | This tiny east-coast village is perched high in the clay-yielding hills that have supplied local potters for about 300 years. A few working potteries are open daily to visitors, who can watch as artisans create bowls, vases, candleholders, and decorative objects—which are, of course, for sale. ✉ *Coggins Hill, Chalky Mount* 💲 *Free.*

★ Cherry Tree Hill

VIEWPOINT | The cherry trees for which this spot was named have long since disappeared, but the view from Cherry Tree Hill, just east of St. Nicholas Abbey greathouse, is still one of the most spectacular in Barbados. Although only about 850 feet above sea level, it is one of the highest points on the island and affords a broad view of the rugged east coast and the entire Scotland District—so named because its rolling hills resemble the moors of Scotland. Today, when approaching from the west, you drive through a majestic stand of mature, leafy mahogany trees. Stop at the crest of the hill for a stunning panoramic view. ■TIP→ **Photo op!** ⊠ *Cherry Tree Hill Rd., Moore Hill.*

Codrington Theological College

BUILDING | An impressive stand of cabbage-palm trees lines the road leading to the coral-stone buildings and serene grounds of Codrington College, the oldest Anglican theological seminary in the western hemisphere, opened in 1745 on a cliff overlooking Conset Bay. The college's benefactor was Christopher Codrington III (1668–1710), a former governor-general of the Leeward Islands, whose antislavery views were unpopular in the plantocracy of the times. You can visit the chapel, stroll the grounds, gaze at the duck pond, enjoy the view, and even have a picnic. ⊠ *Sargeant St., Codrington College* ☎ *246/416–8051* ⊕ *www.codrington.org* ✉ *Donations welcome.*

Farley Hill National Park

NATIONAL/STATE PARK | **FAMILY** | At this national park in northern St. Peter, across from the Barbados Wildlife Reserve, gardens and lawns—along with an avenue of towering palms and gigantic mahogany, whitewood, and casuarina trees—surround the impos-ing ruins of a plantation greathouse built by Sir Graham Briggs in 1861 to entertain royal visitors from England. Partially rebuilt for the filming of *Island in the Sun,* the classic 1957 film starring Har-ry Belafonte and Dorothy Dandridge, the structure was destroyed by fire in 1965. Behind the estate is a sweeping view of the region called Scotland for its rugged landscape. The park has a play-ground and is also the site of festivals and musical events. ⊠ *Hwy. 2* ☎ *246/422–3555* ✉ *$3 per car, pedestrians free.*

Morgan Lewis Windmill

HISTORIC SITE | Built in 1727 of boulders "cemented" in place with a mixture of egg whites and coral dust, the mill was operational until 1945. Today it's the only remaining windmill in Barbados with its wheelhouse and sails intact. The mill was donated to the Barbados National Trust in 1962 and eventually restored to original working specifications in 1998 by millwrights from the United Kingdom. ⊕ *Southeast of Cherry Tree Hill* ☎ *246/426–2421* ⊕ *www.barbadosnationaltrust.org* ✉ *$3, guided tour $5, grounds free* ☉ *Closed Sun.*

St. Nicholas Abbey

HOUSE | The island's oldest greathouse (circa 1650) was named after the original British owner's hometown, St. Nicholas Parish, near Bristol, and Bath Abbey nearby. Its stone-and-wood architec-ture makes it one of only three original Jacobean-style houses still standing in the western hemisphere. Behind the greathouse and

St. Nicholas Abbey is the island's oldest surviving plantation home.

its lush tropical garden is a rum distillery that produces award-winning rum with a 19th-century steam press. It is the only estate-distilled rum in the world (this is the process of growing cane, distilling, and bottling, all done on the same premises). The St. Nicholas Abbey Heritage Railway, introduced in 2018, takes visitors on an hour long steam train ride through the property. Unfortunately this well-curated attraction doesn't fully acknowledge or memorialize the tragedy of slavery and the lives of the enslaved people that would have also called this site home. ✉ *Cherry Tree Hill Rd., Moore Hill* ☎ *246/422–5357* ⊕ *www.stnicholasabbey.com* 🖃 *$23* ⊗ *Closed Sat.*

Beaches

Be cautioned: swimming at east-coast beaches is treacherous, even for strong swimmers, and is *not* recommended. Waves are high, the bottom tends to be rocky, the currents are unpredictable, and the undertow is dangerously strong.

Bathsheba Beach

BEACH—SIGHT | FAMILY | Although unsafe for swimming, the miles of untouched sand along the East Coast Road in St. Joseph Parish are great for beachcombing and wading. Expert surfers from around the world converge on Bathsheba Soup Bowl, at the south end of the beach, each November for the Barbados Independence Pro competition. **Amenities:** none. **Best for:** solitude; sunrise; surfing; walking. ✉ *East Coast Rd., Bathsheba.*

118

★ Cattlewash Beach

BEACH—SIGHT | **FAMILY** | Swimming is unwise at this windswept beach with pounding surf, which follows the Atlantic Ocean coastline in St. Andrew, but you can take a dip, wade, and play in the tidal pools. Barclays Park, a 50-acre public park up the road, has a shaded picnic area. **Amenities:** none. **Best for:** solitude; sunrise; walking. ⊠ *Ermy Bourne Hwy., Cattlewash.*

Restaurants

The Atlantis

$$$ | **CARIBBEAN** | **FAMILY** | For decades, an alfresco lunch on the Atlantis deck overlooking the ocean has been a favorite of both visitors and Bajans. A pleasant atmosphere and good food have always been the draw, with a casually elegant dining room and a top-notch menu that focuses on local produce, seafood, and meats. **Known for:** best place for lunch when touring the east coast; stunning ocean views from your table; West Indian buffet luncheon on Wednesday and Sunday and kids' menu every day. ⑤ *Average main: $29* ⊠ *The Atlantis Historic Inn, Tent Bay* ☎ *246/433–9445* ⊕ *www.atlantishotelbarbados.com.*

Round House

$$$ | **CARIBBEAN** | **FAMILY** | Owners Robert and Gail Manley oversee the menu for guests staying in their historic (1832) manse-turned-inn, as well as tourists enjoying the east coast and Bajans dining out. The lunch menu—served on a deck overlooking the Atlantic Ocean—includes homemade soups and quiches, sandwiches, salads, and pasta. **Known for:** casual alfresco dining overlooking smashing ocean surf; good spot for lunch, served all afternoon, when touring the east coast; Friday night barbecue dinner, biweekly in high season, with live music. ⑤ *Average main: $26* ⊠ *Bathsheba* ☎ *246/433–9678* ⊕ *www.roundhousebarbados.com.*

Acknowledging History

Barbados' tourism product reflects a romanticized perspective of British colonialism without sufficiently acknowledging and engaging with the harsh realities and legacies of the trans-Atlantic slave trade. Barbados can be considered an active archaeological site, and there are many chapters in history still yet to be told. The Barbados Museum, along with other organizations like the Eco Adventures Barbados, are trying to tell that full story, but the country on a whole has a long way to go.

Hotels

The Atlantis Historic Inn

$$ | **B&B/INN** | Renowned for its spectacular oceanfront location, this hotel has been a fixture on the rugged east coast for more than a century. **Pros:** historical and modern blend beautifully; spectacular oceanfront location; popular restaurant. **Cons:** for oceanfront rooms, smashing waves can be noisy at night; no beach for swimming, but there is a pool; remote location, so rental car is advised. ⑤ *Rooms from: $281 ✉ Tent Bay ☎ 246/433–9445 ⊕ www.atlantishotelbarbados.com ⥽ 9 rooms ⦿ Free breakfast.*

★ ECO Lifestyle + Lodge

$ | **B&B/INN** | This sustainable boutique hotel is inspired by its natural surroundings—a cliff overlooking the sea that's thick with palm trees and other tropical foliage. **Pros:** peaceful and relaxing; farm-to-table menu in the small restaurant; yoga, massage, and meditation in the Zen Gully. **Cons:** remote location; some rooms have no air-conditioning; no TV or in-room telephone. ⑤ *Rooms from: $219 ✉ Tent Bay ☎ 246/433–9450 ⊕ www.ecolifestylelodge. com ⥽ 10 rooms ⦿ Free Breakfast.*

Round House Inn

$ | **B&B/INN** | It's hard to tell which is more appealing: the view of the rugged coastline or the magnificent historic (1832) manse strategically perched on the cliff to take advantage of the view. **Pros:** fabulous ocean views; small and intimate; quiet and peaceful—bring a good book. **Cons:** really remote location; no TV (if you care); few on-site activities. ⑤ *Rooms from: $175 ✉ Bathsheba ☎ 246/433–9079 ⊕ www.roundhousebarbados.com ⥽ 4 rooms ⦿ Free breakfast.*

Central Interior

The central interior of Barbados is dotted with small villages and covered with miles and miles of sugarcane. It's also marked by the island's unique cave system, a forested gully, magnificent gardens, and an amazing view of the entire south coast. Whether traveling around the south, east, or west coast, be sure to incorporate this area into your tour.

Sights

★ Coco Hill Forest

FOREST | FAMILY | This lush, 52-acre tropical forest is ideal for nature walks, hiking, and forest bathing, or if you need a break from the beach. The view over the island's east coast is simply breathtaking. Hiking trails are approximately 1½ miles long and should take 1½ hours to complete. **■ TIP→ Hire a guide to share details on the hundreds of tree, plant, and herb species, as well as the history of agriculture in Barbados and the project's mission to regenerate the soils.** Check their Facebook page for the latest tour details. ⊠ *Richmond Rd. , Melvin Hill, Bathsheba* ☎ *246/235–4926* ⊕ *www. facebook.com/cocohillforest* ⊠ *$10.*

Flower Forest Botanical Gardens

GARDEN | FAMILY | It's a treat to meander among fragrant flowering bushes, canna and ginger lilies, puffball trees, and more than 100 other species of tropical flora in a cool, tranquil forest of flowers and other plants. A ½-mile (1-km) path winds through the 53.6-acre grounds, a former sugar plantation; it takes about 30 to 45 minutes to follow the path, or you can wander freely for as long as you wish. Benches throughout provide places to pause and reflect. There's also a snack bar, a gift shop, and a beautiful view of Mt. Hillaby, at 1,100 feet the island's highest point. ⊠ *Hwy. 2, Richmond* ☎ *246/433–8152* ⊕ *www.flowerforestbarbados.com* ⊠ *$15.*

Gun Hill Signal Station

HISTORIC SITE | FAMILY | The 360-degree view from Gun Hill, at 700 feet, was of strategic importance to the 18th-century British army. Using lanterns and semaphore, soldiers here could communicate with their counterparts at the south coast's Garrison and the north's Grenade Hill about approaching ships, civil disorders, storms, or other emergencies. Time moved slowly in those days, and Captain Henry Wilkinson whiled away his off-duty hours by carving a huge lion from a single rock—on the hillside below the tower. Come for a short history lesson but mainly for the view; it's so gorgeous that military invalids were sent here to convalesce. There's a small café for refreshments. ⊠ *Fusilier Rd., Gun Hill* ☎ *246/429–1358* ⊕ *www.barbadosnationaltrust.org/project/gunhill* ⊠ *$6* ⊙ *Closed Sun.*

★ Harrison's Cave

CAVE | FAMILY | This limestone cavern, complete with stalactites, stalagmites, subterranean streams, and a 40-foot underground waterfall, is a rare find in the Caribbean—and one of Barbados's most popular attractions. Tours include a nine-minute video and

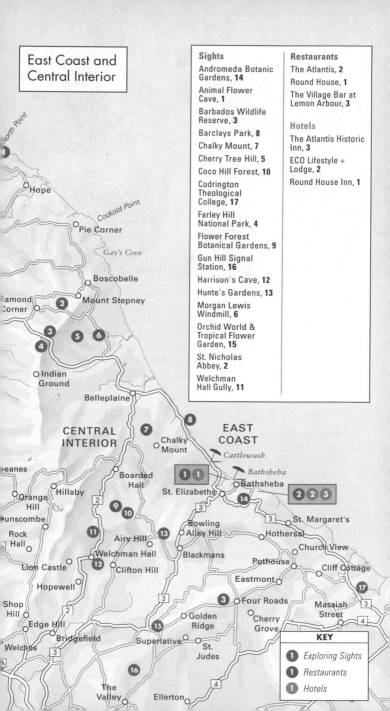

East Coast and Central Interior

Sights

Andromeda Botanic Gardens, **14**

Animal Flower Cave, **1**

Barbados Wildlife Reserve, **3**

Barclays Park, **8**

Chalky Mount, **7**

Cherry Tree Hill, **5**

Coco Hill Forest, **10**

Codrington Theological College, **17**

Farley Hill National Park, **4**

Flower Forest Botanical Gardens, **9**

Gun Hill Signal Station, **16**

Harrison's Cave, **12**

Hunte's Gardens, **13**

Morgan Lewis Windmill, **6**

Orchid World & Tropical Flower Garden, **15**

St. Nicholas Abbey, **2**

Welchman Hall Gully, **11**

Restaurants

The Atlantis, **2**

Round House, **1**

The Village Bar at Lemon Arbour, **3**

Hotels

The Atlantis Historic Inn, **3**

ECO Lifestyle + Lodge, **2**

Round House Inn, **1**

KEY

- **1** *Exploring Sights*
- **1** *Restaurants*
- **1** *Hotels*

The Gun Hill Signal Station lion was carved from a single rock in 1868.

an hour-long underground journey via electric tram. The visitor center has interactive displays, life-size models and sculptures, a souvenir shop, a restaurant, and elevator access to the tram for people with disabilities. Tram tours fill up fast, so book ahead. More intrepid visitors may like the 1½-hour walk-in tour or 4-hour eco-adventure tour, exploring nature trails and some of the cave's natural passages. ⊠ *Allen View, Welchman Hall* ✛ *Off Hwy. 2* ☎ *246/417–3700* ⊕ *www.harrisonscave.com* 🎫 *Tours from $20.*

★ Hunte's Gardens
GARDEN | FAMILY | Horticulturist Anthony Hunte spent two years converting an overgrown sinkhole (caused by the collapse of a limestone cave) into an extraordinary garden environment. Trails lead up, down, and around 10 acres of dense foliage—everything from pots of flowering plants and great swaths of thick ground cover to robust vines, exotic tropical flowers, and majestic 100-year-old cabbage palms that reach for the sun. Benches and chairs, strategically placed among the greenery, afford perfect (and fairly private) vantage points, while classical music plays overhead. Hunte lives on the property and welcomes visitors to his verandah for a glass of juice or rum punch. Just ask, and he'll be happy to tell you the fascinating story of how the gardens evolved. ⊠ *Hwy. 3A, Castle Grant* ☎ *246/433–3333* ⊕ *www.hunt-esgardens-barbados.com* 🎫 *$15.*

★ Orchid World & Tropical Flower Garden.

FOREST | FAMILY | Meandering pathways thread through gardens filled with more than 30,000 colorful orchids and other tropical plants. You'll see Vandaceous orchids attached to fences or wire frames, Schomburgkia and Oncidiums stuck on mahogany trees, Aranda and Spathoglottis orchids growing in a grotto, and Ascocendas suspended from netting in shady enclosures as well as seasonal orchids, scented orchids, and multicolor Vanda orchids. Benches are well placed to rest, admire the flowers, or take in the expansive view of the surrounding cane fields and distant hills of Sweet Vale. Snacks, cold beverages, and other refreshments are served in the café. ⊠ *Hwy. 3B, Groves, Sweet Vale* ☏ *246/433–0306* ⊕ *www.orchidworldbarbados.com* ⊜ *$13* ⊗ *Closed Mon. May 15–Oct. 15.*

Welchman Hall Gully

NATURE PRESERVE | FAMILY | This 1½-mile-long (2-km-long) natural gully is really a collapsed limestone cavern, once part of the same underground network as Harrison's Cave. The Barbados National Trust protects the peace and quiet here, making it a beautiful place to hike past acres of labeled flowers and stands of enormous trees. You can see some interesting birds and troops of native green monkeys. There are some scheduled, free, guided tours, and a guide can be arranged with 24 hours' notice. Otherwise, the 30- to 45-minute walk is self-guided. ⊠ *Welchman Hall* ☏ *246/438–6671* ⊕ *www.welchmanhallgullybarbados.com* ⊜ *$12.*

 Restaurants

★ The Village Bar at Lemon Arbour

$ | CARIBBEAN | Commonly known as Lemon Arbour, this is the place to be on a Saturday afternoon, as Bajans from all walks of life descend on this family-run restaurant and bar overlooking the countryside. Try some "Pudding and souse"—a local dish combining steamed sweet potato (the pudding) and pickled pork (souse)—it tastes better than it sounds! **Known for:** pudding and souse, and other Bajan dishes; relaxed and lively atmosphere; great people watching (it can get quite lively). ⑤ *Average main: $10* ⊠ *Lemon Arbour* ☏ *246/433–3162* ⊗ *Closed Sun.*

Activities

Cricket, football (soccer), polo, and rugby are extremely popular sports in Barbados for participants and spectators alike, with local, regional, and international matches held throughout the year. Check local newspapers for information about schedules and tickets.

Diving and Snorkeling

More than two dozen dive sites lie along the west coast between Maycocks Bay and Bridgetown and off the south coast as far as the St. Lawrence Gap. Certified divers can explore flat coral reefs and see dramatic sea fans, huge barrel sponges, and more than 50 varieties of fish. Nine sunken wrecks are dived regularly, and at least 10 more are accessible to experts. Underwater visibility is generally 80 to 90 feet. The calm waters along the west coast are also ideal for snorkeling. The marine reserve, a stretch of protected reef between Sandy Lane and the Colony Club, contains beautiful coral formations accessible from the beach.

DIVE SITES

On the west coast, **Bell Buoy** is a large, dome-shape reef where huge brown coral tree forests and schools of fish delight all categories of divers at depths ranging from 20 to 60 feet. At **Dottins Reef,** off Holetown, you can see schooling fish, barracudas, and turtles at depths of 40 to 60 feet. **Maycocks Bay,** on the northwest coast, is a particularly enticing site; large coral reefs are separated by corridors of white sand, and visibility is often 100 feet or more. The 165-foot freighter *Pamir* lies in 60 feet of water off Six Men's Bay; it's still intact, and you can peer through its portholes and view dozens of varieties of tropical fish. **Silver Bank** is a healthy coral reef with beautiful fish and sea fans; you may get a glimpse of the *Atlantis* submarine at 60 to 80 feet. Not to be missed is the *Stavronikita,* a scuttled Greek freighter at about 135 feet; hundreds of butterfly fish hang out around its mast, and the thin rays of sunlight filtering down through the water make fully exploring the huge ship a wonderfully eerie experience.

Farther south, **Carlisle Bay** is a natural harbor and marine park just below Bridgetown. Here you can retrieve empty bottles thrown overboard by generations of sailors and see cannons and cannonballs, anchors, and six unique shipwrecks (*Berwyn, Fox, CTrek, Eilon,* the barge *Cornwallis,* and *Bajan Queen*) lying in 25 to 60 feet of water, all close enough to visit on the same dive. The *Bajan*

Queen, a cruise vessel that sank in 2002, is the island's newest wreck.

Dive shops provide a two-hour beginner's "resort" course ($100–$110) followed by a shallow dive, or a weeklong certification course (about $450). Once you're certified, a one-tank dive runs about $70; a two-tank dive is $120. All equipment is supplied, and you can purchase multidive packages. Gear for snorkeling is available (free or for a small rental fee) from most hotels. Snorkelers can usually accompany dive trips for $30 for a one- or two-hour trip. Most dive shops have relationships

with several hotels and offer special dive packages, with transportation, to hotel guests.

Sea Urchin Alert

Black sea urchins lurk on the shallow sea bottom and near reefs, and their venom-filled spines can cause painful wounds. They've even been known to pierce wet suits, so divers should be careful when brushing up against submerged rock walls. Getting several stings might cause muscle spasms and breathing difficulties; victims should get help immediately.

DIVE OPERATORS
★ Barbados Blue
DIVING/SNORKELING | FAMILY | Located within the Hilton Barbados hotel complex at Needham's Point, Barbados Blue offers daily scuba and snorkeling trips to Carlisle Bay Marine Park—think shipwrecks and hawksbill turtles—as well as private boat charters and PADI classes. Scuba and snorkeling gear are available to rent, along with underwater digital cameras, and hotel pickup can be arranged. Added bonuses: the facility is 100% eco-ware, it's the only dive operator with two marine biologists on staff, and your money directly benefits the marine park and a coral restoration project. ⊠ *Hilton Barbados, Aquatic Gap, Garrison* ☎ *246/434–5764, 800/929–7154 in U.S.* ⊕ *www.divebarbadosblue.com.*

Dive Hightide Watersports
SCUBA DIVING | FAMILY | On the west coast, Dive Hightide Watersports offers three dive trips daily—one- and two-tank dives and night reef–wreck–drift dives—for up to eight divers, along with PADI instruction, equipment rental, and free transportation. ⊠ *Coral Reef Club, Hwy. 1, Holetown* ☎ *246/432–0931, 800/970–0016, 800/513–5763* ⊕ *www.divehightide.com.*

Barbados Blue offers snorkeling and diving in Carlisle Bay.

Dive Shop, Ltd

SCUBA DIVING | FAMILY | Next to the marine park on Carlisle Bay, just south of Bridgetown, the island's oldest dive shop offers daily reef and wreck dives, plus beginner classes, certification courses, and underwater photography instruction. Underwater cameras are available for rent. Free transfers are provided between your hotel and the dive shop. ⊠ *Amey's Alley, Upper Bay St., Garrison* ⊹ *Next to Nautilus Beach Apts.* ☎ *246/426–9947* ⊕ *www.divebds. com.*

Reefers & Wreckers Scuba Diving

SCUBA DIVING | FAMILY | The island's most northerly dive shop provides easy access to the north's unspoiled reefs, runs daily trips to dive sites and wrecks all along the west coast and in Carlisle Bay, and offers PADI courses ranging from "discover" to "dive master"—including nitrox, advanced open water, night diver, deep diver, drift diver, and rescue diver. ⊠ *Queen St., Speightstown* ⊹ *Next to Orange St. Grocer* ☎ *246/422–5450* ⊕ *www.reefers-wreckersbarbados.com.*

★ Trident Freedivers

DIVING/SNORKELING | FAMILY | Barbadian Freediving record holder Johanna Loch-Allen offers freediving tours and certification, as well as spearfishing tours and underwater photoshoots. Whether you're a beginner or a more advanced freediver, Johanna shows you the best spots on the island. A popular tour includes spearing the invasive lionfish from the reefs around Barbados, followed by ice cold beers and a barbecue on the beach. If you're feeling really fancy, you can have fresh lionfish ceviche prepared on the spot. ⊠ *Hastings* ☎ *246/234–7778* ⊕ *www.freedivebarbados.com.*

Fishing

Fishing is a year-round activity in Barbados, but prime time is January through April, when game fish are in season. Whether you're a serious deep-sea fisher looking for marlin, sailfish, tuna, and other billfish or you prefer angling in calm coastal waters where wahoo, barracuda, and other smaller fish reside, you can choose from a variety of half- or full-day charter trips departing from The Careenage in Bridgetown. Expect to pay $175 per person for a shared half-day charter; for a private charter, expect to pay $500 to $600 per boat for a four-hour half-day or $950 to $1,000 for an eight-hour full-day charter. Spectators who don't fish are welcome for $50 per person.

Billfisher Deepsea Fishing
FISHING | *Billfisher III*, a 40-foot Viking Sport Fisherman, accommodates up to six passengers with three fishing chairs and five rods. Captain Ralphie White's full-day charters include a full lunch; all trips include drinks and transportation to and from the boat. ⊠ *Bridge House Wharf, Cavans La., The Careenage, Bridgetown* ☎ *246/431–0741* ⊕ *www.greatadventuresbarbados.com.*

Cannon Charters
FISHING | *Cannon II*, a 42-foot Hatteras Sport Fisherman, has three chairs and five rods and accommodates six passengers. Drinks and snacks are complimentary, and lunch is served on full-day charters. ⊠ *The Careenage, Bridgetown* ☎ *246/424–6107* ⊕ *www. fishingbarbados.com.*

High Seas Fishing Charters
FISHING | *Ocean Hunter*, a 42-foot custom-built sportfishing boat, has an extended cockpit that easily accommodates six people. Choose a four-, six-, or eight-hour charter. All tackle and bait are supplied, as well as drinks and snacks. Charter rates include hotel transfers. ⊠ *The Careenage* ☎ *246/233–2598* ⊕ *www.sportfishing-barbados.com.*

Sports Legend: Sir Garfield Sobers

Cricket is more than a national pastime in Barbados. It's a passion. And no one is more revered than Sir Garfield Sobers, the greatest sportsman ever to hail from Barbados and globally acknowledged as the greatest all-round cricketer the game has ever seen. Sobers played his first test match in 1953 at the age of 17 and continually set and broke records until his last test match in 1973.

He was an equally accomplished batsman and bowler. Knighted by Queen Elizabeth II in 1974 for his contributions to the sport, he was honored as a national hero of Barbados in 1999. A bronze statue honoring His Excellency, the Right Honorable Sir Garfield Sobers (or Sir Gary, as he's known locally) dominates the entry to Kensington Oval, the stadium in Bridgetown used mainly for cricket.

Golf

Barbadians love golf, and golfers love Barbados. Courses open to visitors are listed below.

Barbados Golf Club

GOLF | The first public golf course on Barbados, an 18-hole championship course (two returning 9s), was redesigned in 2000 by golf course architect Ron Kirby. The course has hosted numerous competitions, including the European Senior tour in 2003. Several hotels offer preferential tee-time reservations and reduced rates. Cart, trolley, club, and shoe rentals are all available. ⊠ *Hwy. 7, Durants* ☎ *246/538–4653* ⊕ *www.barbadosgolfclub.com* ⊠ *$105 for 18 holes; $65 for 9 holes; 3-, 5-, and 7-day passes $255, $400, $525, respectively* ⅄ *18 holes (2 returning 9s), 6805 yds, par 72.*

★ Country Club at Sandy Lane

GOLF | At this prestigious club, golfers can play the Old Nine or either of two 18-hole championship courses: the Tom Fazio–designed Country Club Course and the spectacular Green Monkey Course, which is reserved for hotel guests and club members. The layouts offer a limestone-quarry setting (Green Monkey), a modern style with lakes (Country Club), and traditional small greens and narrow fairways (Old Nine). Golfers can use the driving range for free. The Country Club Restaurant and Bar, overlooking the 18th hole, is open to the public. Caddies, trolleys, clubs, and shoes are available for rent, as are GPS-equipped carts that alert you to upcoming hazards, give tips on how to play holes, and let you order refreshments. ⊠ *Sandy Lane Hotel, Hwy. 1* ☎ *246/444–2000, 866/444–4080 in U.S.* ⊕ *www.sandylane.com/ golf ⛳ Country Club: $240 for 18 holes ($200 hotel guests); $150 for 9 holes ($130 for guests); 7-day pass $1350 ($1250 for guests). Green Monkey: $390 for 18 holes (guests only). Old Nine: $90 for 9 holes ($75 guests); 7-day pass $560 ($450 guests) ⅄ Green Monkey: 18 holes, 7343 yds, par 72; Country Club: 18 holes, 7060 yds, par 72; Old Nine: 9 holes, 3345 yds, par 36.*

Hiking

Hilly but not mountainous, the island's northern interior and east coast are ideal for hiking.

★ Barbados Hiking Association

HIKING/WALKING | FAMILY | Free walks sponsored by the Barbados National Trust and the Barbados Hiking Association are conducted year-round and are a great way to see the island! Experienced guides group you with others of similar ability on "Stop and Stare" walks, 5 to 6 miles (8 to 10 km); medium hikes, 8 to 10 miles (13 to 16 km); medium-fast hikes, 10 to 12 miles (16 to 19 km); or really fast hikes, 12 to 14 miles (19 to 23 km). Wear loose clothes, sensible shoes, sunscreen, and a hat, and bring a camera and water. Routes and locations change, but each hike is a loop, finishing where it began. Check newspapers, call the Trust, or check the Association's Facebook page for schedules and meeting places. ⊠ *Barbados National Trust, Wildey House, Errol Barrow Hwy., Wildey* ☎ *246/426–2421.*

Sea Excursions

Minisubmarine voyages are enormously popular with families and those who enjoy watching fish but don't wish to get wet. Party boats depart from Bridgetown's Deep Water Harbour for sightseeing and snorkeling or romantic sunset cruises. Prices are $70 to $125 per person for four- or five-hour daytime cruises and $60 to $85 for three- or four-hour sunset cruises, depending on the type of refreshments and entertainment included; transportation to and from the dock is provided. For an excursion that may be less splashy in terms of a party atmosphere—but is definitely splashier in terms of the actual experience—turtle tours allow participants to swim with and feed a resident group of hawksbill and leatherback sea turtles.

Atlantis Submarine

BOATING | FAMILY | This 50-foot, 48-passenger submarine turns the Caribbean into a giant aquarium. The 90-minute voyage (including 45 minutes underwater) takes in wrecks and reefs as deep as 150 feet. Children love the adventure, but they must be at least 3 feet tall. ☒ *Shallow Draught, Bridgetown* ☎ *246/436–8929* ⊕ *www.barbados.atlantissubmarines.com* ⌷ *From $112.*

Cool Runnings Catamaran Cruises

BOATING | FAMILY | Captain Robert Povey, owner of *Cool Runnings* catamaran, skippers a five-hour lunch cruise with stops to swim with the fishes, snorkel with sea turtles, and explore a shallow shipwreck. A four-hour sunset cruise includes swimming, snorkeling, and exploring underwater as the sun sinks. Delicious meals with wine, along with an open bar, are part of all cruises. ☒ *Carlisle House, Carlisle Wharf, Hincks St., Bridgetown* ☎ *246/436–0911* ⊕ *www.coolrunningsbarbados.com* ⌷ *Lunch cruise $95, sunset cruise $85.*

★ Tiami Catamaran Cruises

BOATING | FAMILY | Tiami operates five catamaran party boats for luncheon cruises to a secluded bay for swimming with turtles or for romantic sunset and moonlight cruises. Daytime cruises include buffet lunch, open bar, and three swim/snorkel stops. Evening cruises include a swim/snorkel stop as the sun goes down, buffet dinner, and cocktails. ■**TIP➜ Round-trip hotel transfers are complimentary for all cruises.** ☒ *Shallow Draught, Bridgetown* ☎ *246/430–0900* ⊕ *www.tiamicatamarancruises.com* ⌷ *Lunch cruises from $96, sunset cruises from $71.*

Surfing

The best surfing is at Bathsheba Soup Bowl on the east coast; the Barbados Independence SurfPro championship (an international competition) is held here every November. But the water on the windward (Atlantic Ocean) side of the island is safe only for the most experienced surfers. Surfers also congregate at Surfer's Point, at the southern tip of Barbados near Inch Marlow, where the Atlantic Ocean meets the Caribbean Sea.

Zed's Surfing Adventures

SURFING | FAMILY | This outfit rents surfboards, provides lessons, and offers surf tours including equipment, guide, and transportation to surf breaks appropriate for your experience. Two-hour group lessons are held regularly; a six-hour package includes three lessons and a week's board rental. Surfboard rentals for experienced surfers and private lessons are always available. ✉ *Surfer's Point, Inch Marlowe* ☎ *246/428–7873* ⊕ *www.zedssurf-travel.com* ⌨ *From $80 for lessons, from $25 per hour for board rental.*

Windsurfing and Kiteboarding

Barbados is one of the prime locations in the world for windsurf-ing—and, increasingly, for kiteboarding. Winds are strongest November through April at the island's southern tip, at Silver Sands–Silver Rock Beach, which is where the Barbados Windsurf-ing Championships are held in mid-January. Use of windsurfing boards and equipment as well as instruction are often among the amenities included at larger hotels, and some also rent to nonguests. Kiteboarding is a more difficult sport that requires several hours of instruction to reach proficiency; Silver Sands is about the only location where you'll find kiteboarding equipment and instruction. Stand-up paddling has also become increasingly popular, and most surf shops (and many resorts) offer paddling equipment and instruction.

deAction Surf Shop

WINDSURFING | Directly on Silver Sands–Silver Rock Beach, Brian "Irie Man" Talma's shop stocks a range of rental surfing equip-ment and offers beginner windsurfing, kiteboarding, surfing, and stand-up paddling lessons. Conditions are ideal, with waves off the outer reef and flat water in the inner lagoon. Kiteboarding, which isn't easy, generally involves six hours of instruction broken up into two or three sessions: from flying a small kite to getting the body dragged with a big kite to finally getting up on the board. All equipment is provided. ✉ *Silver Sands–Silver Rock Beach, Silver Sands* ☎ *246/428–2027* ⊕ *www.briantalma.com.*

★ Paddle Barbados

WATER SPORTS | **FAMILY** | Paddle Barbados offers instruction, rentals, stand-up paddle yoga sessions, and tours around the harbor. A quick lesson will get you up on the board and paddling away in about 10 minutes. ✉ *Barbados Cruising Club, Aquatic Gap, Garri-son* ☎ *246/249–2787* ⊕ *www.paddlebarbados.com.*

SAINT LUCIA

Updated by
Jane E. Zarem

⊙ Sights   🍴 Restaurants   🛏 Hotels   🛍 Shopping   🍸 Nightlife
★★★★★   ★★★★★   ★★★★★   ★★★☆☆   ★★★☆☆

WELCOME TO SAINT LUCIA

TOP REASONS TO GO

★ **The Natural Beauty:** Magnificent, lush scenery makes Saint Lucia one of the most beautiful Caribbean islands.

★ **The Romance:** A popular honeymoon spot, Saint Lucia has abundant romantic retreats.

★ **Indulgent Accommodations:** Sybaritic lodging options include an all-inclusive spa resort, a posh sanctuary sandwiched between a mountain and the beach, and two resorts with prime locations between the Pitons.

★ **The Music:** Performers and fans from around the world come for the annual Saint Lucia Jazz & Arts Festival.

★ **The Welcome:** The friendly Saint Lucians love sharing their island and their cultural heritage with visitors.

.

1 Rodney Bay and the North. The lovely harbor has a marina, great restaurants, and a few places to stay. Some of the most luxurious resorts and the only public golf course are at Cap Estate, in the far north.

2 Castries. The lively capital city has an active market and small hotels; lovely resorts are tucked into the coastline.

3 Marigot Bay. Between Castries and Soufrière, the "village" surrounding the man-made lagoon has an active marina, large resorts and small hotels, lots of restaurants, and shopping.

4 Soufrière and the Southwest Coast. The island's oldest town is also the location of the Pitons, the botanical garden, the drive-in volcano, and waterfalls. There's also great resorts and restaurants.

5 Vieux Fort and the East Coast. In and around relatively quiet Vieux Fort—home to the airport and a pair of resorts—you can explore some of the island's unique ecosystems.

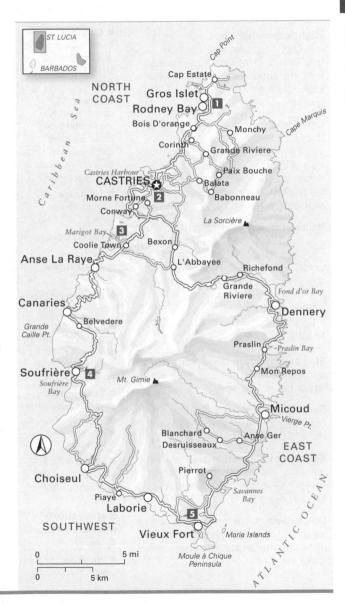

ST. LUCIA

BARBADOS

Cap Point

Cap Estate

NORTH
COAST

Gros Islet 1
Rodney Bay

Bois D'orange

Cape Marquis

Monchy

Corinth

Grande Riviere

Paix Bouche

Castries Harbour

CASTRIES ✪

Balata

Morne Fortune 2

Babonneau

Conway

La Sorcière ▲

Marigot Bay 3

Coolie Town

Bexon

Anse La Raye

L'Abbayee

Richefond

Grande
Riviere

Fond d'or Bay

Canaries

Belvedere

Dennery

Grande
Caille Pt.

Praslin • Praslin Bay

Soufrière 4

Mt. Gimie ▲

Mon Repos

Soufrière
Bay

Micoud

Vierge Pt.

Blanchard

Anse Ger

Desruisseaux

EAST
COAST

Pierrot

Choiseul

Savannes
Bay

Piaye

Laborie 5

SOUTHWEST

Vieux Fort

Maria Islands

ATLANTIC OCEAN

0   5 mi

0   5 km

Moule à Chique
Peninsula

Caribbean Sea

ISLAND SNAPSHOT

WHEN TO GO

High Season: Mid-December through mid-April is the best and most expensive time to visit Saint Lucia. You're guaranteed the most entertainment at resorts, but luxury hotels are often booked far in advance.

Low Season: From August through late October, the weather can be oppressively hot and humid, with a high risk of tropical storms and substantial rain. Some upscale hotels close in September and October; those that are open offer deep discounts.

Value Season: From late April through July and from November through mid-December, hotel prices drop 20% to 50% (except during Saint Lucia Jazz and Carnival). Expect scattered showers but many sun-kissed days and few crowds.

WAYS TO SAVE

Stay at a cozy inn. Small properties are more intimate (and far cheaper) than the typical beach resort.

Shop at open-air markets. Buy local fruits, veggies, spices, souvenirs, and more in Castries.

Take the public minibus. Especially in the north, a jitney journey that costs a dollar or two would be much more expensive by taxi.

Do a full-day tour. Instead of renting a car or taking multiple taxis or minitours, do an attractions blitz with a full-day island tour.

AT A GLANCE

■ **Currency:** Eastern Caribbean dollar; pegged to the U.S. dollar at EC$2.67/$1

■ **Money:** ATMs common but dispense only local currency; major credit cards and U.S. dollars (not coins) widely accepted

■ **Language:** English, Creole patois

■ **Country Code:** ☎1 758

■ **Emergencies:** ☎999

■ **Driving:** On the left

■ **Electricity:** 220v/50 cycles; plugs are U.K. standard, square with three pins

■ **Time:** Same as Eastern time during daylight saving; one hour ahead otherwise

■ **Documents:** A valid passport and a return or ongoing ticket

■ **Major Mobile Companies:** Digicel, FLOW

■ **Websites:** ⊕ www. saintlucianow.com

A verdant, mountainous island halfway between Martinique and St. Vincent, Saint Lucia has evolved into one of the Caribbean's most popular vacation destinations—particularly for honeymooners and other romantics enticed by the island's striking natural beauty, its many splendid resorts and appealing inns, and its welcoming atmosphere.

The capital city of Castries and nearby villages in the northwest are home to 40% of the nearly 182,000 Saint Lucians. This area, Cap Estate and Rodney Bay Village (farther north), Marigot Bay (just south of the capital), and Soufrière (southwestern coast) are the destinations of most vacationers. In central and southwestern areas, dense rain forest, jungle-covered mountains, and vast banana plantations dominate the landscape. A tortuous road follows most of the coastline, bisecting small villages, cutting through mountains, and passing fertile valleys. Petit Piton and Gros Piton, unusual twin peaks that anchor the southwestern coast and rise up to 2,600 feet, are familiar landmarks for sailors and aviators, as well as a UNESCO World Heritage Site. Divers are attracted to the reefs in the National Marine Reserve between the Pitons and extending north past Soufrière, the capital during French colonial times. Most of the natural tourist attractions are in this area, along with several fine resorts and inns.

The pirate François Le Clerc, nicknamed Jambe de Bois (Wooden Leg) for obvious reasons, was the first European "settler." In the late 16th century, Le Clerc holed up on Pigeon Island, just off Saint Lucia's northernmost point, using it as a staging ground for attacking passing ships. Now, Pigeon Island National Landmark is a public park connected by a causeway to the mainland; Sandals Grande Saint Lucian Spa & Beach Resort, one of the largest resorts in Saint Lucia, and the Landings Resort & Spa, a luxury villa community, sprawl along that causeway. Another Sandals, the fourth on Saint Lucia, is expected to open in this same area in 2022.

Like most of its Caribbean neighbors, Saint Lucia was first inhabited by Arawaks and then the Carib people. British settlers attempted to colonize the island twice in the early 1600s, but it wasn't until 1651, after the French West India Company suppressed the local Caribs, that Europeans gained a foothold. For 150 years, battles between the French and the British over the island were frequent, with a dizzying 14 changes in power before the British finally took possession in 1814. The Europeans established sugar plantations, using enslaved people from West Africa to work the fields. By 1838, when the enslaved people were finally emancipated, more than 90% of the population was of African descent—roughly the same proportion as today.

On February 22, 1979, Saint Lucia became an independent state within the British Commonwealth of Nations, with a resident governor-general appointed by the Queen. Still, the island appears to have retained more relics of French influence—notably the island's patois, cuisine, village names, and surnames—than of the British. Most likely, that's because the British contribution primarily involved the English language, the educational and legal systems, and the political structure, whereas the French culture historically had more influence on the arts—culinary, dance, and music.

Except for a small area in the extreme northeast, one main highway circles all of Saint Lucia. The road snakes along the coast, cuts across mountains, makes hairpin turns and sheer drops, and reaches dizzying heights. It takes at least four hours to drive the whole loop. Even at a leisurely pace with frequent sightseeing stops, and whether you're driving or being driven, the curvy roads make it a tiring drive in a single outing.

Between Castries and Cap Estate, in the far north, the road is mainly flat. The area is built up with businesses, resorts, and residences, so the two-lane road is often clogged with traffic—especially just north of **Castries** and around **Rodney Bay Village** but less as you approach Pigeon Island and Cap Estate. Frequent bus service is available on this route.

The West Coast Road between Castries and **Soufrière** (a 1½-hour journey) has steep hills and sharp turns, but it's well marked and incredibly scenic. South of Castries, the road tunnels through Morne Fortune, skirts the island's largest banana plantation (more than 127 varieties of bananas, called "figs" in this part of the Caribbean, grow on the island) and the road to **Marigot Bay,** and then passes through tiny fishing villages. Just north of Soufrière, the road negotiates the island's fruit basket, where most of the mangoes, breadfruit, tomatoes, limes, and oranges are grown. In the mountainous region that forms a backdrop for Soufrière, you will notice 3,118-foot Mt. Gimie (pronounced Jimmy), Saint Lucia's highest peak. Approaching Soufrière, you'll have spectacular views of the Pitons; the plume of smoke wafting out of the thickly forested mountainside just east of Soufrière emanates from the so-called drive-in volcano.

The landscape changes dramatically between the Pitons and **Vieux Fort** on the island's southeastern tip. Along the South Coast Road traveling southeasterly from Soufrière, the terrain starts as steep mountainside with dense vegetation, progresses to undulating hills, and finally becomes rather flat and comparatively arid. Anyone arriving at Hewanorra International Airport, which is in Vieux Fort, and staying at a resort near Soufrière will travel along this route, a journey of about 45 minutes each way.

From Vieux Fort north to Castries, a 1½-hour drive, the East Coast Road twists through Micoud, Dennery, and other coastal villages. It then winds up, down, and around mountains, crosses Barre de l'Isle Ridge, and slices through the rain forest. Much of the scenery is breathtaking. The Atlantic Ocean pounds against rocky cliffs, and acres and acres of bananas and coconut palms blanket the hillsides. If you arrive at Hewanorra and stay at a resort in Marigot Bay, Castries, Rodney Bay, or Cap Estate, you'll travel along the East Coast Road.

Planning

Getting Here and Around

AIR

Saint Lucia's primary gateway is Hewanorra International Airport (UVF) in Vieux Fort, on the island's southern tip. Regional airlines fly into George F. L. Charles Airport (SLU) in Castries, commonly called Vigie Airport and more convenient to resorts in the north.

Taxis are available at both airports, although transfers may be included in your travel package. It's an expensive ride to the north from Hewanorra—$80–$100 for up to four passengers—and $75–$80 to Soufrière.

A helicopter shuttle cuts the transfer time to about 10 minutes, but the cost doubles.

CAR

The 40-mile (64-km) drive between Hewanorra International Airport (UVF) and resorts in the north takes about 90 minutes; between Hewanorra and Marigot Bay, about 60 minutes; and between Hewanorra and Soufrière, about 45 minutes.

A car is more important if you are staying at a small inn or hotel away from the beach. Just keep in mind that driving is on the left, British-style. If you're staying at an all-inclusive beach resort and don't plan to leave for meals, taxis may be the better bet. Privately owned and operated minivans constitute Saint Lucia's bus system, an inexpensive and efficient means of transportation used primarily by locals and a good way to travel between Castries and the Rodney Bay area. Water taxis are also available in some places and can save time. ⇨ *For more information on car travel in Saint Lucia and car rentals, see Car in the Travel Smart chapter.*

Essentials

BEACHES

The sand on Saint Lucia's beaches ranges from golden to black, and the island has some of the best off-the-beach snorkeling in the Caribbean—especially along the western coast north of Soufrière.

Saint Lucia's longest, broadest, and most popular beaches are in the north, which is also the flattest part of this mountainous island and the location of most resorts, restaurants, and nightlife. Many of the island's biggest resorts front the beaches from Choc Bay to Rodney Bay and north to Cap Estate. Elsewhere, tiny coves with inviting crescents of sand offer great swimming and snorkeling opportunities. Beaches are all public, but hotels flank many of the beaches along the northwestern coast. A few secluded stretches of beach on the southwestern coast, south of Marigot Bay and accessible primarily by boat, are popular swimming and snorkeling stops on catamaran day sails or powerboat sightseeing trips. Don't swim along the windward (eastern) coast, as the Atlantic Ocean is too rough—but the views are spectacular. Coconut Bay Beach Resort and Serenity by Coconut Bay, both in Vieux Fort at the southernmost tip of the island, share a beautiful beach facing the Atlantic; the water is rough—but an artificial reef makes it safe for swimming and water sports, especially kitesurfing.

HEALTH AND SAFETY

Dengue, chikungunya, and zika have all been reported throughout the Caribbean. We recommend that you protect yourself from these mosquito-borne illnesses by keeping your skin covered and/or wearing mosquito repellent. The mosquitoes that transmit these viruses are as active by day as they are by night. Beyond that, use sunblock to protect yourself from sunburn, as the sun is more intense than you think. The water in Saint Lucia is safe to drink, although bottled water is always available.

HOTELS

Nearly all of Saint Lucia's resorts and small inns face unspoiled beaches or are hidden away on secluded coves or tucked into forested hillsides in three locations along the calm Caribbean (western) coast. They're in the greater Castries area between Marigot Bay, a few miles south of the city, and Labrelotte Bay in the north; in and around Rodney Bay and north to Cap Estate; and in and around Soufrière on the southwest coast near the Pitons. There's also a pair of resorts in Vieux Fort, near Hewanorra. The advantage of being in the north is that you have access to a wider range of restaurants and nightlife; in the south, you may be limited to hotel offerings—albeit some of the best—and a few other dining options in and around Soufrière.

Beach Resorts: Most people—particularly honeymooners—choose to stay in one of Saint Lucia's many beach resorts, most of which are upscale and fairly pricey. Several are all-inclusive, including three Sandals resorts, two Sunswept resorts (The BodyHoliday and Rendezvous), St. James's Club Morgan Bay Resort & Spa, East Winds Inn, Coconut Bay Beach Resort & Spa and Serenity at Coconut Bay, and Royalton Saint Lucia Resort & Spa. Others may offer an all-inclusive option.

Small Inns: If you are looking for something more intimate and perhaps less expensive, a locally owned inn or small hotel is a good option; it may or may not be directly on the beach.

Villas: Luxury villa communities that operate like hotels are a good alternative for families. Several are in the north in the Cap Estate area.

Hotel reviews have been shortened. For full information, visit Fodors.com.

Luxury villa and condo communities are an important part of the accommodations mix on Saint Lucia, as they can be an economical option for families, other groups, or couples vacationing together. Several communities have opened in recent years, and more are on the way. The villa units themselves are privately owned, but nonowners can rent individual units directly from the property managers for a vacation or short-term stay, much like reserving hotel accommodations. Units with fully equipped kitchens, up to three bedrooms, and as many baths run $200 to $2,500 per night, depending on the size and the season.

Local real-estate agencies will arrange vacation rentals of privately owned villas and condos that are fully equipped. Most private villas are in the hills of Cap Estate in the very north of the island, at Rodney Bay or Bois d'Orange, or in Soufrière among Saint Lucia's natural treasures. Some are within walking distance of a beach.

All rental villas are staffed with a cook who specializes in local cuisine and a housekeeper; in some cases, a caretaker lives on the property and a gardener and night watchman are on staff. All properties have telephones, and most will have Internet access. Telephones may be barred against outgoing overseas calls; plan to use a phone card or calling card. Most villas also have TVs and other entertainment options and/or connectivity. All private villas have a swimming pool; condos share a community pool. Vehicles are generally not included in the rates, but rental cars can be arranged for and delivered to the villa upon request. Linens and basic supplies (such as bath soap, toilet paper, and dish detergent) are included. Pre-arrival grocery stocking can be arranged.

Units with one to nine bedrooms and the same number of baths run $200 to $2,000 per night, depending on the size of the villa, the amenities, the number of guests, and the season. Rates include utilities and government taxes. Your only additional cost will be for groceries and staff gratuities. A security deposit is required upon booking and refunded after departure less any damages or unpaid miscellaneous charges.

RENTAL CONTACTS Blue Sky Luxury. ☎ *758/450–8240* ⊕ *www. blueskyluxurystlucia.com.* **Discover Villas of Saint Lucia.** ✉ *Cap Dr., Cap Estate* ☎ *758/484–3066, 758/450–0002* ⊕ *discovervillasstlucia.com.*

What It Costs in U.S. Dollars			
$	$$	$$$	$$$$
RESTAURANTS			
under $13	$13–$20	$21–$30	over $30
HOTELS			
under $275	$275–$375	$376–$475	over $475

RESTAURANTS

Bananas, mangoes, passion fruit, plantains, breadfruit, okra, avocados, limes, pumpkins, cucumbers, papaya, yams, christophenes (also called chayote), and coconuts are among the fresh fruits and vegetables that grace Saint Lucian menus. The French influence is strong, and most chefs cook with a Creole flair. Resort buffets and restaurant fare include standards like steaks, chops, pasta, and pizza—and every menu lists fresh fish along with the ever-popular lobster.

Caribbean standards include callaloo, stuffed crab back, pepperpot stew, curried chicken or goat, and *lambi* (conch). The national dish of salt fish and green fig—a stew of dried, salted codfish and boiled green banana—is, let's say, an acquired taste. A runner-up in terms of local popularity is *bouyon*, a cooked-all-day soup or stew that combines meat (usually pig tail), "provisions" (root vegetables), pigeon peas, dumplings, broth, and local spices. Soups and stews are traditionally prepared in a coal pot—unique to Saint Lucia—a rustic clay casserole on a matching clay stand that holds the hot coals.

Chicken and pork dishes and barbecues are also popular here. Fresh Caribbean spiny lobster (mainly a tail without front claws) is available in season, which lasts from August through February. As they do throughout the Caribbean, local vendors set up barbecue grills along the roadside, at street fairs, and at Friday-night "jump-ups" and do a bang-up business selling grilled fish or chicken legs, bakes (fried biscuits), and beer—you can get a full meal for less than $10. Most other meats are imported—beef from Argentina and Iowa, lamb from New Zealand. Piton is the local brew; Bounty, the local rum.

Guests at Saint Lucia's many popular all-inclusive resorts take most meals at hotel restaurants—which are generally quite good and, in some cases, exceptional—but it's fun when vacationing to try some of the local restaurants, as well—for lunch when sightseeing or for a special night out.

What to Wear: Dress on Saint Lucia is casual but conservative. Shorts are usually fine during the day, but bathing suits and immodest clothing are frowned upon anywhere but at the beach. Nude or topless sunbathing is prohibited. In the evening the mood is casually elegant, but even the fanciest places generally expect only a collared shirt and long pants for men and a sundress or slacks for women.

NIGHTLIFE

Most resort hotels have entertainment—island music, calypso singers, and steel bands, as well as disco, karaoke, and talent shows—every night in high season and a couple of nights per week in the off-season. Otherwise, Rodney Bay is the best bet for nightlife. The restaurants and bars there attract a crowd nearly every night.

SHOPPING

The island's best-known products are wood carvings, straw mats, clay pottery, and clothing and household articles made from batik and silk-screened fabrics that are designed and produced in island workshops. You can also take home straw hats and baskets and locally grown cocoa, coffee, spices, sauces, and flavorings.

TOURS

Taxi drivers are well informed and can give you a full tour and often an excellent one, thanks to government-sponsored training programs. Full-day island tours cost $140 for up to four people, depending on the route and whether entrance fees and lunch are included; half-day tours, $100. If you plan your own day, expect to pay the driver $40 per hour plus tip.

Island Routes

ADVENTURE TOURS | This Sandals partner offers dozens of adventure tours, including guided, drive-it-yourself dune buggy safaris of Soufrière's natural sites and attractions (six hours, $215). Drivers must be at least 23, have a valid driver's license, and be able to operate a manual transmission. A catamaran cruise down the west coast from Rodney Bay to Soufrière is a less exhausting experience (seven hours, $115). Other tours include hiking, biking, horseback riding, and ziplining adventures; a guided historical tour; and many, many more. ⊠ *Castries* ☎ *877/768–8370 in U.S., 758/455–2000* ⊕ *www.islandroutes.com.*

Jungle Tours

GUIDED TOURS | This company specializes in rain-forest hiking tours in small groups and for all ability levels. You're required only to bring hiking shoes or sneakers and have a willingness to get wet and have fun. The cost is $95 per person and includes lunch, fees, and transportation via an open Land Rover truck. ⊠ *Cas en Bas* ☎ *758/715–3438* ⊕ *www.jungletoursstlucia.com.*

Rainforest Adventures

GUIDED TOURS | **FAMILY** | Ever wish you could get a bird's-eye view of the rain forest? Or at least experience it without hiking up and down miles of mountain trails? Here's your chance. Depending on your athleticism and spirit of adventure, choose a two-hour aerial tram ride, a zipline experience, or both. Either activity guarantees a magnificent view as you peacefully ride above or actively zip through the canopy of the 3,442-acre Castries Waterworks Rain Forest in Babonneau, 30 minutes east of Rodney Bay. On the tram ride, eight-passenger gondolas glide slowly among the giant trees, twisting vines, and dense thickets of vegetation accented by colorful flowers, as a tour guide explains and shares anecdotes about the various trees, plants, birds, and other wonders of nature found in the area. You might even spot a Jacquot parrot! The zipline, on the other hand, is a thrilling experience in which you're rigged with a harness, helmet, and clamps that attach to cables strategically strung through the forest. Short trails connect 18 platforms, so riders come down to earth briefly and hike to the next station before speeding through the forest canopy to the next stop. There's even a nighttime zipline tour. By the way, you can take a guided trail hike, too. ■TIP➔ **Bring binoculars and a camera.** ⊠ *Chassin, Babonneau* ☎ *758/461–5151* ⊕ *www.rainforestadventure.com* ⛿ *$75 tram, $65 zipline, $85 tram and zipline, $45 trail hike.*

St. Lucia Helicopters

AIR EXCURSIONS | How about a bird's-eye view of the island? A 10-minute North Island tour ($120 per person) leaves from the hangar in Castries, continues up the west coast to Pigeon Island, then flies along the rugged Atlantic coastline before returning inland over Castries. The 20-minute South Island tour ($187 per person) starts at Pointe Seraphine and follows the western coastline, circling beautiful Marigot Bay, Soufrière, and the majestic Pitons before returning inland over the volcanic hot springs and tropical rain forest. A complete island tour combines the two and lasts 30 minutes ($231 per person). All tours require a minimum of four passengers; the copter holds six. ⊠ *George F. L. Charles Airport, Island Flyers Hangar, Vigie* ☎ *758/453–6950* ⊕ *stluciahelicopters.com.*

★ St. Lucia National Trust

ECOTOURISM | Among the trust's fascinating Eco-South Tours (located in and around the southeast of Saint Lucia) are a hike through a mangrove forest, a boat trip and trek to Maria Islands Nature Reserve, a native fishing tour on a traditional pirogue, handicraft production, horseback riding, or sea moss harvesting. ⊠ *Pigeon Island National Landmark, Pigeon Island* ☎ *758/452–5005 Maria Islands Interpretation Centre, Vieux Fort, 758/454–5014* ⊕ *slunatrust.org/tours/toureco-south-tours.*

WEDDINGS

Marriage licenses cost $125 with a required three-day waiting period or $200 if the application is made in less than one business day, plus $60 for the associated registrar and certificate fees. There is no residency requirement. You'll need to produce valid passports and original or certified copies of birth certificates and, if applicable, divorce decrees or death certificates. Some resorts offer free weddings when combined with a honeymoon stay.

> ### Rodney Bay,
> ### Then and Now
>
> A mosquito-infested swamp near Reduit Beach was drained and opened up to the sea in the 1970s, creating a beautiful lagoon and ensuring the value of the surrounding real estate for tourism development. Today, Rodney Bay Village is a hive of tourist activity, with hotels, restaurants, much of the island's nightlife—and, of course, Rodney Bay Marina.

The high season runs from mid-December through mid-April and during the annual Saint Lucia Jazz Festival and Carnival events; at other times of the year, hotel rates may be significantly cheaper. December and January are the coolest months, and June through August are the hottest. Substantial rain (more than just a tropical spritz) is more likely from June through November.

Rodney Bay and the North

Hotels, popular restaurants, a huge mall, and the island's only casino surround a natural bay and an 80-acre man-made lagoon named for Admiral George Rodney, who sailed the British navy out of Gros Islet in 1780 to attack and ultimately destroy the French fleet. With 253 slips and a 4½-acre boatyard, Rodney Bay Marina is one of the Caribbean's premier yachting centers; each December, it's the destination of the Atlantic Rally for Cruisers, a transatlantic sailing competition for racing yachts. Yacht charters and sightseeing day trips can be arranged at the marina. Rodney Bay Village is about 15 minutes north of Castries.

⊙ Sights

Pigeon Island National Landmark

BEACH—SIGHT | FAMILY | Jutting out from the northwest coast, Pigeon Island connects to the mainland via a causeway. Tales are told of the pirate Jambe de Bois (Wooden Leg), who once hid out on this 44-acre hilltop islet—a strategic point during the French and British struggles for control of Saint Lucia. Now Pigeon Island is a national park and a venue for concerts, festivals, and family gatherings. There are two small beaches with calm waters for swimming and snorkeling, a restaurant, and picnic areas. Scattered around the grounds are ruins of barracks, batteries, and garrisons that date from 18th-century French and English battles. In the Museum and Interpretative Centre, housed in the restored British officers' mess, a multimedia display explains the island's ecological and historical significance. The site is administered by the Saint Lucia National Trust. ⊠ *Pigeon Island* ☎ *758/452–5005* ⊕ *www.slunatrust.org/sites/pigeon-island-national-landmark* ⊠ *$8.*

★ Splash Island Water Park

AMUSEMENT PARK/WATER PARK | FAMILY | The Eastern Caribbean's first open-water-sports park, installed just off Reduit Beach a dozen or so yards from the sand in front of Bay Gardens Beach Resort, thrills kids and adults alike—but mostly kids. They spend hours on the colorful, inflatable, modular features, which include a trampoline, climbing wall, monkey bars, swing, slide, hurdles, double rocker, and water volleyball net. Children must be at least six, and everyone must wear a life vest. A team of lifeguards is on duty when the park is open. ⊠ *Reduit Beach, Reduit Beach Rd., Rodney Bay* ✛ *Facing Bay Gardens Beach Resort* ☎ *758/457–8532* ⊕ *www.saintluciawaterpark.com* ⊠ *From $13 per hr.*

Beaches

Pigeon Island Beach

BEACH—SIGHT | FAMILY | This small beach within the national landmark, on the northwestern tip of Saint Lucia, has golden sand, a calm sea, and a view that extends from Rodney Bay to Martinique. It's a perfect spot for picnicking, and you can take a break from the sun by visiting the nearby Pigeon Island Museum and Interpretive Centre. **Amenities:** food and drink; toilets. **Best for:** snorkeling; solitude; swimming. ⊠ *Pigeon Island National Landmark, Pigeon Island Causeway, Pigeon Island* ⊠ *$10 park admission.*

★ Reduit Beach

BEACH—SIGHT | FAMILY | Many feel that Reduit (pronounced *red-WEE*) is the island's finest beach. The long stretch of golden sand that frames Rodney Bay is within walking distance of many hotels and restaurants in Rodney Bay Village. Bay Gardens Beach Resort and Mystique St. Lucia by Royalton face the beachfront; Harmony Suites and Ginger Lily hotels are across the road. At Mystique's water-sports center, you can rent sports equipment and beach

Rodney Bay and the North

Caribbean Sea

Sights

Pigeon Island
National Landmark, **1**

Splash Island
Water Park, **2**

Restaurants

Big Chef
Steakhouse, **8**

Buzz
Seafood & Grill, **4**

The Cliff at Cap, **3**

Jacques Waterfront
Dining, **6**

Lil' Chef Prime Sea
Food & Tapas, **7**

The Naked
Fisherman Beach
Bar & Grill, **2**

Orlando's
Restaurant, Rodney
Bay, **5**

Tao, **1**

Ti Bannane, **9**

Quick Bites

Elena's Cafe, **1**

Hotels

Bay Gardens Beach
Resort & Spa, **8**

Bay Gardens
Hotel, **14**

Bay Gardens
Marina Haven
Hotel, **6**

BodyHoliday
Saint Lucia, **1**

Cap Maison, **2**

Coco Palm, **13**

East Winds
Saint Lucia, **15**

Ginger Lily Hotel, **7**

Harbor Club
St. Lucia, **10**

Harmony Marina
Suites, **11**

The Landings
Resort & Spa, **5**

Mystique St. Lucia
by Royalton, **9**

Royalton Saint Lucia
Resort and Spa, **3**

Sandals Grande
St. Lucian, **4**

Starfish St. Lucia, **12**

Pigeon
Island
1

*Pigeon
Island*

Rodney Bay

Trouya

*Labrellotte
Bay*

15

Bois D'orange

Marisule Beach

Corinth

Marisule

Choc Bay
Choc Beach

KEY	
1	*Exploring Sights*
1	*Restaurants*
1	*Quick Bites*
1	*Hotels*

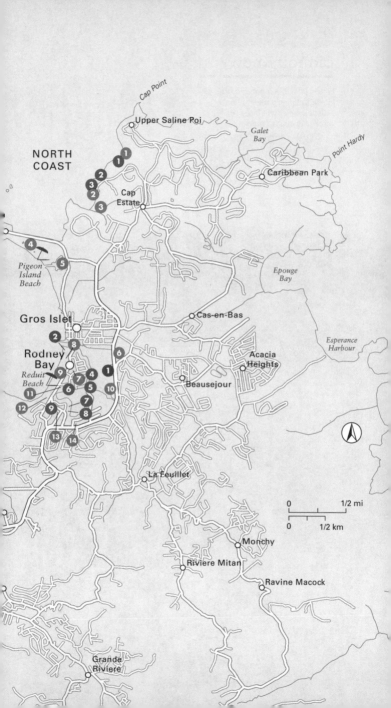

chairs and take windsurfing or waterskiing lessons. Kids (and adults alike) love Splash Island Water Park, an open-water inflatable playground near Bay Gardens Beach Resort with a trampoline, climbing wall, monkey bars, swing, slide, and more. **Amenities:** food and drink; toilets; water sports. **Best for:** snorkeling; sunset; swimming; walking; windsurfing. ⊠ *Rodney Bay.*

🍴 Restaurants

Big Chef Steakhouse

$$$$ | **STEAKHOUSE** | It's not always easy to find a good thick steak outside of a major city—or perhaps Texas!—but Big Chef owners Marc and Rosie Joinville have being delivering mouthwatering steaks (and more) for more than a decade. Chef Rosie trained at London's Cordon Bleu Cooking School, worked all over the world, and has run several restaurants in Saint Lucia, so she knows what she's doing in the kitchen. **Known for:** thick, juicy steaks; chef Rosie's rich desserts; friendly service. $ *Average main: US$36* ⊠ *Waterside Inn, Reduit Beach Ave., opposite Baywalk Mall, Rodney Bay* ☎ *758/450–0210* ⊕ *bigchefsteakhouse.com* ⊘ *No lunch.*

Buzz Seafood & Grill

$$$ | **SEAFOOD** | Opposite the Mystique Royal St. Lucia hotel and Reduit Beach, this dining spot is part of Rodney Bay's "restaurant central." After cool drinks and warm appetizers at the bar, diners make their way to the dining room or garden for some serious seafood or a good steak, West Indian pepperpot stew, spicy Moroccan-style lamb shanks, or simple chicken and chips. The seared yellowfin tuna, potato-crusted red snapper, and seafood Creole are big hits, too. **Known for:** flashy tropical cocktails; indoor and outdoor seating; happy hour every evening. $ *Average main: US$30* ⊠ *Reduit Beach Rd., Rodney Bay* ☎ *758/458–0450* ⊕ *www. facebook.com/buzzrestaurant.*

★ The Cliff at Cap

$$$$ | **ECLECTIC** | High on top of a cliff at the northern tip of Saint Lucia, the open-air dining room at Cap Maison welcomes diners to what executive chef Craig Jones calls "nouveau" French–West Indian cuisine. True, he incorporates local vegetables, fruits, herbs, and spices with the best meats and fresh-caught seafood you'll find on the island; but the technique and presentation—and the service—lean more toward the French. **Known for:** superb dining; panoramic view; daily (pricey) tastings in the wine cellar. $ *Average main: US$36* ⊠ *Cap Maison, Smuggler's Cove Dr., Cap Estate* ☎ *758/457–8681* ⊕ *www.thecliffatcap.com.*

★ Jacques Waterfront Dining

$$$$ | FRENCH | Chef-owner Jacky Rioux creates magical dishes in his waterfront restaurant set within the gardens of Harmony Suites Hotel in Rodney Bay. The cooking is decidedly French, as is Rioux, but fresh produce and local spices create a memorable fusion cuisine. **Known for:** long-standing reputation for quality cuisine; waterfront location; jazz brunch on Sunday. $ *Average main: US$34 ⊠ Harmony Suites Hotel, Reduit Beach Ave., Rodney Bay* ☎ *758/458–1900* ⊕ *www.jacquesrestaurant.com* ☉ *No dinner Sun. No lunch Mon.*

Lil' Chef Prime Seafood & Tapas

$$$ | TAPAS | The sister restaurant to Big Chef Steakhouse, this waterfront spot serves small plates, more than a dozen classic and inspired choices—all come with homemade bread, olives, aioli, olive oil, chutneys, and salsa—as well as full meals like the beef and chorizo burger or coconut steamed fish. Pair your food with a glass (or pitcher) of sangria or perhaps a glass (or bottle) of robust red wine from Spain—and, if your dining partners don't mind, a Cuban cigar. **Known for:** small plates, large portions; harbor view; happy hours and (Friday night) entertainment. $ *Average main: US$24 ⊠ Waterside Inn, Reduit Beach Ave., Rodney Bay* ⊹ *Behind Big Chef Steakhouse* ☎ *758/451–2433* ⊕ *lilchefstlucia.com.*

The Naked Fisherman Beach Bar & Grill

$$$$ | SEAFOOD | The rather sophisticated beachside restaurant at Cap Maison is tucked into a cliff surrounding a crescent of sand at the northern tip of Saint Lucia. During the day, match a glass (or bottle) of excellent wine to an arugula-and-apricot salad, grilled island catch, Caribbean roti, or perfectly cooked Wagyu beef or fish burger with shoestring fries—while staring across the sea as far as Martinique. **Known for:** remote beach location; all-day dining; great wines and great food. $ *Average main: US$35 ⊠ Cap Maison, Smugglers Cove Rd., Cap Estate* ⊹ *On beach, 92 steps down (and back up) from road* ☎ *758/457–8694* ⊕ *nakedfishermanstlucia.com.*

★ Orlando's Restaurant, Rodney Bay

$$$ | CARIBBEAN | Chef Orlando Satchell's second restaurant opened on "restaurant row" in busy Rodney Bay Village in 2020. As in the original Orlando's restaurant in Soufrière, the renowned chef's signature "Share the Love" Caribbean cuisine is the focus here, which means using local ingredients—organic as much as possible. **Known for:** tantalizing dinner menu; small portions and big flavor; fish, pasta, "jerk" dishes, and sandwiches at lunch. $ *Average main: US$28 ⊠ Reduit Beach Ave., Rodney Bay* ☎ *758/489–6211* ⊕ *facebook.com/OrlandosRestaurantRodneyBay/.*

★ Tao

$$$$ | ASIAN FUSION | For a special evening, head for this Cap Estate restaurant on the premises of BodyHoliday Saint Lucia resort. On a second-floor balcony at the edge of Cariblue Beach, you'll enjoy a pleasant breeze and a starry sky while you dine on fusion cuisine—mouthwatering Asian tastes with a Caribbean touch. **Known for:** sophisticated cuisine; top-drawer service; romantic atmosphere. ⑤ *Average main: US$35 ⊠ BodyHoliday Saint Lucia, Cariblue Beach, Cap Estate ☎ 758/450–8551, 758/457–7800 hotel front desk ⊕ www.thebodyholiday.com ⊗ No lunch.*

Ti Bananne

$$$ | CARIBBEAN | FAMILY | Poolside at the Coco Palm hotel, this alfresco bistro and bar attracts mostly hotel guests for breakfast but a wider clientele for lunch and dinner—and happy hour. A live band entertains most evenings and always at the Friday-night Caribbean buffet. **Known for:** easy, breezy dining; friendly bar; poolside snacks. ⑤ *Average main: US$27 ⊠ Coco Palm Resort, Off Reduit Beach Ave., Rodney Bay ☎ 758/456–2800 ⊕ www.coco-resorts. com.*

 Coffee and Quick Bites

Elena's Cafe

$ | CAFÉ | FAMILY | Elena's serves coffee, tea, smoothies, pastries, and other breakfast items at its café in the Baywalk Mall, but homemade gelato is the star of the show. Elena's has a larger restaurant at Rodney Bay Marina, where you can have pizza, burgers, salads, and pasta—and, of course, gelato. **Known for:** several flavors of homemade gelato; quick breakfast stop; beer, wine, and cocktails in the marina restaurant. ⑤ *Average main: US$7 ⊠ Baywalk Mall, Reduit Beach Ave., Rodney Bay ☎ 758/451–0043 ⊕ www.elenascafestlucia.com ⊗ Café closed Sun.*

Hotels

Bay Gardens Beach Resort & Spa

$$$ | RESORT | FAMILY | One of five Bay Gardens properties in Rodney Bay Village, this family-friendly resort has a prime location on beautiful Reduit Beach and its six three-story buildings wrap around a large, lagoon-style pool. **Pros:** kitchenettes are great for families and those who like to self-cater; complimentary passes to Splash Island Water Park just offshore; perfect beach location. **Cons:** cruise passengers with day passes crowd the beach (and beach chairs); plan to eat elsewhere; some rooms a bit tired. ⑤ *Rooms from: US$383 ⊠ Reduit Beach Ave., Rodney Bay*

☎ 758/457–8514, 877/620–3200 in U.S. ⊕ www.baygardensre-sorts.com ↘ 77 rooms ⦿ No meals.

Bay Gardens Hotel

$ | **HOTEL** | Modern, colorful, and surrounded by pretty flower gardens, the hotel is a short walk to beautiful Reduit Beach (shuttle service also available), several popular restaurants, and shopping malls. **Pros:** close to nightspots and shopping; unlimited use of Bay Gardens Beach Club loungers and nonmotorized water sports; complimentary passes to Splash Island Water Park. **Cons:** not beachfront, although there's a beach shuttle; heavy focus on business travelers; on the main road, so noise may be an issue for some rooms. ⑤ Rooms from: US$206 ⊠ Castries–Gros Islet Hwy., Rodney Bay ☎ 758/457–8010, 877/620–3200 in U.S. ⊕ www.baygardensresorts.com ↘ 87 rooms ⦿ Free breakfast.

Bay Gardens Marina Haven Hotel

$ | **HOTEL** | Across the road from Rodney Bay Marina, this small hotel is a short drive from Reduit Beach via a free hourly shuttle service and guestrooms are large and bright with either a garden or pool view. **Pros:** comfortable and affordable; friendly, accommodating staff; relaxing atmosphere. **Cons:** near but not on the beach; close to busy road; go elsewhere for meals. ⑤ Rooms from: US$126 ⊠ Rodney Bay Marina, Castries-Gros Islet Hwy., Rodney Bay ☎ 758/456–8500, 800/088–5104 in U.S. ⊕ baygardensresorts.com/marina-haven ↘ 35 rooms ⦿ No meals.

★ BodyHoliday Saint Lucia

$$$$ | **RESORT** | At this adults-only wellness resort on picturesque Cariblue Beach—where daily treatments are included in the rates—you can customize your own "body holiday" online even before you leave home. **Pros:** special rates for solo travelers; all rooms have at least a partial ocean view; interesting activities, such as archery, include free instruction. **Cons:** expensive (but includes a lot of amenities); lots of steps to the spa, though you can get a lift; no room service. ⑤ Rooms from: US$1088 ⊠ Cariblue Beach, Cap Estate ☎ 758/457–7800, 800/544–2883 ⊕ www.thebodyholiday.com ↘ 155 rooms ⦿ All-inclusive.

★ Cap Maison

$$$ | **RESORT** | **FAMILY** | Prepare to be spoiled by the doting staffers at this intimate villa resort—the luxurious service includes unpacking (if you wish) and a personal butler for any little needs that arise. **Pros:** private and elegant with outstanding service; cocktails with a view at Cliff Bar or surf side at Rock Maison; rooftop plunge pools in most suites. **Cons:** air-conditioning in bedrooms only; 92 steps to the beach; meals are expensive (but delicious) with few nearby options. ⑤ Rooms from: US$470 ⊠ Smuggler's

*Cove Dr., Cap Estate ☎ 758/457–8670, 888/765–4985 in U.S.
⊕ www.capmaison.com ⇌ 49 rooms ⦿ Free breakfast.*

Coco Palm

$ | HOTEL | FAMILY | This popular hotel in Rodney Bay Village over-
looks an inviting pool and a separate cozy guesthouse, Kreole
Village, at the edge of the property. **Pros:** swim-up rooms; nightly
poolside entertainment; walk to all of the Rodney Bay Village
action. **Cons:** not directly on the beach; skip the all-inclusive
package, as good restaurants are nearby; nightly music can be
loud (until 10). *$ Rooms from: US$129 ⊠ Off Reduit Beach Ave.,
Rodney Bay ☎ 758/456–2800 ⊕ www.coco-resorts.com ⇌ 103
rooms ⦿ Free breakfast.*

East Winds Saint Lucia

$$$$ | RESORT | Guests keep returning to this small, all-inclusive
resort on a secluded beach halfway between Castries and Rodney
Bay, where 7 acres of botanical gardens surround 13 duplex
gingerbread-style cottages, three ocean-view rooms, and a suite.
Pros: lovely beach; excellent dining; peaceful and quiet. **Cons:** not
the best choice for kids, though they're welcome; very expensive;
six-night minimum. *$ Rooms from: US$1015 ⊠ La Brelotte Bay,
Gros Islet ☎ 758/452–8212 ⊕ www.eastwinds.com ⇌ 30 suites
⦿ All-inclusive.*

Ginger Lily Hotel

$ | B&B/INN | A small, family-owned hotel with its own restaurant
and swimming pool, Ginger Lily is in the midst of the Rodney
Bay Village scene and across the street from Reduit Beach. **Pros:**
across the street from Reduit Beach and Splash Island Water Park;
large rooms, large bathrooms; clean and comfortable. **Cons:** few
on-site activities; air-conditioning is unreliable; breakfast is just
barely continental. *$ Rooms from: US$150 ⊠ Reduit Beach Ave.,
Rodney Bay ☎ 758/458–0300 ⊕ www.facebook.com/gingerlilyho-
tel ⇌ 11 rooms ⦿ Free breakfast.*

Harbor Club St. Lucia

$ | HOTEL | FAMILY | Part of the Curio Collection by Hilton, this
modern hotel located at Rodney Bay Marina is convenient, full
of amenities, and reasonably priced. **Pros:** stunning location; free
ferry to Reduit Beach; some swim-up rooms. **Cons:** housekeeping
only every other day; restaurant food inconsistent; outside noise
in roadside rooms. *$ Rooms from: US$138 ⊠ Rodney Bay Marina,
Castries-Gros Islet Hwy., Rodney Bay ☎ 758/731–2900 ⊕ www.
theharborclub.com ⇌ 115 rooms ⦿ Free breakfast.*

Harmony Marina Suites

$ | HOTEL | Guests at this inexpensive, adults-only hotel are generally scuba divers, boaters, or others who don't need luxury but appreciate comfort and want to be on the waterfront. **Pros:** marina location with waterfront suites; walk to restaurants, nightspots, and shopping; easy access to Reduit Beach. **Cons:** most rooms are fairly basic; bathrooms need renovating; waterfront rooms can be a little noisy. ⑤ *Rooms from: US$80 ⊠ Flamboyant Dr., Rodney Bay ⊕ Off Reduit Beach Ave.* ☎ *758/452–8756, 888/790–5264 in U.S.* ⊕ *www.harmonymarinasuites.net* ⊋ *30 rooms* ⦿⍽ *No meals.*

★ The Landings Resort & Spa

$$$$ | RESORT | FAMILY | On 19 acres along the Pigeon Point Causeway at the northern edge of Rodney Bay, this villa resort surrounds a private, 17-slip marina where guests can dock their own yachts, literally, at their doorstep. **Pros:** spacious, beautifully appointed units; perfect for yachties, couples, families, even business travelers; kids' club and playground. **Cons:** town-house atmosphere; little hike to beach from some rooms; all-inclusive option carries surcharges for some menu items and premium drinks. ⑤ *Rooms from: US$863 ⊠ Pigeon Island Causeway, Gros Islet* ☎ *758/458–7300, 866/252–0689 in U.S.* ⊕ *www.landingsstlucia.com* ⊋ *188 rooms* ⦿⍽ *Free Breakfast.*

Mystique St. Lucia by Royalton

$$ | RESORT | FAMILY | This beautifully situated all-suites resort on Saint Lucia's best beach caters to every whim—for the whole family. **Pros:** great location on Reduit Beach; two suites equipped for guests with disabilities; convenient to Rodney Bay restaurants, clubs, and shops. **Cons:** get your snacks at the nearby supermarket; rooms ready for a little TLC; food and extras are pricey. ⑤ *Rooms from: US$295 ⊠ Reduit Beach Ave., Rodney Bay* ☎ *758/457–3131* ⊕ *www.mystiqueresorts.com* ⊋ *96 rooms* ⦿⍽ *No meals.*

Royalton Saint Lucia Resort and Spa

$$$$ | ALL-INCLUSIVE | FAMILY | This huge all-inclusive resort on 60 acres overlooking pretty Smuggler's Cove is divided into three distinct sections—a family-friendly area, the Diamond Club with exclusive amenities, and the Hideaway adults-only oasis. **Pros:** plenty of food, fun, and features; beautiful sandy beach; supervised kids' club plus a hangout for teens. **Cons:** rooms near a pool can be noisy; open-concept bathrooms may not be to your liking; at the tip of the island and far from Saint Lucia's attractions. ⑤ *Rooms from: US$497 ⊠ Smugglers Cove Rd., Cap Estate* ☎ *758/731–1000, 877/744–8371 in U.S.* ⊕ *www.royaltonresorts.com/royalton-saint-lucia* ⊋ *352 rooms* ⦿⍽ *All-inclusive.*

★ Sandals Grande St. Lucian

$$$$ | **RESORT** | Perched on the narrow Pigeon Island Causeway at Saint Lucia's northern tip, Sandals Grande offers panoramic views of Rodney Bay on one side and the Atlantic Ocean on the other. **Pros:** grand accommodations, especially the over-the-water bungalow suites; 12 restaurants and countless activities; free scuba for certified divers. **Cons:** really long ride (at least 90 minutes) from/to Hewanorra, but transfers are complimentary; beach can be crowded; while romantic, it's not peaceful or quiet. ⑤ *Rooms from: US$758* ⊠ *Pigeon Island Causeway, Pigeon Island* ☎ *758/455–2000* ⊕ *www.sandals.com/grande-st-lucian* ⇅ *301 rooms* ⦿❘ *All-inclusive.*

Starfish St. Lucia

$ | **ALL-INCLUSIVE** | **FAMILY** | This large, family-friendly resort at the south end of Reduit Beach is surrounded on three sides by gardens, and since it's all-inclusive and reasonably priced—with lots of possibilities for entertainment—it's a viable choice for an economical family vacation. **Pros:** directly on the beach; daily supervised programs for kids; nightly entertainment. **Cons:** beach is fairly narrow here; buffet food uninspiring and other restaurants cost extra; cumbersome process to buy premium drinks. ⑤ *Rooms from: US$240* ⊠ *Reduit Beach Ave., Rodney Bay* ☎ *758/457–3000, 877/957–4051 in U.S.* ⊕ *www.starfishresorts. com/resort/saint-lucia* ⇅ *140 rooms* ⦿❘ *All-inclusive.*

🍸 Nightlife

CASINOS

Treasure Bay Casino

CASINOS | Saint Lucia's only (so far) casino has more than 800 slot and video poker machines, 22 gaming tables (poker, blackjack, roulette, and craps), and a sports bar with 28 screens. It's open 24 hours a day, every day! ⊠ *Baywalk Mall, Reduit Beach Ave., Rodney Bay* ✛ *Just off Castries–Gros Islet Hwy.* ☎ *758/459–2901* ⊕ *treasurebay.com.*

DANCE CLUBS

Most dance clubs with live bands have a cover charge of $10–$20 (EC$25–EC$50), and the music usually starts at 11 pm.

Ultra Lounge

DANCE CLUBS | It's open all afternoon, but nights are when partygoers come to hang out, sip drinks, munch tapas, and dance in an ultra-contemporary atmosphere. ⊠ *Reduit Beach Ave., Rodney Bay* ☎ *758/458–5872* ⊕ *www.facebook.com/ultraloungeslu/.*

Bananas

More than 10,000 Saint Lucian banana farmers produced 134,000 tons of the familiar fruit in the early 1990s, most of which were exported to Europe. By 2005, when the Caribbean nations had lost their preferential treatment in the European market, fewer than 2,000 banana farmers were producing about 30,000 tons. Nevertheless, you'll still see bananas growing throughout Saint Lucia, especially in the rural areas around Babonneau in the northeast and south of Castries near Marigot Bay. As you pass by the banana fields, you'll notice that the fruit is wrapped in blue plastic. That's to protect it from birds and insects—because there's no market for an imperfect banana.

Verve

BARS/PUBS | At what is considered the hottest party spot in Rodney Bay Village, you can dance to the DJ's awesome vibes (and sometimes live bands) every night until 2 am (or later). ⊠ *Reduit Beach Ave., Rodney Bay* ☎ *758/450–1934* ⊕ *www.facebook.com/Vervestlucia.*

STREET PARTIES
★ **Gros Islet Jump-Up**

THEMED ENTERTAINMENT | The island's largest street party is a Friday-night ritual. Huge speakers set up on the street blast Caribbean music all night long. Sometimes there are live bands. When you take a break from dancing, you can buy barbecue fish or chicken, rotis (turnovers filled with meat and/or vegetables), beer, and soda from villagers who set up grills along the roadside. It's the ultimate carnival fête. ⊠ *Dauphin St., Gros Islet* ✛ *Off Castries–Gros Islet Hwy.*

Shopping

CLOTHING AND TEXTILES
Sea Island Cotton Shop

CLOTHING | High-quality T-shirts, clothing and resort wear, and colorful souvenirs are sold at reasonable prices and duty free. ⊠ *Baywalk Mall, Reduit Beach Ave., Rodney Bay* ✛ *Off Castries–Gros Islet Hwy.* ☎ *758/458–4220* ⊕ *www.seaislandsaintlucia.com.*

SHOPPING MALLS
Baywalk Mall

SHOPPING CENTERS/MALLS | FAMILY | With more than 45 stores and a half-dozen restaurants, this two-level complex boasts boutiques,banks, a beauty salon, jewelry and souvenir stores, a large supermarket (great for snacks, picnic items, or a bottle of wine), a playground for kids, and the island's only (so far) casino. ⊠ *Rodney Bay Ave., Rodney Bay* ☎ *758/452–6666* ⊕ *www.baywalkslu.com.*

J. Q.'s Shopping Mall

SHOPPING CENTERS/MALLS | Along with boutiques, restaurants, and other businesses that sell services and supplies, a large supermarket is the focal point here. J. Q.'s has another location in Vieux Fort. ⊠ *Corner Gros Islet Hwy. and Rodney Bay Village Strip* ☎ *758/458–0700* ⊕ *www.shopjqmall.com.*

Castries

Castries, a busy commercial city that wraps around sheltered Castries Harbour, is Saint Lucia's capital; Castries Quarter, which stretches over 30 square miles, is home to some 70,000 residents. Morne Fortune rises sharply to the south of the city, creating a dramatic green backdrop. The charm of Castries lies almost entirely in its current liveliness rather than its history, because four fires between 1796 and 1948 destroyed most of the colonial buildings. Freighters (exporting bananas, coconut, cocoa, mace, nutmeg, and citrus fruits) and cruise ships come and go frequently, making Castries Harbour one of the Caribbean's busiest ports.

Castries and the north are the most developed parts of Saint Lucia. The roads are straight, mostly flat, and easy to navigate. Rodney Bay Marina and most of the island's resorts, restaurants, and nightspots are north of Castries, and the beaches in the north are some of the island's best. Pigeon Island, one of the island's most important historical sites, is at the island's northwestern tip. Marigot Bay, about 15 minutes south of the city, is both a yacht haven and a lovely destination for landlubbers.

 Sights

Antillia Brewing Company

WINERY/DISTILLERY | Antillia brews handcrafted wheat beers, stout, and specialty ales in its brewery at Odsan Industrial Park. You can take a tour of the brewery, but it's easier (and more fun) to enjoy a pint or two—or a flight—at the company's Antillia Beer Garden, adjacent to the cruise terminal at Pointe Seraphine. ⊠ *Odsan Industrial Park, Pointe Seraphine, Castries* ☎ *758/458–0844* ⊕ *www.facebook.com/antilliabrewing/.*

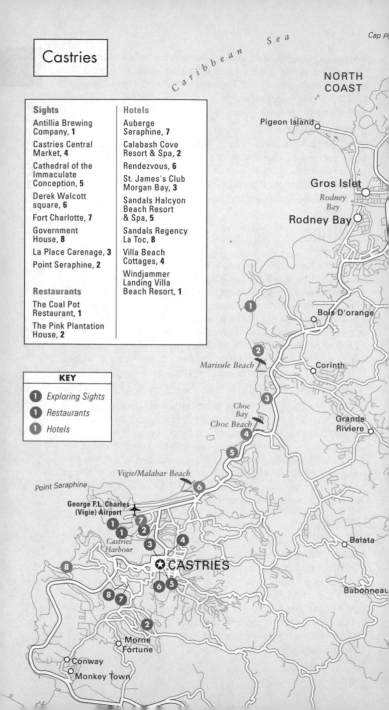

Castries

Sights

Antillia Brewing Company, **1**

Castries Central Market, **4**

Cathedral of the Immaculate Conception, **5**

Derek Walcott square, **6**

Fort Charlotte, **7**

Government House, **8**

La Place Carenage, **3**

Point Seraphine, **2**

Restaurants

The Coal Pot Restaurant, **1**

The Pink Plantation House, **2**

Hotels

Auberge Seraphine, **7**

Calabash Cove Resort & Spa, **2**

Rendezvous, **6**

St. James's Club Morgan Bay, **3**

Sandals Halcyon Beach Resort & Spa, **5**

Sandals Regency La Toc, **8**

Villa Beach Cottages, **4**

Windjammer Landing Villa Beach Resort, **1**

KEY

1 *Exploring Sights*

1 *Restaurants*

1 *Hotels*

Caribbean Sea

Cap P

NORTH COAST

Pigeon Island

Gros Islet

Rodney Bay

Rodney Bay

Bois D'orange

Marisule Beach

Corinth

Choc Bay
Choc Beach

Grande Riviere

Vigie/Malabar Beach

Point Seraphine

George F.L. Charles (Vigie) Airport

Castries Harbour

☆ CASTRIES

Balata

Babonneau

Morne Fortune

Conway

Monkey Town

★ Castries Central Market

MARKET | FAMILY | Under a brilliant orange roof, this bustling market is at its liveliest on Saturday morning, when farmers bring their produce and spices to town, as they have for more than a century. (It's closed Sunday.) Next door to the produce market is the **Craft Market,** where you can buy pottery, wood carvings, handwoven straw articles, and innumerable souvenirs, trinkets, and gew-gaws. At the **Vendors' Arcade,** across Peynier Street from the Craft Market, you'll find still more handicrafts and souvenirs. ✉ *55 John Compton Hwy., Castries.*

Cathedral of the Immaculate Conception

LOCAL INTEREST | Directly across Laborie Street from Derek Walcott Square stands Castries's Roman Catholic cathedral, which was built in 1897. Though it appears rather somber on the outside, the interior walls are decorated with colorful murals reworked by St. Lucian artist Dunstan St. Omer just prior to Pope John Paul II's visit in 1985. This church has an active parish and is open daily for both public viewing and religious services. ✉ *Micoud St., Castries.*

Derek Walcott Square

PLAZA | FAMILY | The city's green oasis, bordered by Brazil, Laborie, Micoud, and Bourbon streets and formerly called Columbus Square, was renamed to honor the late Derek Walcott, the hometown poet who won the 1992 Nobel Prize in Literature and one of two Nobel laureates from Saint Lucia. (The late Sir W. Arthur Lewis won the 1979 Nobel Prize in Economics.) Some of the 19th-century buildings that have survived fire, wind, and rain can be seen on Brazil Street, the square's southern border. On the Laborie Street side, there's a huge, 400-year-old samaan (monkey pod) tree with leafy branches that shade a good portion of the square. ✉ *Bordered by Brazil, Laborie, Micoud, and Bourbon Sts., Castries.*

Fort Charlotte

ARCHAEOLOGICAL SITE | Begun in 1764 by the French as the Citadelle du Morne Fortune, Fort Charlotte was completed after 20 years of battling and changing hands. Its old barracks and batteries are now government buildings and local educational facilities, but you can drive around and look at the remains of redoubts, a guard-room, stables, and cells. You can also walk up to the Inniskilling Monument, a tribute to the 1796 battle in which the 27th (Inniskill-ing) Regiment of Foot wrested the Morne from the French. At the military cemetery, first used in 1782, faint inscriptions on the tombstones tell the tales of French and English soldiers who died in Saint Lucia. Six former governors of the island are also buried here. From this point atop Morne Fortune, you have a beautiful

Dunstan St. Omer

The murals of Dunstan St. Omer (1927–2015), one of Saint Lucia's leading artists—if not *the* leading artist—adorn many walls and churches throughout the island, and his paintings and portraits are prized both locally and internationally. St. Omer is best known for frescoing the walls of the **Cathedral of the Immaculate Conception** in Castries with the images of black saints, just prior to a visit by Pope John Paul II in 1985. St. Omer also designed Saint Lucia's national flag. A 2004 recipient of the St. Lucia Cross, the nation's highest award, he inspired generations of youngsters for more than 30 years as an art instructor in the public schools. St. Omer was also the father of nine children, two of whom—Luigi and Julio—inherited their father's talent and have followed in his footsteps.

view of Castries Harbour, Martinique farther north, and the Pitons to the south. ⊠ *Morne Fortune.*

Government House
HOUSE | The official residence of the governor-general—and one of the island's few remaining examples of Victorian architecture—is perched high above Castries, halfway up Morne Fortune (Hill of Good Fortune), which forms a backdrop for the capital city. Morne Fortune has also seen more than its share of *bad* luck, including devastating hurricanes and four fires that leveled Castries. Within Government House is **Le Pavillon Royal Museum,** which houses important historical photographs and documents, artifacts, crockery, silverware, medals, and awards; original architectural drawings of the house are displayed on the walls. Note that you must make an appointment to visit. ⊠ *Morne Fortune* ☎ *758/452–2481* 🖃 *Free.*

La Place Carenage
STORE/MALL | On the south side of the harbor near the pier and markets is a duty-free shopping complex with a handful of shops and a café. It's busiest when a cruise ship is in port. ⊠ *Jeremie St., Castries* ☎ *758/453–2451.*

Pointe Seraphine
STORE/MALL | This duty-free shopping complex is on the north side of the harbor, about a 20-minute walk or 2-minute cab ride from the city center; a launch ferries passengers across the harbor when cruise ships are in port. Pointe Seraphine's attractive Spanish-style architecture houses more than 20 upscale duty-free

shops, a tourist information kiosk, a taxi stand, and car-rental agencies. The shopping center is adjacent to a cruise-ship pier and is busiest when ships are in port. ⊠ *Castries Harbour, Castries* ☎ *758/457–3425* ⊕ *www.pointeseraphine.lc* ⊗ *Closed Sun. (unless a ship is in port).*

Beaches

Vigie/Malabar Beach

BEACH—SIGHT | FAMILY | This 2-mile (3-km) stretch of lovely white sand runs parallel to the George F. L. Charles Airport runway in Castries and continues on past the Rendezvous resort, where it becomes Malabar Beach. In the area opposite the airport departure lounge, a few vendors sell refreshments. **Amenities:** food and drink. **Best for:** swimming. ⊠ *Castries* ⊹ *Adjacent to George F. L. Charles Airport runway.*

 Restaurants

★ The Coal Pot Restaurant

$$$$ | FRENCH | Popular since it opened in 1968, this tiny waterfront restaurant overlooks pretty Vigie Cove. Come for a light lunch—perhaps a bowl of creamy pumpkin soup, Greek salad with chicken or shrimp, or broiled fresh fish—or enjoy an exquisite French-inspired dinner under the stars. **Known for:** outstanding cuisine and service; picturesque harbor views; repeat customers who love the place. ⑤ *Average main: US$32* ⊠ *Seraphine Rd., Vigie* ☎ *758/452–5566* ⊗ *Closed Sun. No lunch Sat.*

★ The Pink Plantation House

$$$ | CARIBBEAN | A 140-year-old, pretty-in-pink, French Colonial plantation house is the setting for authentic French Creole cuisine—the inspiration of local artist Michelle Elliott, whose ceramics and paintings are displayed for sale in a cozy room set up as a gift shop. Diners enjoy grilled fish, steak, rack of lamb, jumbo shrimp, or chicken breast matched with interesting homemade sauces and accompanied by steamed rice, fried plantains, sautéed vegetables, breadfruit/sweet potato balls, local peas, and christophene (chayote) gratin. **Known for:** scenic garden setting; historic environment; excellent regional cuisine. ⑤ *Average main: US$25* ⊠ *Chef Harry Dr., Morne Fortune* ☎ *758/452–5422* ⊗ *Closed Sat.*

Hotels

Auberge Seraphine

$ | **HOTEL** | This small, family-run inn is a good choice for those look-ing for convenient accommodations, but don't require a beach-front location, on-site activities, or special amenities. **Pros:** close to Vigie airport, Vigie marina, and Castries; nice view of the harbor activity from rooms and the pool deck; attractive price. **Cons:** rooms are fairly basic but comfortable; rather isolated in terms of walking anywhere; no on-site activities other than a swim in the pool. ⑤ *Rooms from: US$160* ⊠ *Vielle Bay, Vigie* ☎ *758/456–3000* ⊕ *www.aubergeseraphine.com* ⌁ *24 rooms* ⑩ *No meals.*

★ Calabash Cove Resort & Spa

$$ | **RESORT** | The luxurious suites and Balinese-inspired cottages at this inviting boutique resort spill gently down a tropical hillside to a secluded beach on Bonaire Bay, just south of Rodney Bay. The private cottages, constructed of mahogany, stone, and other natural materials, all face the sea to take advantage of the sunset. **Pros:** stylish, sophisticated, and friendly atmosphere; great food served in lovely alfresco setting; wedding parties can reserve the entire resort. **Cons:** the long, bone-crunching dirt road to the entrance; steps to the cottages and beach may be difficult for those with mobility issues; few on-site activities. ⑤ *Rooms from: US$300* ⊠ *Bonaire Estate, Marisule Estate* ⌖ *Off Castries–Gros Islet Hwy., south of Rodney Bay* ☎ *758/456–3500, 800/917–2683 in U.S.* ⊕ *www.calabashcove.com* ⌁ *26 rooms* ⑩ *Free Breakfast.*

Rendezvous

$$$$ | **RESORT** | Romance is alive and well at this easygoing, all-in-clusive, boutique resort (for couples only) that stretches along the dreamy white sand of Malabar Beach at the end of the George F. L. **Pros:** very convenient to Castries and Vigie Airport; popular wed-ding venue; attentive, accommodating staff. **Cons:** no room TVs, if that matters; occasional flyover noise from nearby airport; beach can be crowded, especially on weekends. ⑤ *Rooms from: US$875* ⊠ *Malabar Beach, Vigie* ☎ *758/457–7900, 800/544–2883 in U.S.* ⊕ *www.theromanticholiday.com* ⌁ *100 rooms* ⑩ *All-inclusive.*

★ Sandals Halcyon Beach Resort & Spa

$$$$ | **RESORT** | This is the most intimate and low-key of the three Sandals resorts on Saint Lucia; like the others, it's beachfront, all-inclusive, for couples only, and loaded with amenities and activities—including personalized butler service in some suites. **Pros:** all the Sandals amenities in a more intimate setting; lots of dining and activity choices; exchange privileges (including golf) at other Sandals properties. **Cons:** it's Sandals, so it's a theme property that's not for everyone; small and popular, so book well in advance; rooms at back of property, nearest the main road, can be noisy at night. $ *Rooms from: US$615* ⊠ *Choc Bay, Choc* ☎ *758/453–0222, 888/726–3257* ⊕ *www.sandals.com/halcyon-beach* ⊅ *169 rooms* ⧟⧟ *All-inclusive.*

Sandals Regency La Toc

$$$$ | RESORT | The second-largest of the three Sandals on Saint Lucia, this resort distinguishes itself with a 9-hole executive-style golf course (for Sandals guests only); like the others, though, this Sandals is all-inclusive and for couples only. **Pros:** lots to do—never a dull moment; complimentary airport shuttle; on-site 9-hole golf course. **Cons:** somewhat isolated location on a bluff west of Castries; expert golfers will prefer Sandals St. Lucia Golf & Country Club; lots of hills and steps. $ *Rooms from: US$615* ⊠ *La Toc Rd., Castries* ☎ *758/452–3081, 888/726–3257* ⊕ *www.sandals. com/regency-la-toc* ⅄ *9 holes, 3141 yds, par 33* ⊅ *331 rooms* ⧟⧟ *All-inclusive.*

St. James's Club Morgan Bay

$$$$ | RESORT | FAMILY | Singles, couples, and families enjoy tons of sports and activities at this all-inclusive resort on 22 secluded acres surrounding a stretch of white-sand beach. **Pros:** six restaurants, six bars, four pools, four tennis courts, and more; children's club with organized activities; free waterskiing, sailing, and tennis lessons. **Cons:** huge resort can be very busy, especially when full; relatively small beach given resort's size; Wi-Fi only in some rooms and for a fee. $ *Rooms from: US$790* ⊠ *Choc Bay, Choc* ☎ *758/457–3700, 866/830–1617* ⊕ *www.stjamesclubmorganbay. com* ⊅ *345 rooms* ⧟⧟ *All-inclusive.*

Villa Beach Cottages

$$ | HOTEL | Tidy housekeeping cottages with gingerbread-laced facades are steps from the beach at this family-run establishment 3 miles (5 km) north of the airport in Castries. **Pros:** just feet from the water; beautiful sunsets from your balcony; peaceful and quiet environment. **Cons:** close quarters; rent a car, as you'll go out for meals (or groceries); beach is quite narrow and pools are small. $ *Rooms from: US$290* ⊠ *John Compton (Castries-Gros Islet) Hwy., Choc* ☎ *758/450–2884, 866/542–1991 in U.S.* ⊕ *www. villabeachcottages.com* ⊅ *20 rooms* ⧟⧟ *No meals.*

Windjammer Landing Villa Beach Resort

$$ | RESORT | FAMILY | Mediterranean-style villas—which are as appropriate for a family or group vacation as for a romantic getaway—climb the hillside on one of Saint Lucia's prettiest bays. **Pros:** lovely, spacious units with seating areas and kitchenettes; amazing sunset views from every villa; five restaurants, four bars, in-villa dining, room service … you choose. **Cons:** far from main road, so you'll need a car if you plan to leave the property often; meal and bar costs add up fast unless you choose the all-inclusive option; some villa sitting rooms are open-air, meaning no air-conditioning and occasional insects. $ *Rooms from: US$287* ✉ *Trouya Point Rd., La Brellotte Bay, Bois d'Orange* ☎ *758/456–9000, 877/522–0722 in U.S.* ⊕ *www.windjammer-landing.com* ⇄ *331 units* ❍| *Free Breakfast.*

🛍 Shopping

Along the harbor in Castries, rambling structures with bright-orange roofs cover several open-air markets that are open from 6 am to 5 pm Monday through Saturday. Saturday morning is the busiest and most colorful time to shop.

For more than a century, farmers' wives have gathered at the **Castries Market** to sell produce—which you can enjoy on the island but, alas, can't bring to the United States. You can, however, take spices (such as cocoa sticks or balls, turmeric, cloves, bay leaves, ginger, peppercorns, cinnamon sticks, vanilla beans, nutmeg, and mace), as well as locally bottled hot-pepper sauces—all of which cost a fraction of what you'd pay back home. The adjacent **Craft Market** has aisles and aisles of baskets and other handmade straw work, rustic brooms made from palm fronds, wood carvings, leather work, clay pottery, and souvenirs—all at affordable prices. The **Vendors' Arcade,** across the street from the Craft Market, is a maze of stalls and booths where you can find handicrafts among the T-shirts and costume jewelry.

Duty-free shopping areas are at **Pointe Seraphine,** an attractive Spanish-motif complex on Castries Harbour with a dozen shops, and **La Place Carenage,** an inviting three-story complex on the opposite side of the harbor.

CLOTHING AND TEXTILES

Howelton Estate

CLOTHING | This arts-and-crafts shop and studio (formerly Caribelle Batik), high atop Morne Fortune, is named for the old Victorian mansion in which the enterprise is housed. Craftspeople demonstrate the art of batik and silk-screen printing, which you can buy in the shop—along with chocolate products, coconut oil products, and gift items, all made in Saint Lucia. There's a terrace where you can have a cool drink and a garden full of tropical orchids and lilies. You can also take a tour of the estate. ✉ *Howelton House, Old Victoria Rd., Morne Fortune* ☎ *758/452–3785* ⊕ *www.howelton-estate.com.*

HANDICRAFTS
Eudovic's Art Studio
ART GALLERIES | This workshop, studio, and art gallery has wall plaques, masks, and abstract figures hand-carved by sculptor Vincent Joseph Eudovic from local mahogany, red cedar, and eucalyptus wood. ⊠ *West Coast Rd., Goodlands, Morne Fortune* ☎ *758/452–2747* ⊕ *www.eudovicart.com.*

AREAS AND MALLS
Gablewoods Mall
SHOPPING CENTERS/MALLS | **FAMILY** | This mall has about 35 shops that sell groceries, wines and spirits, jewelry, clothing, crafts, books and overseas newspapers, music, souvenirs, household goods, and snacks. ⊠ *Sunny Acres, Gros Islet Hwy., Choc Bay, Castries* ⊹ *A couple miles north of downtown Castries* ☎ *758/453–7752* ⊕ *www.facebook.com/ Shops-at-Gablewoods-Mall-1816458811898957/.*

Marigot Bay

This is one of the prettiest natural harbors in the Caribbean. In 1778, British admiral Samuel Barrington sailed into this secluded bay-within-a-bay and, the story goes, covered his ships with palm fronds to hide them from the French. Today this small community, just 4 miles (7 km) south of Castries, is a favorite anchorage for boaters and a peaceful destination for landlubbers, with a luxury resort, several small inns and restaurants, and a marina village with a snack shop, grocery store, and boutiques. A 24-hour ferry (EC$5 round-trip) connects the bay's two shores—a voyage that takes a minute or so each way.

Sights

St. Lucia Distillers Group of Companies
WINERY/DISTILLERY | St. Lucia Distillers, which produces the island's own Bounty and Chairman's Reserve rums, offers 90-minute Rhythm of Rum tours that cover the history of sugar, the background of rum, a detailed description of the distillation process, colorful displays of local architecture, a glimpse at a typical rum shop, Caribbean music, and a chance to sample the company's rums and liqueurs. The distillery is at the Roseau Sugar Factory in the Roseau Valley, on the island's largest banana plantation a few miles south of Castries and not far from Marigot. Reservations for the tour are essential. ⊠ *Roseau Sugar Factory, West Coast Rd.,*

Roseau Valley, Marigot Bay ☎ *758/456–3148* ⊕ *www.saintluci-arums.com* 🖘 *$10* ⊘ *Closed weekends.*

Beaches

Marigot Beach (*La Bas Beach*)
BEACH—SIGHT | **FAMILY** | Calm waters rippled only by passing yachts lap a sliver of sand on the north side of Marigot Bay adjacent to the Marigot Beach Club & Dive Resort, across the bay from Marigot Bay Resort & Marina, and a short walk from Mango Beach Inn. Studded with palm trees, the tiny beach on extremely picturesque Marigot Bay is accessible by a ferry (EC$5 round-trip) that operates continually from one side of the bay to the other, with pickup at the Marina Village dock. You can find refreshments at adjacent or nearby restaurants. **Amenities:** food and drink; toilets; water sports. **Best for:** swimming; sunset. ⊠ *Marigot Bay.*

 Restaurants

★ **Chateau Mygo House of Seafood**
$$$ | **SEAFOOD** | **FAMILY** | Walk down a garden path to Chateau Mygo (a colloquial corruption of "Marigot") or sail up on your boat, pick out a table on the deck of this popular dockside restaurant, and soak up the waterfront atmosphere of what may be the Caribbean's prettiest bay. The tableau is mesmerizing—and that's at lunch, when you can order a sandwich, burger, roti, fish- or chicken-and-chips, salads, or grilled fish or savory coconut chicken with peas and rice and vegetables. **Known for:** casual waterside dining on Marigot Bay; local seafood (and other) specialties; live local music and dancing (weekly). ⑤ *Average main: US$25* ⊠ *Marigot Bay* ☎ *758/458–3947* ⊕ *www.chateaumygo.com.*

DOOlittle's Restaurant + Bar
$$$ | **SEAFOOD** | **FAMILY** | Named for the protagonist in the original (1967) *Dr. Doolittle* movie, part of which was filmed in Marigot Bay, this indoor-outdoor restaurant at Marigot Beach Club & Dive Resort is on the north side of the bay. **Known for:** casual atmosphere; close to the beach; evening entertainment. ⑤ *Average main: US$28* ⊠ *Marigot Beach Club & Dive Resort, Marigot Bay* ✛ *North side of bay* ☎ *758/451–4974* ⊕ *www.marigotbeachclub.com.*

Coffee and Quick Bites

Hurricane Hole Bar & Restaurant

$$ | CAFÉ | FAMILY | Join the yachties and nearby hotel guests for breakfast, lunch, afternoon tea, a casual evening meal, cocktails or a cold drink, or just dessert at this café in the Marina Village on Marigot Bay. Eat in (well, outside on the dock), get it to go, or select something quickly from the grab 'n' go counter. **Known for:** alfresco dining at the marina; all-day menu; quick service. $ *Average main: US$20 ⊠ Marina Village, Marigot Bay* ☎ 758/458–5300 ⊕ *www.marigotbayresort.com.*

🛏 Hotels

Mango Beach Inn

$ | B&B/INN | When the Marigot Bay ferry delivers you to the dock across the bay, a small gate opens to a stone staircase that leads through a jungle of trees and flowers to this delightful, tidy little B&B. **Pros:** spectacular views of Marigot Bay; beach, restaurants, and activities nearby; lovely hosts and personalized service. **Cons:** tiny garden rooms; only showers in the bathrooms; steps to the inn may be difficult for anyone with mobility issues. $ *Rooms from: US$240 ⊠ North side of bay, Marigot Bay* ☎ 758/485–1621 ⊕ *www.mangobeachmarigot.com* ➪ *6 rooms* ⊚| *Free Breakfast.*

★ Marigot Bay Resort & Marina

$$$$ | RESORT | FAMILY | Five miles (8 km) south of Castries, this ultrachic—yet laid-back—villa resort climbs the hillside overlooking what author James Michener called "the most beautiful bay in the Caribbean." Bedrooms are exquisitely decorated in a contemporary style with dark Balinese furniture, creamy upholstery accented with colorful cushions, a comfy bed with pillow-top mattress, and dark hardwood flooring. **Pros:** ground-level units for those with difficulty negotiating stairs; complimentary hourly treats at the pool; oversize villa accommodations. **Cons:** car recommended to explore beyond Marigot Bay; nearby beach is tiny, so head to Anse Cochon; while meals are good, à la carte dining is pricey. $ *Rooms from: US$540 ⊠ Marigot Bay ✛ South side of bay, overlooking marina* ☎ 758/458–5300 ⊕ *www.marigotbayresort.com* ➪ *124 rooms* ⊚| *No meals.*

Marigot Beach Club & Dive Resort

$ | RESORT | FAMILY | Divers love this place, and everyone loves the location facing the little palm-studded beach at Marigot Bay. Some accommodations are right on the beachfront; others are on the hillside with a sweeping view of the bay. **Pros:** deeply discounted rates off-season; beautiful views of Marigot Bay from every room; good casual dining with live entertainment on Saturday night. **Cons:** adjacent beach is tiny; hillside rooms require a trek; general maintenance issues. ⑤ *Rooms from: US$260* ✉ *Marigot Bay* ☎ *758/451–4974* ⊕ *www.marigotbeachclub.com* ➴ *36 rooms* ❍❘ *No meals.*

Shopping

AREAS AND MALLS
Marigot Marina Village
SHOPPING CENTERS/MALLS | FAMILY | There are shops and services here for boaters and landlubbers alike, including a bank, grocery store, business center, art gallery, assortment of boutiques, a restaurant, and a casual café. ✉ *Bayside, next to Marigot Bay Resort, Marigot Bay* ☎ *758/458–5300* ⊕ *www.marigotbayresort. com/marina/marina-village.*

Soufrière and the Southwest Coast

Soufrière, the oldest town in Saint Lucia and the island's historic French colonial capital, was founded by the French in 1746 and named for its proximity to the volcano of the same name. The wharf is the center of activity in this sleepy town (population, about 9,000), particularly when a ship anchors in pretty Soufrière Bay. French colonial influences are evident in the second-story verandas, gingerbread trim, and other appointments of the wooden buildings that surround the market square. The market building itself is decorated with colorful murals.

The site of much of Saint Lucia's renowned natural beauty, Soufrière is also the destination of most sightseeing trips. This is where you can get up close to the landmark Pitons and visit the "drive-in" volcano, botanical gardens, working plantations, waterfalls, and countless other examples of the natural beauty for which Saint Lucia is deservedly famous.

Sights

★ Diamond Falls Botanical Gardens and Mineral Baths
HOT SPRINGS | These splendid gardens are part of Soufrière Estate, a 2,000-acre land grant presented by King Louis XIV in 1713 to three Devaux brothers from Normandy in recognition of their services to France. The estate is still owned by their descendants; Joan Du Boulay Devaux maintains the gardens. Bushes and shrubs bursting with brilliant flowers grow beneath towering trees

and line pathways that lead to a natural gorge. Water bubbling to the surface from underground sulfur springs streams downhill in rivulets to become Diamond Waterfall, deep within the botanical gardens. Through the centuries, the rocks over which the cascade spills have become encrusted with minerals tinted yellow, green, and purple. Near the falls, mineral baths are fed by the underground springs. King Louis XVI of France provided funds in 1784 for the construction of a building with a dozen large stone baths to fortify his troops against the Saint Lucian climate. It's claimed that the future Joséphine Bonaparte bathed here as a young girl while visiting her father's plantation nearby. During the Brigand's War, just after the French Revolution, the bathhouse was destroyed. In 1930 André Du Boulay had the site excavated, and two of the original stone baths were restored for his use. Outside baths were added later. For a small fee, you can slip into your swimsuit and soak for 30 minutes in one of the outside pools; a private bath costs slightly more. ⊠ *Soufrière Estate, Diamond Rd., Soufrière* ☎ *758/459–7155* ⊕ *www.diamondstlucia.com* ⊠ *$7, public bath $6, private bath $7.*

Edmund Forest Reserve

FOREST | FAMILY | Dense tropical rain forest that stretches from one side of Saint Lucia to the other, sprawling over 19,000 acres of mountains and valleys, is home to a multitude of exotic flowers, trees, plants, and rare birds—including the brightly feathered Jacquot parrot. The Edmund Forest Reserve, on the island's western side, is most easily accessed from the road to Fond St. Jacques, which is just east of Soufrière. A trek through the verdant landscape, with spectacular views of mountains, valleys, and the sea beyond, can take three or more hours. The ranger station at the reserve entrance is a 30-minute drive from Soufrière and 90 minutes or more from the northern end of Saint Lucia. You'll need a four-wheel-drive vehicle to drive inland to the trailhead, which can take another hour. The trek itself is a strenuous hike, requiring stamina and sturdy hiking shoes. Your hotel can help you obtain permission from the St. Lucia Forestry Department to access reserve trails and to arrange for a naturalist or forest officer guide—necessary because the vegetation is so dense. ⊠ *Soufrière* ☎ *758/468–5649 Forestry Dept.* ⊠ *Nature trails $10, guide $25.*

★ Fond Doux Estate

FARM/RANCH | FAMILY | One of the earliest French estates established by land grants (1745 and 1764), this plantation still produces cocoa, citrus, bananas, coconuts, and vegetables on 135 hilly acres within the UNESCO World Heritage Site of Soufrière. The restored 1864 plantation house is still in use, as well. A 90-minute

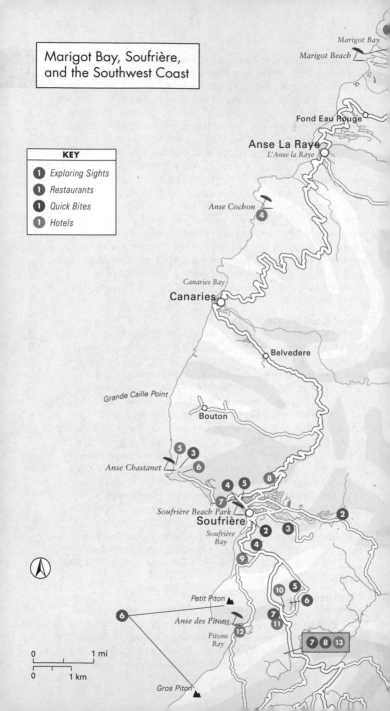

Marigot Bay, Soufrière, and the Southwest Coast

KEY

- 1 *Exploring Sights*
- 1 *Restaurants*
- 1 *Quick Bites*
- 1 *Hotels*

Marigot Bay

Marigot Beach

Fond Eau Rouge

Anse La Raye
L'Anse la Raye

Anse Cochon 4

Canaries Bay
Canaries

Belvedere

Grande Caille Point

Bouton

5 3
6
Anse Chastanet

4 5
8

7
Soufrière Beach Park
Soufrière
Soufrière Bay

2 3
4

9

10 5
6

2

6
Petit Piton

7
11

Anse des Pitons
12
Pitons Bay

7 8 13

Gros Piton

0 | | 1 mi

0 | | 1 km

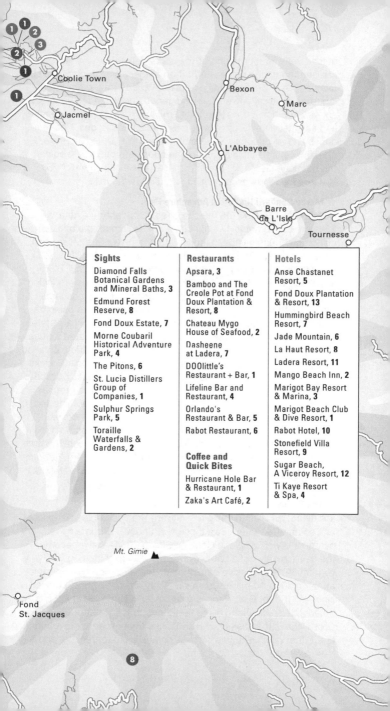

Coolie Town

Bexon

Marc

Jacmel

L'Abbayee

Barre
da L'Isle

Tournesse

Sights	Restaurants	Hotels
Sights	**Restaurants**	**Hotels**
Diamond Falls Botanical Gardens and Mineral Baths, **3**	Apsara, **3**	Anse Chastanet Resort, **5**
Edmund Forest Reserve, **8**	Bamboo and The Creole Pot at Fond Doux Plantation & Resort, **8**	Fond Doux Plantation & Resort, **13**
Fond Doux Estate, **7**	Chateau Mygo House of Seafood, **2**	Hummingbird Beach Resort, **7**
Morne Coubaril Historical Adventure Park, **4**	Dasheene at Ladera, **7**	Jade Mountain, **6**
The Pitons, **6**	DOOlittle's Restaurant + Bar, **1**	La Haut Resort, **8**
St. Lucia Distillers Group of Companies, **1**	Lifeline Bar and Restaurant, **4**	Ladera Resort, **11**
Sulphur Springs Park, **5**	Orlando's Restaurant & Bar, **5**	Mango Beach Inn, **2**
Toraille Waterfalls & Gardens, **2**	Rabot Restaurant, **6**	Marigot Bay Resort & Marina, **3**
		Marigot Beach Club & Dive Resort, **1**
	Coffee and Quick Bites	Rabot Hotel, **10**
	Hurricane Hole Bar & Restaurant, **1**	Stonefield Villa Resort, **9**
	Zaka's Art Café, **2**	Sugar Beach, A Viceroy Resort, **12**
		Ti Kaye Resort & Spa, **4**

Mt. Gimie

Fond
St. Jacques

guided walking tour begins at the cocoa *fermentary*, where you can see the drying process. You then follow a trail through the cultivated area, where a guide points out various fruit- or spice-bearing trees, tropical flowers, and indigenous birds (and their unique songs). Additional trails lead to old military ruins, a religious shrine, and a vantage point for viewing the spectacular Pitons. Cool drinks and an optional Creole buffet lunch are served after the tour. Souvenirs, including just-made chocolate sticks, are sold at the boutique. ⊠ *Vieux Fort Rd., Château Belair* ☎ *758/459–7545* ⊕ *www.fonddouxresort.com* ⊠ *$25, $40 with lunch.*

★ Morne Coubaril Historical Adventure Park

FARM/RANCH | FAMILY | On the site of an 18th-century estate, a 250-acre land grant in 1713 by Louis XIV of France, the original plantation house has been rebuilt and a farmworkers' village has been re-created. Both do a good job of showing what life was like for both the owners (a single family owned the land until 1960) and those who did all the hard labor over the centuries producing cotton, coffee, sugarcane, and cocoa. Cocoa, coffee, coconuts, manioc, and tropical fruits are still grown on the estate using traditional agricultural methods. On the 45-minute Historical Estate Tour, guides show how coconuts are opened and roasted for use as oil and animal feed and how cocoa is fermented, dried, crushed by dancing on the beans, and finally formed into chocolate sticks. Manioc roots (also called cassava) are grated, squeezed of excess water, dried, and turned into flour used for baking. The grounds are lovely for walking or hiking, and the views of mountains and Soufrière Bay are spellbinding. More adventurous visitors will enjoy ziplining past Petit Piton and through the adjacent rain forest—or a two-hour horseback ride on a trail to the beach. ⊠ *West Coast Rd., Soufrière* ⊹ *2 miles (3 km) south of Soufrière Harbour* ☎ *758/712–5808* ⊕ *www.mornecoubarilestate.com* ⊠ *$11 estate tour, $75 zipline, $120 horseback ride.*

★ The Pitons

HISTORIC SITE | Rising precipitously from the cobalt-blue Caribbean just south of Soufrière Bay, these two unusual mountains—named a UNESCO World Heritage Site in 2004—have become the iconic symbol of Saint Lucia. Covered with thick tropical vegetation, the massive outcroppings were formed by a volcanic eruption 30 to 40 million years ago. They are not identical twins, since 2,619-foot Gros Piton is taller and 2,461-foot Petit Piton is broader. It's possible to climb the Pitons, but it's a strenuous trek. Gros Piton is the easier climb and takes about four hours round-trip. Either climb requires permission and a guide; register at the base of Gros Piton. ⊠ *Soufrière.*

The Devaux family has owned Diamond Falls Botanical Gardens and Mineral Baths since 1713; the minerals in the sulfurous water cascading over the waterfall have stained the underlying rocks, making them sparkle—like diamonds.

★ Sulphur Springs Park

HOT SPRINGS | FAMILY | As you approach Sulphur Springs Park and the crater of the "drive-in volcano," your nose will pick up a strong scent emanating from more than 20 belching pools of murky water, crusty sulfur deposits, and other multicolor minerals baking and steaming on the surface. You don't actually drive all the way in. Rather, you drive within a few hundred feet of the gurgling, steaming mass and then walk behind your guide (whose service is included in the admission price) around a fault in the substratum rock. (Don't worry... the volcano hasn't erupted since the 1700s, probably because it continues to let off steam.) Following the fascinating, educational half-hour tour, you're welcome to take a quick dip in the nearby hot, mineral-rich bathing pools—they can also be pretty stinky on a hot day, but your skin (and joints) will thank you! ■**TIP→ You can rinse off under the waterfall.** ⊠ *Malgretoute, Soufrière ✛ Off West Coast Rd., south of town* ☏ *758/714–8900* ⊕ *sulphurspringstlucia.com* ⊠ *$9 tour, $5 bath, $13 combo; from $120 for half- or full-day tours with hotel transportation.*

Toraille Waterfalls & Gardens

BODY OF WATER | FAMILY | A mile or so inland from Soufrière and a stone's throw from the road through Fond St. Jacques, Toraille Waterfall cascades over a cliff and down about 50 feet to a pool. You're invited to don your bathing suit (changing rooms are available) and take a refreshing plunge or let the falling water massage your back and shoulders. A nature trail leads through the surrounding lush tropical gardens. ☏ *758/459–7527* ⊕ *www. toraillewaterfall.com* ⊠ *$4.*

Beaches

★ Anse Chastanet

BEACH—SIGHT | FAMILY | In front of the resort of the same name and Jade Mountain, this palm-studded, dark-sand beach just north of Soufrière Bay has a backdrop of green mountains, brightly painted fishing skiffs bobbing at anchor, calm waters for swimming, and some of the island's best reefs for snorkeling and diving right from shore. Anse Chastanet Resort's gazebos are among the palms; its dive shop, restaurant, and bar are on the beach and open to the public. The mile-long dirt road from Soufrière, though, is a challenge even for taxi drivers, given its (by design) state of disrepair. **Amenities:** food and drink; parking (no fee); toilets; water sports. **Best for:** snorkeling; sunset; swimming. ⊠ *Anse Chastanet Rd., Soufrière ✛ 1 mile (1½ km) north of Soufrière.*

★ **Anse Cochon**

BEACH—SIGHT | FAMILY | This dark-sand beach in front of Ti Kaye Resort & Spa is accessible by boat or by jeep via Ti Kaye's mile-long, tire-crunching access road—and then 166 steps down to the beach. The calm water and adjacent reefs, part of the National Marine Reserve, are superb for swimming, diving, and snorkeling. Most catamaran cruises to Soufrière stop here on the northbound leg so that day-trippers can take a quick swim. Moorings are free, and boaters and swimmers can enjoy refreshments at Ti Kaye's beach bar. Snorkeling equipment is available ($10) at the dive shop on the beach. **Amenities:** food and drink; toilets; water sports. **Best for:** snorkeling; swimming. ⊠ *Off West Coast Rd., Anse La Raye* ⊹ *3 miles (5 km) south of Anse la Raye.*

★ **Anse des Pitons** (*Sugar Beach, Jalousie Beach*)

BEACH—SIGHT | The white sand on this crescent beach, snuggled between the Pitons, was imported years ago and spread over the natural black sand. Accessible through the Sugar Beach, a Viceroy Resort, or by boat, Anse des Pitons (Sugar Beach, Jalousie Beach) offers crystal-clear water for swimming, excellent snorkeling and diving, and breathtaking scenery—you're swimming right between the Pitons, after all. The underwater area here is protected as part of the National Marine Reserve. Neighboring resorts Ladera and Boucan provide shuttle service to the beach. **Amenities:** food and drink; toilets; water sports. **Best for:** snorkeling; sunset; swimming. ⊠ *Val des Pitons, Soufrière* ⊹ *3 miles (5 km) south of Soufrière.*

Soufrière Beach Park

BEACH—SIGHT | FAMILY | The stretch of beachfront on Soufrière Bay was designated Soufrière Beach Park in spring 2019. Formerly called Hummingbird Beach, the new park stretches in front of Hummingbird Beach Resort. The park offers beachgoers a restaurant, spa, smoothie bar, beach bar, pizzeria, souvenir shop, outdoor showers, and a tourism information center. You can also rent nonmotorized water sports equipment. **Amenities:** food and drink; parking (no fee); showers; toilets; water sports. **Best for:** snorkeling; sunset; swimming. ⊠ *Bridge Rd., Soufrière.*

🍴 Restaurants

Apsara

$$$ | INDIAN | India has had an important influence on the Caribbean islands, from the heritage of their people to the colorful madras plaids and the curry flavors that are a staple of Caribbean cuisine. At night, Anse Chastanet's Trou au Diable restaurant transforms into Apsara, an extraordinarily romantic, candlelit, beachfront

Amazing views at Dasheene restaurant in the Ladera Resort

dining experience with modern Indian cuisine. **Known for:** exotic cuisine in an island setting; accessible by land or water; chef visits with diners at table to discuss cuisine. $ *Average main: US$26* ✉ *Anse Chastanet, 1 Anse Chastanet Rd., Soufrière* ☎ *758/459–7000* ⊕ *www.apsarastlucia.com* ⊘ *Closed Tues. No lunch.*

Bamboo and The Creole Pot at Fond Doux Plantation & Resort
$$$ | **CARIBBEAN** | **FAMILY** | The small, rustic pair of restaurants are two of the most popular spots to enjoy a Creole lunch when touring the natural sights in and around Soufrière. Bamboo offers à la carte options at both lunch and dinner while the Creole Pot has a buffet lunch of stewed chicken, grilled fish, rice and beans, macaroni and cheese, caramelized plantains, figs (green bananas), breadfruit balls, purple yams, salad, and more. **Known for:** farm to table Creole cuisine; natural environment; plantation tours before or after your meal. $ *Average main: US$25* ✉ *Fond Doux Eco Resort, West Coast Rd., Château Belair* ☎ *758/459–7545* ⊕ *fond-douxresort.com/dining.*

★ Dasheene
$$$ | **CARIBBEAN** | The terrace restaurant at Ladera Resort has breathtaking, close-up views of the Pitons and the sea between them, especially beautiful at sunset. The atmosphere is casual by day and magical at night. **Known for:** fresh, stylish island cuisine; Pitons views; live local music every evening. $ *Average main: US$30* ✉ *Ladera Resort, West Coast Rd., Soufrière* ✛ *3 miles (5 km) south of Soufrière* ☎ *758/459–6623* ⊕ *www.ladera.com/dining.*

Lifeline Bar and Restaurant

$$$ | CARIBBEAN | The cheerful restaurant-bar in the Humming-bird Beach Resort specializes in French creole cuisine. Try fresh seafood or chicken seasoned with local herbs and accompanied by fresh-picked vegetables from the Hummingbird's garden. **Known for:** authentic Caribbean food; great in-town, on-the-beach location; a favorite for three decades. $ *Average main: US$25* ⊠ *Hummingbird Beach Resort, Anse Chastanet Rd., Soufrière* ☎ *758/459–7232* ⊕ *www.facebook.com/ Humming-Bird-Beach-Resort-St-Lucia-845981815423509.*

Orlando's Restaurant & Bar

$$$$ | CARIBBEAN | A man on a mission, chef Orlando Sachell opened his original restaurant in downtown Soufrière to present his "Share the Love" (or STL) style of Caribbean cooking. Breakfast and lunch are served here, and dinner is served at his second Orlando's Restaurant, which opened in Rodney Bay in 2020. **Known for:** star chef yet always accommodating; exquisite small plates and excellent wine; casual courtyard dining. $ *Average main: US$38* ⊠ *Bridge St., Soufrière* ☎ *758/459–5955* ⊕ *www. facebook.com/Orlandos.Restaurant.Soufriere.St.Lucia/* ☉ *Closed Tues. No dinner.*

★ Rabot Restaurant

$$$$ | CARIBBEAN | Aah … chocolate! Here on the Rabot Estate, a working cocoa plantation, that heavenly flavor is infused into just about every dish—cacao gazpacho or citrus salad with white chocolate dressing for starters. **Known for:** "pioneering" cacao cuisine; open-air dining room with Pitons views; sunset at the bar with a cacao Bellini. $ *Average main: US$38* ⊠ *Rabot Hotel, Rabot Estate, West Coast Rd., Soufrière* ⊹ *3 miles (5 km) south of Soufrière* ☎ *758/459–7966* ⊕ *hotelchocolat.com/uk/boucan/ restaurant.html.*

☕ Coffee and Quick Bites

★ Zaka's Art Café

$ | CAFÉ | FAMILY | Stop in for a chat and a cup of coffee—and, of course, Zaka's rather brilliant artwork. In his studio in nearby Malgretoute, artist and craftsman Simon "Zaka" Gajhadhar (and his team of local artists and wood carvers) fashion totems and masks from driftwood, branches, and other environmentally friendly wood sources—taking advantage of the natural nibs and knots that distinguish each piece. **Known for:** coffee; hand-carved wood art;. $ *Average main:* ⊠ *26 Maurice Mason St., Soufrière* ☎ *758/457–1504* ⊕ *zaka-art.com* ▬ *No credit cards.*

Hotels

Anse Chastanet Resort

$$$$ | RESORT | Spectacular, individually designed rooms—some with fourth walls wide open to the stunning Pitons view—peek out of the thick rain forest that cascades down a steep hillside to the beach. **Pros:** great location for divers; the open-wall Pitons views; attractive room furnishings and artwork. **Cons:** no pool; air-conditioning only in beachfront rooms; steep hillside not conducive to strolling or to guests with walking or cardiac issues. ⑤ *Rooms from: US$660* ⊠ *1000 Anse Chastanet Rd., Soufrière* ☎ *758/459–7000, 800/223–1108 in U.S.* ⊕ *www.ansechastanet. com* ⤴ *49 rooms* ⦿ *No meals.*

★ Fond Doux Plantation & Resort

$$$ | RESORT | FAMILY | At this laid-back "eco resort" on one of Soufrière's most active agricultural plantations, nine historic homes salvaged from all around the island have been rebuilt on the 135-acre estate and refurbished as guest accommodations with luxury bathrooms and period furniture, and surrounded by dense tropical foliage and marked trails that meander through the property. **Pros:** an exotic, eco-friendly experience; striking location on an 18th-century plantation; free beach shuttle. **Cons:** no room TVs; no air-conditioning; a car is advised, as local sights are a few miles away. ⑤ *Rooms from: US$395* ⊠ *Fond Doux Estate, Soufrière* ⊹ *4 miles (7 km) south of Soufrière* ☎ *758/459–7545* ⊕ *www. fonddouxresort.com* ⤴ *16 rooms* ⦿ *Free breakfast.*

Hummingbird Beach Resort

$ | B&B/INN | Unpretentious and welcoming, this delightful little inn on Soufrière Harbour has simply furnished rooms—a traditional motif emphasized by four-poster beds and African wood sculptures—in small seaside cabins. **Pros:** local island hospitality; lovely gardens; good food. **Cons:** few amenities—but that's part of the charm; late-night beach party music can be a nuisance; beach out front is rather narrow. ⑤ *Rooms from: US$150* ⊠ *Anse Chastanet Rd., Soufrière* ☎ *758/459–7232* ⊕ *www.facebook.com/Humming-Bird-Beach-Resort-St-Lucia-845981815423509* ⤴ *10 rooms* ⦿ *Free breakfast.*

★ Jade Mountain

$$$$ | RESORT | This premium-class, premium-priced, adults-only hotel is an architectural wonder perched on a picturesque mountainside overlooking the Pitons and the Caribbean. **Pros:** access to Anse Chastanet beach, water sports, restaurants, and spa; huge in-room pools; open fourth wall with Pitons views in every "sanctuary". **Cons:** sky-high rates; no air-conditioning (except in one "sky suite"); not recommended for anyone with physical disabilities. $ Rooms from: US$1635 ✉ Anse Chastanet, Anse Chastanet Rd., Soufrière ☎ 758/459–4000, 800/223–1108 in U.S. ⊕ www. jademountain.com ⤳ 29 rooms ⦿ No meals.

La Haut Resort

$ | B&B/INN | FAMILY | "La Haut" is French for "the height," so it's all about the view—the Pitons, of course—plus the appeal of staying in an intimate and affordable family-run inn. **Pros:** lovely for weddings and honeymoons but also for families; stunning Pitons views; complimentary fresh fruit daily. **Cons:** no air-conditioning in some rooms; spotty Wi-Fi access; vehicle recommended. $ Rooms from: US$200 ✉ West Coast Rd., Colombette, Soufrière ⊹ Just north of Soufrière ☎ 758/459–7008, 866/773–4321 in U.S. ⊕ www.lahaut.com ⤳ 17 rooms ⦿ Free breakfast.

★ Ladera Resort

$$$$ | RESORT | The elegantly rustic Ladera Resort, perched 1,000 feet above the sea directly between the two Pitons, is one of the most sophisticated small inns in the Caribbean but, at the same time, takes a local, eco-friendly approach to furnishings, food, and service. **Pros:** excellent cuisine at Dasheene; hand-hewn furniture makes each room unique; open fourth walls and private plunge pools provide breathtaking views. **Cons:** communal infinity pool is small; steep drops make this the wrong choice for people with physical disabilities; no air-conditioning (but breezy, so no real need). $ Rooms from: US$840 ✉ Rabot Estate, Soufrière–Vieux Fort Hwy., Soufrière ⊹ 3 miles (5 km) south of town ☎ 758/459–6600, 844/785–8242 in U.S. ⊕ www.ladera.com ⤳ 37 rooms ⦿ No meals.

★ Rabot Hotel

$$$$ | HOTEL | Anyone who loves chocolate will love this themed boutique hotel just south of Soufrière and within shouting distance of the Pitons. **Pros:** pool with a view and daily beach shuttle service; chocolate lover's dream; self-guided trail walks and cocoa tours throughout the estate. **Cons:** no air-conditioning, but naturally breezy; no TV, but a preloaded iPod and free Wi-Fi; no children 18 or under. $ Rooms from: US$761 ✉ Rabot Estate, West Coast Rd., Soufrière ⊹ 2 miles (3 km) south of Soufrière ☎ 758/459–7966 ⊕ www.thehotelchocolat.com/uk/rabothotel.html ⤳ 14 rooms ⦿ Free breakfast.

Stonefield Villa Resort

$$ | RESORT | The 18th-century plantation house and cottage-style villas that dot this 26-acre family-owned estate, a former lime and cocoa plantation that spills down a tropical hillside, afford eye-popping views of Petit Piton. **Pros:** quiet, natural, very private

setting; beautiful pool; great sunset views from villa decks. **Cons:** car recommended to go off-site; fitness facility could use air-conditioning; no room TVs. ⑤ *Rooms from: US$319* ✉ *West Coast Rd., Soufrière* ✛ *1 mile (1½ km) south of Soufrière* ☎ *758/459–7037, 800/420–5731 in U.S.* ⊕ *www.stonefieldresort.com* ↪ *17 villas* ⑩ *Free breakfast.*

★ Sugar Beach, A Viceroy Resort

$$$$ | **RESORT** | **FAMILY** | Located in Val des Pitons, the steep valley between the Pitons and the most dramatic 100 acres in Saint Lucia, magnificent private villas are tucked into the dense tropical foliage that covers the hillside and reaches down to the sea. **Pros:** exquisite accommodations, scenery, service, and amenities; huge infinity pool; complimentary Wi-Fi and use of iPad during stay. **Cons:** very expensive; fairly isolated, so a meal plan makes sense; rental car advised. ⑤ *Rooms from: US$768* ✉ *Val des Pitons, Soufrière* ✛ *2 miles (3 km) south of town* ☎ *800/235–4300 in U.S., 758/456–8000* ⊕ *www.viceroyhotelsandresorts.com/sugarbeach* ↪ *96 rooms* ⑩ *No meals.*

★ Ti Kaye Resort & Spa

$$$ | **RESORT** | Rustic elegance is not an oxymoron at this upscale, adults-only cottage community that spills down a hillside above fabulous Anse Cochon beach. **Pros:** great for a wedding, honeymoon, or getaway (adults only); excellent dining at Kai Manje; on-site dive shop. **Cons:** those 166 steps down to (and up from) the beach; room TV costs extra; location is far from anywhere—rent a car to get around. ⑤ *Rooms from: US$441* ✉ *Anse Cochon, off West Coast Rd., Anse La Raye* ✛ *Halfway between Anse la Raye and Canaries* ☎ *758/456–8101, 888/300–7026 in U.S.* ⊕ *www.tikaye.com* ↪ *33 cottages* ⑩ *Free breakfast.*

Nightlife

STREET PARTIES

Anse la Raye Seafood Friday

THEMED ENTERTAINMENT | **FAMILY** | For a taste of Saint Lucian village life, head for this street festival, held every Friday night beginning at 6:30. The main street in this tiny fishing village—about halfway between Castries and Soufrière—is closed to vehicles, and residents prepare what they know best: fish cakes, grilled or stewed fish, hot bakes (biscuits), roasted corn, boiled crayfish, and lobster (grilled before your eyes). Prices range from a few cents for a fish cake or bake to $10 or $15 for a whole lobster. Walk around, eat, chat with locals, and listen to live music until the wee hours. ✉ *Main St., Anse La Raye* ✛ *Off West Coast Rd.*

Shopping

The Batik Studio

CLOTHING | FAMILY | The superb batik sarongs, scarves, and wall panels sold here are designed and created on-site by the shop's proprietor, Joan Alexander Stowe. ⊠ *Hummingbird Beach Resort, Anse Chastanet Rd., Soufrière* ☎ *758/459–7985.*

Choiseul Art Gallery

CRAFTS | Leo and Hattie Barnard, who came to Saint Lucia from England, offer paintings and handmade greeting cards that capture the beauty of the island, along with books Hattie and souvenirs, palm crafts, and wood carvings made locally by Leo and others. ⊠ *River Doree, La Fargue* ☎ *758/715–5740* ⊕ *choiseulartgallery.com* ⊙ *Closed Sun., Mon., Aug., and Sept.*

Vieux Fort and the East Coast

Vieux Fort, on the southeastern tip of Saint Lucia, is the island's second-largest town (Castries, the only "official" city) and the location of Hewanorra International Airport, which serves all commercial jet aircraft arriving on and departing from the island.

Although less developed for tourism than the island's north and west, the area around Vieux Fort and points north along the east coast are home to some of Saint Lucia's unique ecosystems and interesting natural attractions. From the Moule à Chique Peninsula, the island's southernmost tip, you can see much of Saint Lucia to the north and the island of Saint Vincent 21 miles (34 km) to the south. This is where the waters of the clear Caribbean Sea blend with those of the deeper blue Atlantic Ocean.

◉ Sights

Barre de l'Isle Forest Reserve

FOREST | FAMILY | Saint Lucia is divided into eastern and western halves by Barre de l'Isle ridge. A mile-long (1½-km-long) trail cuts through the reserve, and four lookout points provide panoramic views. Visible in the distance are Mt. Gimie (Jimmy), immense green valleys, both the Caribbean Sea and the Atlantic Ocean, and coastal communities. The trailhead is a half-hour drive from Castries. It takes about an hour to walk the trail—an easy hike—and another hour to climb Mt. LaCombe Ridge. Permission from the St. Lucia Forestry Department is required to access the trail in Barre de l'Isle; a naturalist or forest officer guide will accompany

Saint Lucia's Two Nobel Laureates

Sir W. Arthur Lewis won the Nobel Memorial Prize in Economic Science in 1979. Born in Saint Lucia in 1915, Lewis graduated with distinction from the London School of Economics and went on to earn a PhD in industrial economics. His life interest—and his influence—was in economic development and the transformation and expansion of university education in the Caribbean. Lewis died in 1991 and was buried on the grounds of Sir Arthur Lewis Community College on Morne Fortune in Saint Lucia.

Sir Derek Walcott was born in Castries in 1930. He was a writer, playwright, and water-color painter. *Omeros*—an epic poem about his journey around the Caribbean, the American West, and London—contributed to his winning the Nobel Prize in Literature in 1992. He taught poetry and drama in the United States, Canada, and England and gave lectures and readings throughout the world. In 2016 he was honored by Queen Elizabeth II as the Knight Commander of the Order of Saint Lucia. Walcott died in 2017 and is also buried on Morne Fortune.

you. ⊠ *Micoud Hwy., Ravine Poisson* ✢ *Midway between Castries and Dennery* ☎ *758/468–5649 Forestry Dept.* 🎫 *$20, $10 for the guide* ☞ *Call weekdays 8:30–4:30.*

Mamiku Gardens

GARDEN | One of Saint Lucia's loveliest botanical gardens surrounds the hilltop ruins of the Micoud Estate. Baron Micoud, an 18th-century colonel in the French army and governor-general of Saint Lucia, deeded the land to his wife, Madame de Micoud, to avoid confiscation by the British during one of the many times when Saint Lucia changed hands. Locals abbreviated her name to "Ma Micoud," which, over time, became Mamiku. (The estate did become a British military outpost in 1796, but shortly thereafter was burned to the ground by slaves during the Brigand's War.) The estate is now primarily a banana plantation, but the gardens themselves—including several secluded or "secret" gardens—are filled with tropical flowers and plants, delicate orchids, and fragrant herbs. ⊠ *Micoud Rd., Praslin* ✢ *Off Micoud Hwy., south of Praslin* ☎ *758/455–3729* ⊕ *www.mamikugardens.com* 🎫 *$8, guided tour $10* ☞ *Guided tours must be booked at least 3 days in advance.*

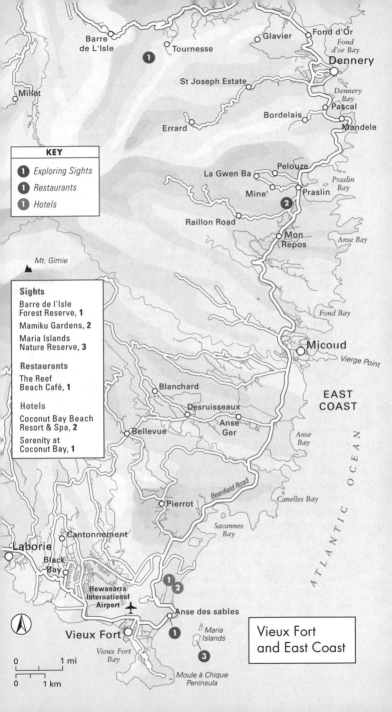

KEY

- 1 *Exploring Sights*
- 1 *Restaurants*
- 1 *Hotels*

Sights

Barre de l'Isle
Forest Reserve, **1**

Mamiku Gardens, **2**

Maria Islands
Nature Reserve, **3**

Restaurants

The Reef
Beach Café, **1**

Hotels

Coconut Bay Beach
Resort & Spa, **2**

Serenity at
Coconut Bay, **1**

Vieux Fort
and East Coast

0 — 1 mi
0 — 1 km

Embracing Kwéyòl

English is Saint Lucia's official language, but most Saint Lucians speak Kwéyòl—a French-based Creole language—for informal conversations among themselves. Primarily a spoken language, Kwéyòl in its written form doesn't look at all like French.

A similar version of the Creole language, or patois, is spoken on nearby Dominica. Otherwise, the Saint Lucian Kwéyòl is quite different from that spoken in other Caribbean islands that have a French and African heritage, such as Haiti, Guadeloupe, and Martinique—or elsewhere, such as Louisiana, Mauritius, and Madagascar. The Kwéyòl spoken in Saint Lucia and Dominica is mostly unintelligible to people from those other locations—and vice versa.

Saint Lucia embraces its Creole heritage by devoting the month of October each year to celebrations that preserve and promote Creole culture, language, and traditions. In selected communities throughout the island, events and performances highlight Creole music, food, dance, theater, native costumes, church services, traditional games, folklore, native medicine—a little bit of everything, or *tout bagay*, as you say in Kwéyòl.

Creole Heritage Month culminates at the end of October with all-day events and activities on Jounen Kwéyòl Entenasyonnal, or International Creole Day, which is recognized by all countries that speak a version of the Creole language.

Maria Islands Nature Reserve

ISLAND | FAMILY | Two tiny islands in the Atlantic Ocean off Saint Lucia's southeastern coast make up the reserve, which has its own interpretive center. The 25-acre Maria Major and the 4-acre Maria Minor are inhabited by two rare species of reptiles: the colorful Zandoli Terre ground lizard and the harmless Kouwes grass snake. They share their home with frigate birds, terns, doves, and other wildlife. There's a small beach for swimming and snorkeling, as well as an undisturbed forest, a vertical cliff covered with cacti, and a coral reef for snorkeling or diving. The St. Lucia National Trust offers tours, including a local fishing boat trip to the islands, by appointment only; bring your own picnic lunch, as there are no facilities. ⊠ *Vieux Fort* ☎ *758/454–5014 for tour reservations* ⊕ *slunatrust.org/sites/maria-island-nature-reserve* 🎟 *$35.*

Restaurants

The Reef Beach Café
$$ | **CARIBBEAN** | **FAMILY** | Situate yourself at a table under a shady tree for an early breakfast, casual beachside lunch or dinner (try the ribs), or just chill with drinks and snacks. The café is part of The Reef complex, which includes four tiny rooms for overnight stays and a popular kitesurfing and windsurfing venue. **Known for:** fast, friendly service and consistently good food; close to the airport and convenient for a preflight meal; fun to watch the surfers (wind or kite). $ *Average main: US$15* ⊠ *Anse de Sable Beach/ Sandy Beach, Vieux Fort* ☎ *758/454–3418* ⊕ *reefstlucia.com* ⊗ *No dinner Mon.*

🛏 Hotels

Coconut Bay Beach Resort & Spa
$$$ | **RESORT** | **FAMILY** | Coconut Bay is a sprawling (85 acres), family-friendly, seaside retreat minutes from Hewanorra International Airport. **Pros:** separate section for families with kids; excellent kitesurfing; five minutes from the airport. **Cons:** bathrooms have showers only; rough surf beyond the reef; nothing else nearby. $ *Rooms from: US$378* ⊠ *Off Micoud Hwy., Vieux Fort* ☎ *758/459–6000, 833/300–0146 in U.S.* ⊕ *www.cbayresort.com* ⇨ *250 rooms* ⦿ *All-inclusive.*

★ Serenity at Coconut Bay
$$$$ | **ALL-INCLUSIVE** | This upscale-yet-casual, private-yet-social, couples-only enclave is tucked into a corner of the expansive oceanfront gardens surrounding sister property, Coconut Bay Beach Resort. **Pros:** perfect choice for a romantic interlude, honeymoon, or anniversary; five minutes from Hewanorra International Airport; full access to all of Coconut Bay Beach Resort's restaurants/activities. **Cons:** remote location vis-à-vis island sights/ outside activities; long walk or shuttle to the resort's beach; very expensive even with special offers. $ *Rooms from: US$2525* ⊠ *Eau Piquant, Vieux Fort* ✛ *Adjacent to Coconut Bay Beach Resort & Spa* ☎ *758/459–6068, 877/252–0304 in U.S.* ⊕ *serenityatcoconutbay.com* ⇨ *36 rooms* ⦿ *All-inclusive.*

🛍 Shopping

Vieux Fort Plaza, near Hewanorra International Airport in Vieux Fort, is the main shopping center in the southern part of Saint Lucia. You'll find a bank, supermarket, bookstore, and clothing boutiques.

Activities

Biking

Although the terrain is pretty rugged, a tour operator has put together a fascinating bicycle tour that appeals to both novice riders and those who enjoy a good workout. The bike tour costs $60 per person.

Bike St. Lucia

BICYCLING | Small groups of mountain bikers are accompanied on jungle biking tours along 8 miles (13 km) of groomed trails—with naturally occurring challenges (such as rocks and roots) and a few mud holes to challenge purists—that meander through the remnants of the 18th-century Anse Mamin Plantation, part of the 600-acre Anse Chastanet Estate in Soufrière. Stops are made to explore the French colonial ruins, study the beautiful tropical plants and fruit trees, have a picnic lunch, and take a dip in a river swimming hole or at the beach. There's an orientation loop for learning or brushing up on off-road riding skills, and there are beginner, intermediate, and advanced tracks. If you're staying in the north, you can arrange a tour that includes transportation to the Soufrière area and lunch at Anse Chastanet Resort. ⊠ *Anse Mamin Plantation, Anse Chastanet Adventure Center, Soufrière* ☏ *758/459–7755* ⊕ *www.bikestlucia.com.*

Boating and Sailing

Rodney Bay and Marigot Bay are centers for bareboat or crewed yacht charters. Their marinas offer safe anchorage, shower facilities, restaurants, groceries, and maintenance for yachts sailing the waters of the eastern Caribbean. Charter prices range from $1,900 to $10,000 or more per week, depending on the season and the type and size of vessel, plus about $400 more per day if you want a skipper and cook. Some boat charter companies do not operate in August and September—the height of the hurricane season.

Bateau Mygo

BOATING | **FAMILY** | Choose a monohull or catamaran sailboat or a luxury power yacht for your half-, full-, or two-day cruise along the west coast, or charter by the week and explore neighboring islands. ⊠ *Chateau Mygo, Marigot Bay* ✛ *Adjacent to Marina Village* ☏ *758/721–7007* ⊕ *www.sailsaintlucia.com.*

Cocoa Tea

The homemade chocolate balls or sticks that vendors sell in the market are formed from locally grown and processed cocoa beans. Saint Lucians use the chocolate to make cocoa tea—a beverage that actually originated in Soufrière but has since become a popular drink wherever cocoa is grown throughout the Caribbean. The chocolate is grated and steeped in boiling water, along with a bay leaf and cinnamon stick. Sugar is added, along with a little milk or cream and some vanilla. Some people add nutmeg, as well, and some cornstarch to make it thicker and more filling. Cocoa tea began as a breakfast treat but is now enjoyed with a slice of bread as a snack or even as a dessert. Be sure to bring some chocolate sticks or balls home with you. One sniff and you won't be able to resist buying a few.

Destination St. Lucia Ltd. (*DSL*)

BOATING | FAMILY | For its bareboat yacht charters, DSL's vessels include two catamarans (42 and 44 feet) and several monohulls ranging in length from 32 to 46 feet. ⊠ *Rodney Bay Marina, Rodney Bay* ☎ *758/452–8531* ⊕ *www.dsl-yachting.com.*

The Moorings St. Lucia

BOATING | FAMILY | Bareboat and crewed catamarans and monohulls are available for charter. You can also plan a one-way sail through the Grenadines, either picking up or dropping off at the company's facility in Grenada. ⊠ *Rodney Bay Marina, Rodney Bay* ☎ *758/451–4357, 888/350–3575 in U.S.* ⊕ *www.moorings.com.*

Diving and Snorkeling

You'll find on-site dive shops at several resorts, including BodyHoliday St. Lucia, Sandals Grande, Royal St. Lucia, and Rendezvous in the north; Marigot Bay Resort and Ti Kaye farther south; and Anse Chastanet and Sugar Beach, A Viceroy Resort, in Soufrière. Nearly all dive operators, regardless of their own location, provide transportation from Rodney Bay, Castries, Marigot Bay, or Soufrière. Depending on the season, the particular trip, and whether you rent or have your own gear, prices range from about $40 for a one-tank shore dive and $90 for a two-tank boat dive to $225 to $320 for a six-dive package over three days and $350 to $500 for a 10-dive package over five days—plus a Marine Reserve permit fee of $5 to $15, depending on the number of days. Dive shops provide instruction for all levels (beginner, intermediate, and advanced). For beginners, a resort course (pool training), followed by one open-water dive, runs from about $20 to $160, depending on the number of days and dives included. Snorkelers are generally welcome on dive trips and usually pay $60 to $75. All prices usually include taxi/boat transfers, refreshments, and equipment.

Anse Chastanet, near the Pitons on the southwest coast, is the best beach-entry dive site. The underwater reef drops from 20 feet to nearly 140 feet in a stunning coral wall.

A 165-foot freighter, *Lesleen M,* was deliberately sunk in 60 feet of water near **Anse Cochon** to create an artificial reef; divers can explore the ship in its entirety and view huge gorgonians, black coral trees, gigantic barrel sponges, lace corals, schooling fish, angelfish, sea horses, spotted eels, stingrays, nurse sharks, and sea turtles.

Anse La Raye, midway up the west coast, is one of Saint Lucia's finest wall and drift dives and a great place for snorkeling.

At the **Pinnacles,** four coral-encrusted stone piers rise to within 10 feet of the surface.

Superman's Flight is a dramatic drift dive along the steep walls beneath the Pitons. At the base of **Petit Piton** a spectacular wall drops to 200 feet, where you can view an impressive collection of huge barrel sponges and black coral trees; strong currents ensure good visibility.

DIVE OPERATORS
Dive Fair Helen
SCUBA DIVING | FAMILY | In operation since 1992 and owned by a Saint Lucian environmentalist, this PADI dive center offers half- and full-day excursions on two custom-built dive boats to wreck, wall, and marine reserve areas, as well as night dives and instruction. ⊠ *Marina Village, Marigot Bay* ☎ *758/451–7716* ⊕ *www. divefairhelen.com.*

Island Divers
DIVING/SNORKELING | FAMILY | At the edge of the National Marine Park, with two reefs and an offshore wreck accessible from shore, this dive shop at Ti Kaye Resort & Spa offers guided shore dives ($40), boat dives, PADI certification, equipment rental, and an extensive list of specialty courses. Hotel transfers available. ⊠ *Ti Kaye Resort & Spa, Off West Coast Rd., Anse La Raye* ⊹ *Between Anse la Raye and Canaries* ☎ *758/456–8110* ⊕ *www.tikaye. com/diving.*

A large brain coral off the coast of Saint Lucia

Scuba Steve's Diving

SCUBA DIVING | FAMILY | Operating out of a LEED Platinum-certified building at Rodney Bay Marina, Saint Lucia's state-of-the-art dive center has a purpose-built training pool, fully equipped classrooms for adult and junior instruction (beginner or PADI-certified), fully equipped compressors, equipment rental and storage, guided dives, and two specialized dive boats that accommodate 10 and 15 divers, respectively. Dive trips include lunch, drinks, and hotel transfers (north of Castries). ⊠ *Rodney Bay Marina, Castries-Gros Islet Hwy., Rodney Bay* ☎ *758/450–9433* ⊕ *www.scubastevesdiving.com.*

Scuba St. Lucia

SCUBA DIVING | FAMILY | Daily (and nightly) beach and boat dives and resort and certification courses are available from this PADI 5 Star facility located on Anse Chastanet, and they also have underwater photography and snorkeling equipment. Transportation from the north of the island can be arranged. ⊠ *Anse Chastanet Resort, Anse Chastanet Rd., Soufrière* ☎ *758/459–7755, 800/223–1108 in U.S.* ⊕ *www.scubastlucia.com.*

Fishing

Among the deep-sea creatures you can find in Saint Lucia's waters are dolphin (the fish, also called dorado or mahi-mahi), barracuda, mackerel, wahoo, kingfish, sailfish, and white and blue marlin. Sportfishing is generally done on a catch-and-release basis, but the captain may permit you to take a fish back to your hotel to be prepared for your dinner. Neither spearfishing nor collecting live fish in coastal waters is permitted. Half- and full-day deep-sea fishing excursions can be arranged at Vigie Marina. A half day of fishing runs about $75 to $90 per person to join a scheduled party; a private charter will cost from about $570 to $1,500 for up to six or eight people, depending on the size of the boat and the length of time. Beginners are welcome.

Captain Mike's

FISHING | FAMILY | Named for Captain Mike Hackshaw and run by his family, Bruce and Andrew, this operation has a fleet of power-boats (31 to 46 feet) that accommodate up to eight passengers for half- or full-day sportfishing charters (tackle and cold drinks are supplied). Customized sightseeing or whale/dolphin-watching trips (from $55 per person) can also be arranged for four to six people. ⊠ *Vigie Marina, Vigie* ☎ *758/452–7044* ⊕ *www.captmikes.com.*

Hackshaw's Boat Charters

FISHING | FAMILY | In business since 1953, this company runs group and private deep-sea sports fishing charters on *Blue Boy,* a 31-foot Bertram; *Limited Edition,* a 47-foot custom-built Buddy Davis; and *Party Hack,* a 64-foot double-deck power catamaran used for bot-tom fishing, as well as for snorkeling, whale-watching, and party cruises. *Bandi t,* a 34-foot speed boat for adventure cruising, and *Lady Anne,* a 50-foot catamaran used for snorkeling, touring, and sunset cruises, complete the fleet. ⊠ *Vigie Marina, Seraphine Rd., Vigie* ☎ *758/453–0553* ⊕ *www.hackshaws.com.*

Golf

Saint Lucia has only one 18-hole championship course: **Sandals St. Lucia Golf & Country Club at Cap Estate. Sandals Regency La Toc Golf Resort and Spa** has a 9-hole executive-style course for its guests.

Sandals St. Lucia Golf & Country Club at Cap Estate

GOLF | FAMILY | Saint Lucia's only public course is at the island's northern tip and features broad views of both the Atlantic and the Caribbean, as well as many spots adorned with orchids and bromeliads. Wind and the demanding layout present challenges. The Cap Grill serves breakfast, lunch, and light meals until 7 pm; the Sports Bar is a convivial meeting place all day long. You can arrange lessons at the pro shop and perfect your swing at the 350-yard driving range. Carts are mandatory and cost $50; club and shoe rentals are available. Reservations are essential. ⊠ *Cap Estate* ☎ *758/450–8523* ⊕ *www.sandals.com/golf/st-lucia* ⛳ *$175 for 18 holes, $135 for 9 holes* ⅄. *18 holes, 6744 yards, par 71.*

The Des Cartiers Rain Forest Trail is a 1-mile (2-km) loop.

Hiking

The island is laced with trails, but you shouldn't attempt the more challenging ones—especially those that are deep in the rain forest—without a guide.

St. Lucia Forestry Department

HIKING/WALKING | **FAMILY** | Trails under this department's jurisdiction include the Barre de L'Isle Trail (just off the highway, halfway between Castries and Dennery), the Forestiere Trail (20 minutes east of Castries), the Des Cartiers Rain Forest Trail (west of Micoud), the Edmund Rain Forest Trail and Enbas Saut Waterfalls (east of Soufrière), the Millet Bird Sanctuary Trail (east of Marigot Bay), and the Union Nature Trail (north of Castries). Most are two-hour hikes on 2-mile (3-km) loop trails; the bird-watching tour lasts four hours. The Forestry Department charges $25 for access to the hiking trails ($10 for nature trails), and provides guides ($20 to $30, depending on the hike) who explain the plants and trees that you'll encounter and keep you on the right track. Seasoned hikers climb the Pitons, the two volcanic cones rising 2,461 feet and 2,619 feet from the ocean floor, just south of Soufrière. Casual hiking is recommended only on Gros Piton, which offers a steep but safe trail to the top. The first half of the hike is moderately difficult; reaching the summit is challenging and should be attempted only by those who are physically fit. The view from the top is spectacular. Tourists are also permitted to hike Petit Piton, but the second half of the hike requires a good deal of rock climbing, and you'll need to provide your own safety equipment. Hiking either Piton requires permission from the Forestry Department and a knowledgeable guide. ⊠ *Union Forestry Complex, Union, Castries* ☎ *758/468–5649, 758/489–0136 for Pitons permission* ⊕ *www. forestryeeunit.blogpost.com.*

Tet Paul Nature Trail

HIKING/WALKING | Climb the natural "stairway" for a stunning 360-degree view of Saint Lucia including the entire southern coast (and neighboring St. Vincent in the distance), Mt. Gimie in the island's center, the Pitons on the nearby west coast, and as far north as Martinique on a clear day. This St. Lucia Heritage Site, just 10 minutes from downtown Soufrière, is an easy-to-moderate, 45-minute hike, with stops along the way to observe the scenery and a picnic area. ⊠ *West Coast Rd., Soufrière* ✛ *3 miles (5 km) south of town behind Fond Doux Plantation* ☎ *758/723–2930* ⊕ *www.tetpaulnaturetrail.com* ✆ *$10 entry fee includes guide.*

Horseback Riding

Creole horses, a breed native to South America and popular on Saint Lucia, are fairly small, fast, sturdy, and even-tempered animals suitable for beginners. Established stables can accommodate all skill levels. They offer countryside trail rides, beach rides with picnic lunches, plantation tours, carriage rides, and lengthy treks. Prices run about $40–$75 for a guided ride and $65–$120 for a beach ride with swimming (with your horse), depending on the distance and how long you're in the saddle. Local people sometimes appear on beaches with their steeds and offer 30-minute rides for $15 to $20; ride at your own risk.

Atlantic Shores Riding Stables

HORSEBACK RIDING | **FAMILY** | Two-hour trail rides roam along the beach, three-hour treks roam the countryside, and private rides can be arranged. Beginners and children are welcome. ⊠ *Micoud Hwy., Savannes Bay, Vieux Fort* ☎ *758/454–8660* ⊕ *www.atlantic-ridingstables.com.*

Morne Coubaril Estate

HORSEBACK RIDING | **FAMILY** | Horseback riding and ziplining are just two of the activities at Morne Coubaril Historical Adventure Park, a historic plantation in Soufrière. Tour the estate atop your steed, noting the views of Soufrière Bay and Petit Piton, ride through hillside trails to the beach and swim with your horse, or take the longer tour through the rain forest to the volcano and sulphur springs. ⊠ *West Coast Rd., Malgretoute* ✛ *2 miles (3 km) south of town* ☎ *758/712–5808* ⊕ *www.mornecoubarilestate.com.*

Trim's National Riding Stable

HORSEBACK RIDING | **FAMILY** | At the island's oldest riding stable there are four riding sessions per day, both beach tours and trail rides, plus riding lessons, party rides, pony rides, and horse-and-carriage tours to Pigeon Island. ⊠ *Cas en Bas* ☎ *758/450–8273* ⊕ *www.horserideslu.50megs.com.*

Kitesurfing

Kitesurfers congregate at Anse de Sables (Sandy) Beach in Vieux Fort, at the southeastern tip of Saint Lucia, to take advantage of the blue-water and high-wind conditions that the Atlantic Ocean provides.

Aquaholics

LOCAL SPORTS | **FAMILY** | There's no better place to kitesurf—or learn to kitesurf—than on a beautiful, crescent-shape bay at the northeastern tip of Saint Lucia, where the Atlantic Ocean meets the Caribbean Sea and the trade winds are consistent from November to June. ⊠ *Cas-En-Bas Beach, Cotton Bay, Cap Estate* ☎ *758/726–0600* ⊕ *www.aquaholicsstlucia.com.*

The Reef Kite + Surf

WINDSURFING | **FAMILY** | This water-sports center offers equipment rental and lessons from certified instructors. Kitesurfing equipment rents for $70 half day, $90 full day. The three-hour starter costs $220, including equipment and safety gear; the one-hour taster, $50. Kitesurfing is particularly strenuous, so participants must be excellent swimmers and in good health. ⊠ *The Reef Beach Café, Sandy Beach, Micoud Hwy., Vieux Fort* ☎ *758/454–3418* ⊕ *www.stluciakitesurfing.com.*

Sea Excursions

A day sail or sea cruise from Rodney Bay or Vigie Cove to Soufrière and the Pitons is a wonderful way to see Saint Lucia and a great way to get to the island's distinctive natural sites. Prices for a full-day sailing excursion to Soufrière run about $110 per person and include a land tour to the Diamond Botanical Gardens, lunch, a stop for swimming and snorkeling, and a visit to pretty Marigot Bay. Add ziplining, if you wish! Half-day cruises to the Pitons, three-hour whale-watching tours, and two-hour sunset cruises along the northwest coast will cost about $50 per person.

Captain Mike's

WHALE-WATCHING | FAMILY | With 20 species of whales and dolphins living in Caribbean waters, your chances of sighting some are very good on these 3½-hour whale- and dolphin-watching trips ($55 per person) aboard Captain Mike's *Free Willie*, a 60-foot Defender. ⊠ *Vigie Marina, Ganthers Bay, Castries* ☎ *758/452–7044* ⊕ *www.captmikes.com.*

★ Carnival Sailing

BOATING | FAMILY | Carnival Sailing has eight party catamarans that accommodate from 30 to 170 passengers and they run a variety of trips along the coast to Soufrière—tours, entrance fees, lunch, and drinks included. Prices vary for the menu of day tours, adventure tours, sunset cruises, and private charters. ⊠ *Reduit Beach Ave., Rodney Bay* ☎ *758/452–5586* ⊕ *carnivalsailing.com.*

Mystic Man Ocean Adventures

BOATING | FAMILY | The glass-bottom boat, sailing, catamaran, deep-sea fishing, snorkeling, and/or whale- and dolphin-watching tours are all great family excursions; there's also a sunset cruise. Most trips depart from Soufrière. ⊠ *Bay St., Soufrière* ✛ *On bay front* ☎ *758/459–7783, 800/401–9804* ⊕ *www.mysticmantours.com.*

Sea Spray Cruises

BOATING | FAMILY | Sail down the west coast from Rodney Bay to Soufrière on *Mango Tango* (a 52-foot catamaran), *Jus Tango* (a 65-foot catamaran), Go Tango (an 80-foot double-deck catamaran), *Calypso Cat* (a 42-foot double-deck power catamaran), or *Tango* (a 78-foot power catamaran). The all-day Tout Bagay (a little bit of everything) tour includes a visit to the sulfur springs, drive-in volcano, and Morne Coubaril Estate. The view of the Pitons from the water is majestic. You'll have lunch and drinks onboard, plenty of music, and an opportunity to swim at a remote beach. ⊠ *Rodney Bay Marina, Rodney Bay* ☎ *758/458–0123* ⊕ *www.seaspraycruises.com.*

Index

Photo Credits

Front Cover: Viviane Teles [Description: Barbados Bottom Bay Beach.]. **Back cover, from left to right:** Walleyelj/Dreamstime.com, Vlad61/Shutterstock, NAPA/Shutterstock. **Spine:** PHB.cz (Richard Semik)/Shutterstock. **Interior, from left to right:** jangeltun (1). zstock/Shutterstock (2). **Chapter 1: Experience Barbados and Saint Lucia:** mbrand85/Shutterstock (6-7). Simon Dannhauer/Shutterstock (8). Evaulphoto | Dreamstime.com (9). Mikael Lamber (9). clarkography / Shutterstock (10). This image and talent depicted is the property of the Barbados Tourism Marketing Inc. (10). Anna Jedynak/Shutterstock (10). Tiraspr | Dreamstime.com (10). jwebb/iStockphoto (11). Solarisys/Shutterstock (11). Provided by the Barbados Tourism Authority/Jim Smith (12). LJ7753/Shutterstock (12). Sandy Lane Hotel (12). M. Timothy O'Keefe / Alamy (13). nick.thompson/Shutterstock (16). Simon Dannhauer/Shutterstock (16). evenfh/Shutterstock (16). Walleyelj | Dreamstime.com (16). Filip Fuxa/Shutterstock (17). Courtesy of Anse Chastanet Resort (18). Four Oaks/Shutterstock (18). Courtesy of Anse Chastanet Resort (18). Courtesy of Barbados Tourism Marketing, Inc (18). Barbados Tourism Marketing, Inc (19). Courtesy of Serenity at Coconut Bay (20). Courtesy of Ti Kaye (20). Macduff Everton/Courtesy of Jade Mountain (20). Courtesy of The Sandpiper (20). Courtesy of Ladera (21). Simon Dannhauer/Shutterstock (28). **Chapter 2: Travel Smart:** Frank Fell Media/Shutterstock (29). **Chapter 3: Barbados:** Irishka777 | Dreamstime.com (55). This image and talent depicted is the property of the Barbados Tourism Marketing Inc. (61). Miltudog | Dreamstime.com (73). Wollwerth | Dreamstime.com (75). Ingolf Pompe / age fotostock (94). Roy Riley / Alamy (96). graham tomlin/Shutterstock (108). Provided by the Barbados Tourism Authority/Mike Toy (110-111). Provided by the Barbados Tourism Authority/Ronnie Carrington (115). St. Nicholas Abbey (117). Styve Reineck/Shutterstock (122). Kiera Bloom @Barbados Blue (126). World Pictures / age fotostock (130). **Chapter 4: Saint Lucia:** Colin Sinclair / age fotostock (133). Ian Cumming / age fotostock (150-151). Ian Cumming / age fotostock (159). Helene Rogers / age fotostock (164). fokke baarssen/Shutterstock (170). Ian Cumming / age fotostock (179). Courtesy of Ladera (182). Stephen Frink Collection / Alamy (195). M. Timothy O'Keefe / Alamy (197). **About Our Writers:** All photos are courtesy of the writers.

*Every effort has been made to trace the copyright holders, and we apologize in advance for any accidental errors. We would be happy to apply the corrections in the following edition of this book.